The Nature of Money

The Nature of Money

Geoffrey Ingham

polity

First published in 2004 by Polity Press Ltd

Polity Press
65 Bridge Street
Cambridge CB2 1UR, UK

Polity Press
350 Main Street
Malden, MA 02148, USA

A catalogue record for this book is available from the British Library.

Library of Congress Cataloging-in-Publication Data

Ingham, Geoffrey K.
   The nature of money / Geoffrey Ingham.
      p. cm.
Includes bibliographical references.
   ISBN 0–7456–0996–1—ISBN 0–7456–0997–X (pbk.)
1. Money. 2. Money—Philosophy. 3. Money—Social aspects. 4. Capitalism. I. Title.

HG220.A2I584 2004
332.4—dc22

2003017409

Typeset in 10.5 on 12 pt Times
by Kolam Information Services Pvt. Ltd, Pondicherry, India
Printed and bound in Great Britain by MPG Books, Bodmin, Cornwall

For further information on Polity, visit our website: www.polity.co.uk

Contents

Preface

This book is the result of my long-standing impatience with the disciplinary boundaries of the social sciences in modern academia. Not only have they become sharper, but there is also greater specialization and fragmentation into 'sub-fields' and esoteric niches. Since the division of intellectual labour in the early twentieth century, I believe that there has been a loss of understanding of how the world works. This belief is based on direct experience over a period of almost forty years in the University of Cambridge.

Using the economist Leijonhufvud's (1973) whimsical classification of the social science tribes – Econs, Sociogs and PolScis – I explained in an earlier paper on money that after initiation in the Sociog tribe, I lived for almost twenty-five years with the Econs in the Faculty of Economics (Ingham 2000b). I became interested in money, and I asked some of their tribal elders for guidance. What is money? Some answered that money, as such, was not really as important as (my) common sense might suggest. I was not convinced, and, in particular, I could not accept the orthodox economic conception of money as a 'neutral veil'. General equilibrium theory's inability to find an essential analytical place for money in its sophisticated mathematical models seemed even more puzzling. I had reached an impasse.

Several years later, I contracted to write an introductory text on the sociology of the basic institutions of the capitalist economy. The first chapter on money has now, several years later, grown into this book. However, this time round, one of the more heterodox Econ elders in Cambridge, Geoff Harcourt, pointed me in the direction of a much more congenial post-Keynesian literature. His assistance gave me the start I needed; I could not have begun without his help. I went back to Keynes's *A Treatise on Money* (1930) and realized for the first time that parts of the first two chapters were unwittingly, but thoroughly, 'sociological'. In effect, chapter 2 describes the social relations of production of bank credit-money. At the same time, I came across the reissue of Schumpeter's posthumous *History of Economic Analysis* (1994 [1954]). As a graduate student in Cambridge in the early 1960s, I had read parts of this wonderfully erudite and intellectually engaging work. It is probably better for being unfinished and unedited by Schumpeter: one can see the process of thinking with all the doubts, inconsistencies and contradictions. As a guide to the history of the economic analysis of money (and much more), it is unmatched.

Lacking the framework of a formal economics education has enabled me to write this unorthodox book; on the other hand, it has posed obvious problems. Deciphering the lexicons and idioms of the different traditions was slow going – 'endogenous' and 'exogenous' money took a little time to unravel! (Exogenous to what? At one time I thought that I could find at least three meanings. The reader will be pleased to hear that they do not appear in this final version.) Here again, I must thank Geoff Harcourt; he was the bridge without which I would not have been able to travel between the two tribes. He is always willing to answer my questions and suggest even more reading. The recommendation of the work of the economists John Smithin and Randall Wray has proved invaluable. It is gratifying to know that they in turn have taken an interest in mine. Attention to detail is not my strongest suit. Consequently, I have very good reason to be especially grateful for the highly professional expertise, and forbearance, of Sarah Dancy and her editorial team.

Polity has waited patiently a very long time for this partial fulfilment of the original contract. It is for others to judge whether it was in vain.

Part I

Concepts and Theories

Introduction

Gladstone, speaking in a parliamentary debate on Sir Robert Peel's Bank Act of 1844 and 1845, observed that even love has not turned more men into fools than has meditation on the nature of money.

Marx 1970: 64

I know of only three people who really understand money. A professor at another university; one of my students; and a rather junior clerk at the Bank of England.

Attributed to Keynes, quoted in Lietaer 2001: 33

Money's Puzzles and Paradoxes

Money is one of our essential social technologies; along with writing and number, it was a foundation for the world's first large-scale societies in the ancient Near East during the third millennium BC, and today it literally does make the globalized world 'go round'. Money plays this indispensable role by performing the familiar list of functions of the economic textbook.[1] It is a *medium of exchange*, *store of value*, *means of unilateral payment* (*settlement*), and *measure of value* (*unit of account*).[2] Each is fundamental for the continuance of routine life in the modern world.

In the first place, as Adam Smith and the classical economists made clear, a medium of exchange makes for the efficient operation of the division of labour and exchange of products that creates the 'wealth of nations'. This indirect multilateral exchange is a means of 'translating the work of the farmer into the work of the barber ... [money] is action at a distance' (McLuhan 1964: 10). Secondly, and perhaps most remarkably, money is able to store abstract value, as pure purchasing power, for longer periods than is necessary for any particular exchanges. The consequences of this property define the freedom and flexibility of the modern world. As Simmel explained, a feudal lord could demand specifically a quantity of honey and poultry from his serfs and thereby directly determine their labour. 'But the moment he imposes merely a money levy the peasant is free, insofar as he can decide whether to keep bees or cattle or anything else' (Simmel 1978 [1907]: 285–6). With money, decisions can be deferred, revised, reactivated, cancelled; it is 'frozen desire' (Buchan 1997). But, '[a]ll of these consequences are dependent on what is, in principle, the most important fact of all, the possibility of monetary calculation' (Weber 1978: 80–1). This third attribute of money, as a measure of value (money of account), enables the calculation of actual and potential costs and benefits, profits and losses, debts, prices. In short, money is the basis for the progressive rationalization of social life – a process that began, as we shall see, in those empires of ancient Mesopotamia.

However, money should not be seen simply as a useful instrument; it has a dual nature. Money does not merely have functions – that is to say, beneficial consequences for individuals and the social and economic system. In Mann's (1986) terminology, money is not only 'infrastructural' power, it is also 'despotic' power. In other words, money expands human society's capacity to get things done, but this power can be appropriated by particular interests. This is not simply a question of the possession and/or control of *quantities* of money – the power of wealth. Rather, as we shall see, the actual process of the *production* of money in its different forms is inherently a source of power. For example, modern capitalist money is bank credit-money that is produced on the basis of credit ratings that reinforce and increase existing levels of inequality by imposing differential interest rates. In the most general terms, as Weber contended, money is a weapon in the struggle for economic existence. Moreover, the dual elements in the nature of money can also be contradictory, in that particular interests' advantages may undermine the public benefits. This is a familiar theme in the ultra-liberal economic critique of the government's debt-financed spending that gives it an interest in inducing inflation to reduce the real value of the debt. These issues will be explored throughout the book.

Only a very little probing into these well-known observations reveals long-standing puzzles and paradoxes. Perhaps the greatest paradox is that such a commonplace as money should give rise to so much bewilderment, controversy and, it must be said, error. It is not well understood. Arguably, one of the most brilliant conceptual thinkers in economics in the twentieth century struggled unsuccessfully for forty years to finish his 'money book'. Midway through my own difficulties, I was dismayed to discover that Joseph Schumpeter, according to one of his close Harvard colleagues, was never able to get 'his ideas on money straightened out to his own satisfaction' (quoted in Earley 1994: 342).[3] I know what he meant.

Let us start to reveal the puzzles that lie behind everyday familiarity with money by looking more closely at the textbook list of functions. Leaving aside for the moment economic analysis's misleading implication that the functions *explain* the existence and nature of money, the presence of multiple attributes in the list raises two questions. Do *all* the functions have to be performed before 'moneyness' is established? If not, which are the definitive functions? In short, how is money to be uniquely specified? For 2,000 years or so, money was identified by the integration of the four functions in the form of coin (and later in notes directly representing coin) – that is, 'money proper' in the late nineteenth-century Cambridge economists' lexicon. The value of the coin (or note) was either the embodiment or direct representation of a valuable commodity. As we shall see, this common-sense designation of money, as a tangible object, persists, and has led to widespread confusions – for example, that electronic money heralds the 'end of money'. But a closer inspection of the coinage era reveals that matters are not quite so simple. For much of this long period, coins were not stamped or inscribed with any numerical value – that is, they did not bear any unit of account. This meant that the coin's nominal 'monetary' value and bullion value could and did vary considerably. The sovereign usually assigned the nominal values of coins in accordance with a declared money of account. In medieval Europe, for example, changes in the value of money were mainly the result of the alteration of the nominal unit of account by the king in relation to an 'imaginary' standard of value – 'crying' the coinage up or down, not the alteration of its precious metallic content. Furthermore, many units of money of account – such as the 'pound' of pounds, shillings and pence – were never minted as coin (Einaudi 1953 [1936]). Similarly, guineas continued as a money of account – that is, for pricing goods and debt contracts – for centuries after the coins had ceased to circulate.

'Cash' – portable things that we take to be money – is still used in 85 per cent of all transactions, but now amounts to only 1 per cent of the total value of monetary transactions (*The Guardian*, 17 April 2000). In other words, actual media of exchange are now a relatively insignificant element of most monetary systems; but consciousness of money is still formed to a significant extent by the small-scale transactions. The euro's introduction in the form of notes and coins is dated from 2002, but it had existed as a means of setting prices, contracting debts, and as a means of payment for over a year before it was embodied in these media of exchange. As we shall see, these considerations do not exhaust the logical and conceptual problems of the list of money's attributes and functions. In short, the question is: where is the quality of 'moneyness' located?

There are, in very general terms, two quite different answers to this question. As Schumpeter observed, there are 'only two theories of money which deserve the name ... the commodity theory and the claim theory. From their very nature they are incompatible' (Schumpeter, quoted in Ellis 1934: 3). Most orthodox economic theory focuses on the concept of money essentially as a *medium of exchange*. This has three meanings that are not always carefully distinguished. Money is either itself an exchangeable commodity (for example, gold coin), or it is a direct symbol of such a commodity (convertible note), or it may be the symbolic representation (*numéraire*) of a commodity standard – cow, barrel of oil, value of a 'basket' of commodities.[4] In this view, money is seen as the universal commodity, in that it is exchangeable for all others. It should be noted that in this conception 'moneyness' is somewhat tautologically 'exchangeability' – that is, the most 'liquid' commodity. It is at least strongly implied that all other qualities and functions in the conventional list – that is, money of account, means of payment, store of value – follow from, or can be subsumed under, medium of exchange. In sharp contrast, a heterodox 'nominalist' argument maintains that money 'in the full sense of the term can only exist in relation to Money of Account' (Keynes 1930: 3). (As we shall see, this nominalism is closely linked to the notion that money consists in 'claims' and 'credits', not merely tradable objects or their symbols.) In this conception, an abstract money of account is logically anterior to money's forms and functions; it provides all the most important advantages that are attributed to money in general and a medium of exchange in particular. Money of account makes possible prices and debt contracts, which are all that are required for extensive multilateral exchange to take place. Money accounting, with or without an actual 'money stuff' (in the anthropologists' lexicon), is the means of translating the work of the barber into that of the farmer and of producing action at both spatial and temporal distance. In this conception money is abstract – but an abstraction from what?

The crux of the matter, as we shall see, is whether a uniform value standard of the medium of exchange can be established without the *prior* existence of an abstract measure (money of account). In the orthodox economic account, a scale for the measurement of value (money of account) arises spontaneously from Adam Smith's primeval 'truck barter and exchange'. The most exchangeable commodity becomes money which is then counted to make a measure of value, or money of account. However, this raises a fundamentally important problem that will be explored later. Could myriad barter exchanges based on individual subjective preferences produce an agreed scale of values? Can the 'idea' of money – that is, as a measure of value – be derived, as Jevons, the late nineteenth-century economist, famously argued, from individually rational solutions to the 'inconveniences' of barter? How are inter-subjective hierarchies of value produced from subjective preferences? Posed in this way, the question of money becomes one of the fundamental questions of sociological and economic theory.[5]

The most startling paradox, which provided the original impetus for this study, is the fact that the mainstream, or orthodox, tradition of modern economics does not attach much theoretical importance to money (see Smithin 2003 for an overview of this mainstream tradition). Two assumptions in orthodox economics account for this counter-intuitive position; both are fundamentally mistaken. First, as we have noted, it is maintained that money is a commodity. Obviously, since the demise of precious metal currencies and/or standards of value, it is no longer argued that money need consist of a material with an intrinsic exchange-value. But for modern economic theory, money is a commodity in the sense that it can be *understood*, like any other commodity, by means of the orthodox methodology of microeconomics – 'supply and demand', 'marginal utility' and so on. The *analytical* structure of the modern orthodox economic analysis of money is derived fundamentally from the original Aristotelian commodity theory in which money is conceptualized as a 'thing' that acts as a medium of exchange because it possesses value (see chapter 1 for an outline of Aristotle's theory). In this conception, although 'cash' is now reduced to insignificance, there can, nevertheless, be a 'stock', or 'quantity' of 'things' that 'circulate' or 'flow' with varying 'velocity'. But, as we shall see, these metaphors are as misleading as the underlying theory on which they are based. As Schumpeter quipped, the velocity of money may be so great that it finds itself in two places at the same time (Schumpeter 1994 [1954]: 320). Even in this orthodox view, money has to be, at the very least, a rather special commodity. For example, apart from the many other considerations that we shall encounter, the production of the supply of money is always subject to rigorous control, and is not permitted to respond freely to demand.

(The severity of the punishments meted out to counterfeiters is testimony to the rigour.) The scarcity of money is always the result of very
carefully constructed social and political arrangements. As the populist US presidential candidate William Jennings Bryan explained in the
late nineteenth-century debate on the gold standard, 'if you want more
wheat you can go out and raise wheat ... but if the people want more
money they cannot bring money into existence' (*The First Battle*, 1897,
quoted in Jackson 1995: 18).

The 'neutrality' of money is the second paradoxical tenet held by
orthodox economic theory. As we shall see in chapter 1, it is held that
money is a 'neutral veil' over the workings of the 'real' economy. It is
neutral in the long run because, it is argued, variation in its quantity
can affect only the level of prices and not output and growth in the
economy. Indeed, money is not even accorded an analytical place in
some of the most prestigious mathematically sophisticated models of
the economy – such as Arrow–Debreu's general equilibrium. In short,
I shall contend that mainstream economics cannot provide a satisfactory explanation of money's existence and functions; that is to say,
orthodox economics has failed to *specify* the nature of money.

Moreover, this has not been, as they say, a mere 'academic' problem. In anticipation of the discussion in chapter 1, we might refer to
one or two of the difficulties that have followed from the application
of the 'neutral veil' conception and the 'quantity theory' to 'monetarist' policy. In the late 1970s and early 1980s, it was thought that
regulating the quantity of money in circulation could control inflation,
as it was believed occurred under the gold standard. It failed. In the
first place, it should be noted that there was an apparent contradiction
in the insistence that something without efficacy (the 'neutral veil')
should be rigorously controlled. This was resolved with the time-
honoured distinction between the short and long runs. In the long
run, equilibrium between the quantities of money and goods would
prevail. But short-run harmful disequilibria in which the supply of
money outran the supply of goods, causing a rise in the price level,
could occur and should be eradicated. However, as we shall see, it
soon became apparent that monetarists could not reach agreement on
what 'money' was and precisely how it got into the economy. Regardless of any other practical or operational problems, controlling a
quantity of something that could not be clearly identified was well
nigh impossible. Within a short time, measures of money proliferated
in those countries whose governments practised monetarism – numerous Ms were progressively introduced from M_0 (notes and coins and
cheques) to M_{10} and beyond. But they were all measures of what?
Furthermore, it became evident that the imperfectly identified and

measured quantities of money did not seem to be as closely related to prices as the basic quantity theory maintained.

As a practical policy doctrine, monetarism was very short-lived – it scarcely lasted a decade in the USA and UK from the late 1970s. But, as we shall see, the underlying theory on which it was based has been retained in mainstream economic theory by attributing the anomalies in the relation between quantities of money and prices to *short-run*, temporary and analytically *ad hoc* factors. Consequently, the very same conception of money persists as the theoretical underpinning of a different kind of monetary policy, in which quantitative money aggregates are no longer considered to be important. Quantity theory's axiom of long-run monetary neutrality in the equilibrium of nominal money and real economic variables remains the ostensible foundation for policy, but no longer gives guidance to practical action (Issing 2001). In short, the relationship between the orthodox conception of money in economic analysis and practical monetary policy is now tenuous to the point of incoherence.

More recently, as I have already hinted, the same orthodox analytical framework has led to the conjecture that advances in communication and information technology will replace money in the operation of economic systems (see chapter 9). Even the governor of the Bank of England has entertained the idea that such an 'end of money' could render central banks redundant (King 1999). As we shall see, these conjectures are as profoundly mistaken as earlier monetarism, and the error stems just as directly from the same confusion over the nature of money. To identify *forms* of money and their *circulation* with the quality of 'moneyness' is to misunderstand the phenomenon. It is a basic category error, which, as we shall see, has persisted since the classical Greek commodity theory of metallic coinage. This misidentification of money has produced enormous analytical difficulties and quite bizarre intellectual contortion in orthodox economics' treatment of the so-called dematerialization of money since the late nineteenth century.

Yet, the other social and historical sciences have fared no better in the analysis of money. As a direct consequence of the division of intellectual labour in the social sciences after the methodological dispute (*Methodenstreit*) of the early part of the twentieth century, they have been unable to provide a more satisfactory account. In the mistaken belief that it is essentially an 'economic' phenomenon, the other social sciences have abnegated all responsibility for the study of money, by either simply ignoring it or uncritically accepting orthodox economic analysis (Ingham 1998). Modern sociology is almost entirely concerned with very general descriptions of the *consequences* of money for 'modern' society (Giddens 1990), its 'social meanings' (Zelizer 1994), and, more indirectly, with the Marxist problem of 'finance capital'. As Randall Collins (1979) perceptively observed, modern sociology appears to have neglected money because it is not 'sociological enough'. Money's existence has been taken for granted. A recent revival of interest in the subject only serves to highlight the longer-term neglect (Dodd 1994; Zelizer 1994; Leyshon and Thrift 1997; Ingham 1996a, 1999, 2000a, 2000b, 2001, 2002; Hart 2000). There are, as we shall see, a very few notable exceptions (for example, Carruthers and Babb 1996). Aside from reiterating the obvious importance of 'trust', sociology has not addressed the problem of the actual nature of money, how it functions and how it is produced and maintained as a *social institution*. For example, an otherwise exemplary and important work, Fligstein's *The Architecture of Markets: An Economic Sociology of the Twenty-First Century Capitalist Societies*, (2001), does not contain any discussion of what I shall argue is the pivotal institution of modern capitalism. There is not even an entry for 'money' in the index.

It is very significant that the analysis of money was a prominent issue in the *Methodenstreit* that shaped the disciplinary divisions in the social sciences in the late nineteenth and early twentieth centuries. As we have noted, Schumpeter referred at the time to the incompatibility of the theories of money that were held by the opposing sides. As we shall see, the 'claim' or 'credit' theories of money had existed, at least since the fifteenth century, as alternatives to the dominant Aristotelian commodity conception. They were favoured and developed further by the historians and sociologists who were scorned by the economic theorists in the *Methodenstreit*. Unfortunately, sociology was subsequently unable to develop this important early work. Picking up the threads a century later, what follows in this book may be seen, in part, as an exercise in the 'intellectual archaeology' of the social sciences. But of course this can only be the beginning; the aim must be to construct an adequate theory of the nature of money as a social phenomenon.

An Outline of Contents

A theory of money should provide satisfactory answers to three closely related questions: What is money? Where does it come from, or how does it get into society? How does it get or lose its value? Part I examines the answers given by the main traditions in the social sciences. Chapter 1, 'Money as a Commodity and "Neutral" Symbol of

Commodities', outlines the development of the analysis of money to be found in mainstream or orthodox economics. Here I elaborate my contention that this understanding of money is deficient, because it is quite unable to specify money – that is to say, how money differs from other commodities. It follows that if the question of what money is cannot be answered, then the other two – where it comes from and how it gets or loses value – are also likely to be unsatisfactory. Indeed, the question of how money gets into society has been dismissed as irrelevant by one branch of orthodoxy. As Milton Friedman famously remarked, economics might just as well assume that money is dropped by helicopter and then proceed with the analysis of the effects of different quantities on the price level. The quantity theory of money is deeply infused in both the academic and the common-sense answer to the third question of how money gets or loses its value. But I shall argue that there are good grounds for challenging the presumption of direct, linear causation between the quantity of money and the level of prices. Chapter 2, 'Abstract Value, Credit and the State', attempts to draw together the strands in the alternative conception of money which Schumpeter identified and which have occupied what Keynes referred to as the 'underworld' of monetary analysis. This account has two aims. The first is to make heterodoxy's commonalities more explicit and to trace their linkages. The second is to make more explicit what I take to be the inherently sociological nature of these nominalist, credit and state theories of money. Chapter 3, 'Money in Sociological Theory', is not a comprehensive survey. Rather, I wish, first, to illustrate deleterious effects of the narrowly economic conception of money (both neoclassical and Marxist) on modern sociology and, secondly, to rebalance the exegetical accounts of Simmel and Weber on money. Their work on the actual process of the production of money, as opposed to its effects and consequences, was informed by the Historical School's analysis. I intend to restore and use it. These extended analytical critiques form the basis for chapter 4 in which the 'Fundamentals of a Theory of Money' are sketched. This is organized in relation to the three basic questions referred to above. In effect, I shall attempt to reclaim the study of money for sociology. But it is not my intention simply to perpetuate the existing disciplinary divisions; nor do I advocate that a 'sociological imperialism' replace economics' hegemony in these matters. Throughout this work, 'sociological' is construed in what is today a rather old-fashioned Weberian manner in which, as Collins (1986) has persuasively argued, the social/cultural, economic and political 'realms' of reality are each, at one and the same time, amenable to 'social/cultural', 'economic' and, above all, 'political' analysis.

Moreover, by a 'sociology of money' I intend more than the self-evident assertion that money is produced socially, is accepted by convention, is underpinned by trust, has definite social and cultural consequences and so on. Rather, I shall argue that money *is* itself a social relation; that is to say, money is a 'claim' or 'credit' that is constituted by social relations that *exist independently of the production and exchange of commodities*. Regardless of any *form* it might take, money is essentially a provisional 'promise' to pay, whose 'moneyness', as an 'institutional fact', is assigned by a description conferred by an abstract money of account. Money is a social relation of credit and debt denominated in a money of account. In the most basic sense, the possessor of money is owed goods. But money also represents a claim or credit against the issuer – monarch, state, bank and so on. Money has to be 'issued'. And something can only be issued *as money* if it is capable of cancelling *any* debt incurred by the issuer. As we shall see, orthodox economics works from different premises, and typically argues that if an individual in a barter exchange does not have the pig to exchange for the two ducks, it would be possible to issue a document of indebtedness for one pig. This could be held by the co-trader and later handed back for cancellation on receipt of a real pig. Is the 'pig IOU' money? Contrary to orthodox economic theory, it will be argued that it is not, and, moreover, that such hypothetical barter could not produce money. Rather, I will argue that for money to be the most exchangeable commodity, it must first be constituted as *transferable debt* based on an abstract money of account. More concretely, a state issues money, as payment for goods and services, in the form of a promise to accept it in payment of taxes. A bank issues notes, or allows a cheque to be drawn against it as a claim, which it 'promises' to accept in payment by its debtor. Money cannot be said to exist without the simultaneous existence of a debt that it can discharge. But note that this is not a particular debt, but rather *any* debt within a given monetary space. Money may *appear* to get its ability to buy commodities from its equivalence with them, as implied by the idea of the purchasing power of money as measured by a price index. But this misses out a crucial step: the *origin* of the power of money in the promise between the issuer and the user of money – that is, in the issuer's self-declared debt, as outlined above. The claim or credit must also be enforceable.[6] Monetary societies are held together by networks of credit/debt relations that are underpinned and constituted by sovereignty (Aglietta and Orlean 1998). Money *is* a form of sovereignty, and as such it cannot be understood without reference to an authority.

This preliminary sketch of an alternative sociological analysis of money's properties and logical conditions of existence informs the historical and empirical analysis in Part II. Having rejected orthodox economics' conjectural explanations of money's historical origins, an alternative is presented in chapter 5, 'The Historical Origins of Money and its Pre-capitalist Forms'. First, the origin of money is not sought by looking for the early use of tradable commodities that might have developed into proto-currencies, but rather, following the great Cambridge numismatist Philip Grierson, by looking behind forms of money for the very idea of a measure of value (money of account). This again takes up and builds on the nineteenth-century Historical School's legacy, and adds from more recent scholarship. The second part of the chapter, which discusses early coinage and its development to its sophistication in the Roman Empire, has two aims. The first is to cast doubt on the almost universally accepted axiom in orthodox economic analysis that the quantity of precious metal in coins was directly related to the price of commodities – that is to say, for example, that debasing the coinage caused inflation. The second theme resurrects another contentious issue from the *Methodenstreit* – the question of whether the ancient world was 'capitalist'. At the time, the economic theorists argued that their explanatory models applied universally across time and space; 'economic man' and his practices were to be found throughout history. The Historical School, including Weber, argued otherwise, and I elaborate their case with a more monetary interpretation of pre-capitalist history. Chapter 6, 'The Development of Capitalist Credit-Money', pursues the theme by arguing that capitalism's distinctive structural character is to be found in the production of *credit-money*. Capitalism is founded on the social mechanism whereby private debts are 'monetized' in the banking system. Here the act of lending creates deposits of money. This did not occur in the so-called banks of the ancient and classical worlds. Aside from its extended application of the theoretical framework, this chapter is also intended as a correction of the standard sociological account of the rise of capitalism. Here there is an overwhelming tendency to adhere to a loosely Marxist understanding in terms of the relations of *production* combined with a cultural element taken from *The Protestant Ethic and the Spirit of Capitalism*. One-sided emphasis on this book has led to a quite grotesque distortion of Weber's work (Ingham 2003). Chapter 7, 'The Production of Capitalist Credit-Money', involves a partial break with the historical narrative, to present a tentative 'ideal type' of the contemporary structure of social and political relations that produce and constitute capitalist credit-money. Again, I attempt to draw out the implicit sociology in some of the more heterodox economic accounts of the empirical 'stylized facts' involved in credit-money creation. As far as I am aware, no such analysis exists, and this chapter constitutes little more than a pointer to future research. Attention is drawn to the 'performative' role of orthodox economic theory in the social production of the 'fiction of an invariant standard' (Mirowski 1991). Case studies of three types of monetary disorder comprise chapter 8. The purpose is to illustrate the difference between the orthodox economic conception of money and the one being presented here. Orthodoxy has difficulty in accounting for monetary disorder, because of its commitment to the notions of money's neutrality and of long-run equilibrium as the normal state of affairs. If, however, money is seen as a social relation that expresses a balance of social and political forces, and there is no presumption that such a balance entails a normal equilibrium, then monetary disorder and instability are to be expected. The rise and fall of the 'great inflation' of the 1970s, the protracted Japanese deflation of the 1990s, and Argentina's chronic inability to produce viable money are examined. Chapter 9 again provides empirical examples to illustrate the approach. The first is a critique of the many recent conjectures that the impact of technical change (e-money, etc.) might bring about the 'end of money'. These are the result of the fundamental and widespread category error whereby 'moneyness' is identified with a particular 'form' of money. The second looks at the claims that local barter schemes, using information technology, might significantly encroach or even supersede formal money. Thirdly, the different analytical approaches to the eurozone single currency experiment are examined. A short Conclusion attempts to tie the argument and analysis together.

1

Money as a Commodity and 'Neutral' Symbol of Commodities

There can be no unerring measure of either length, of weight, of time or of *value* unless there be some object *in nature* to which the standard itself can be referred.

David Ricardo in Sraffa 1951: 401, emphasis added

Monetary facts...have no direct significance for economic welfare. In this sense money clearly is a veil. It does not comprise any of the essentials of economic life.

Pigou 1949: 14

[E]ven in the most advanced industrial economies, if we strip exchange down to its barest essentials and peel off the obscuring layer of money, we find that trade between individuals or nations largely boils down to barter.

Samuelson 1973: 55

The late nineteenth-century theorists who established the method-ology of modern economics held to one version or another of the commodity theory of money. 'Money proper' referred to either pre-cious metal or its convertible paper symbol. Money was essentially material and tangible; it could be stored and passed from hand to hand – it circulated. The accepted theory of money was the theory of the gold standard. Money in this sense was distinguished from credit, regardless of whether the latter was understood as the practice of the book clearance of debits and credits in the banking system or the issue of circulating credit instruments – such as bills of exchange and promissory notes.

But the theory at the heart of the new economic science was in fact very old. Many of the most influential seventeenth- and eighteenth-century political economists – Locke, Petty, Hume, Cantillon – subscribed to the essentials of Aristotle's explanation of the evolution and functions of money. A little later, 'Adam Smith substantially ratified it' (Schumpeter 1994 [1954]: 290). Late nineteenth-century economists simply incorporated the well-established theory of precious metal coinage into their theories of marginal utility and supply and demand.

Moreover, despite the subsequent disappearance of all forms of precious metal money (either as actual currency or as a non-circulating standard of value), the fundamental assumptions of modern orthodox economic thinking remain grounded in this earliest known theory of the origins and functions of money. I shall argue that this intellectual provenance is the root cause of the significant deficiencies in mainstream economic thinking on the nature of money. Aristotle had produced an *ethical critique* of the pursuit of 'value' as an end in itself in the form of money, as opposed to the satisfaction of wants and the gaining of utility by the production and exchange of commodities.[1] This critique was derived from his conception of an idealized 'natural' economy that was neither capitalist nor market-based. He was concerned with how money *ought* to be used in a society whose 'moral ethos was unfavourable to the values of commerce' (Meikle 2000: 167). It is therefore not surprising that theories implicitly based on his analysis have proved to be a very poor guide to the money of the modern capitalist world.

The Meta-theoretical Foundations of Orthodox Monetary Analysis

The theorems of modern economic micro-economics that deductively model the decision making of rational utility-maximizing individuals and the exchanges between them are derived from a stylized conception of a simple trading economy in which exchange ratios of commodities express their 'real' values. The model comprises *object–object relations* (exchange ratios between commodities, or the 'production function') and *individual agent–object relations* (individual acts of utility calculation, or the 'utility function'). (For similar distinctions, see Ganssmann 1988; Weber 1978: 66–9.) Together, *object–object* and *agent–object* relations constitute what Schumpeter described as the 'real' economy.

> Real analysis proceeds from the principle that all the essential phenomena of economic life are capable of being described in terms of goods and services, of decisions about them, and of relations between them. Money enters the picture only in the modest role of a technical device that has been adopted in order to facilitate transactions ... so long as it functions normally, it does not affect the economic process, which behaves in the same way as it would in a barter economy: this is essentially what the concept of Neutral Money implies. Thus, money has been called a 'garb' or 'veil' of the things that really matter ... Not only can it be discarded whenever we are analyzing the fundamental features of the economic process but it must be discarded just as a veil must be drawn aside if we are to see the face behind it. Accordingly, money prices must give way to the exchange ratios between the commodities that are the really important thing 'behind' money prices. (Schumpeter 1994 [1954]: 277)[2]

Other than the 'higgling' to arrive at a mutually agreed exchange, *agent–agent*, or *social, relations* form no part of the model (Ganssmann 1988). It is assumed that a continuous process of 'higgling' is able to transform the myriad bilateral exchange ratios between all the different commodities, based on individual preferences, into a single price for any uniform good. Money, in the form of a highly liquid commodity, may be introduced into the model to 'lubricate' the process of exchange. As a commodity, the medium of exchange can have an exchange ratio with other commodities. Or, as a symbol, it can *directly* represent real commodities. It is in this sense that money is a 'neutral veil' that has no efficacy other than to overcome the 'inconveniences of barter' which, in the late nineteenth-century formulation, result from the absence of a 'double coincidence of wants'. In his influential *Money and the Mechanism of Exchange* (1875), Jevons illustrated these deficiencies with two examples. The first tells how a French opera singer, Mlle Zelie, on tour in the South Pacific, had a contract to receive payment of one third of receipts. After one concert, her share comprised quantities of pigs, turkeys, chickens, coconuts and other tropical fruits. She could not consume them and, instead, provided a feast for the local population. In the second illustration, Jevons recounts how Wallace, the naturalist and protagonist of evolutionary theory, had to go hungry in the Malay Archipelago during the 1850s. Despite a general abundance of available food, Wallace's party, on occasion, did not have anything that was acceptable in barter for it.

As we have noted, two slightly different versions of the basic orthodox conception of the medium of exchange may be distinguished. The
medium of exchange may be either an actual commodity that maintains an exchange rate with other commodities or, as in Walrasian
general equilibrium theory, a symbol of a 'representative' commodity
or 'basket' of commodities. The Walrasian device of an arbitrarily
assigned *numéraire* (symbolic representation of existing commodity
values) enables the modelling of an exchange economy in which the
market 'clears' (Allington 1987) – that is to say, an equilibrium where
prices are reached at which no goods remain unsold. Further analytical assumptions of instantaneous – that is, 'timeless' – multilateral
trades under conditions of certainty and perfect information are made
in order render this 'general equilibrium' amenable to a precise mathematical expression. But these conditions also render money redundant – particularly as a store of value and means of final payment, or
settlement. As a leading exponent of such theorizing explains:

> The most serious challenge that the existence of money poses to the
> theorist is this: the best model of the economy cannot find room for it.
> The best-developed model is, of course, the Arrow–Debreu version of a
> Walrasian general equilibrium. A world in which all conceivable con-
> tingent future contracts are known neither needs nor wants intrinsically
> worthless money. (Hahn 1982: 1)

In Walras's equation, the *numéraire* is not explained; rather, it is
simply introduced along with the 'auctioneer' in order to render the
model operational – that is to say, to get the bidding started.[3] But
money does no more than lubricate the transaction process. It is not
an autonomous force – it does not make a difference to the level of
economic activity and welfare; it merely enables us, according to Mill,
to do more easily that which we could do without it.

This conception of money runs as a continuous thread through the
development of orthodox economic analysis. Hume's essay *Of Money*
(1752) more or less paraphrases Aristotle: 'Money is not, properly
speaking, one of the objects of commerce, but only an instrument . . . It
is none of the wheels of trade: It is the oil which renders the motion of
the wheels smooth and easy' (quoted in Jackson 1995: 3). In the late
nineteenth century, Alfred Marshall affirmed the orthodoxy that
money is no more than a device by which the 'gigantic system of barter'
is carried out. As the third epigraph to this chapter tells us, one of the
most influential economists of all time would have us believe that
money is an 'obscuring layer' over the economic exchange in modern
capitalism that 'largely boils down to barter' (Samuelson 1973: 55).[4]

Despite money's status as a 'neutral veil', the fact that it was seen as a commodity enabled the new economic methodology to provide a theory of its origins as a medium of exchange. Menger's (1892) rational choice analysis of the evolution of money remains the basis for today's neoclassical explanations (Dowd 2000; Klein and Selgin 2000). Money is the unintended consequence of individual economic rationality. In order to maximize their barter options, traders hold stocks of the most tradable commodities, which, consequently, become *media of exchange* – beans, cigarettes.[5] Coinage is explained with the further conjecture that precious metals have additional advantageous properties – such as durability, divisibility, portability, etc. Metal is weighed and minted into uniform pieces, and the commodity becomes money. (Thus, the commodity theory is sometimes referred to as the 'metallist' theory of money (see Schumpeter 1994 [1954]; Goodhart 1998).) In short, all orthodox economic accounts of money are *commodity-exchange* theories. Both money's historical origins and logical conditions of existence are explained as the outcome of economic exchange in the market that evolves as a result of individual utility maximization.

Quantity Theory and the Value of Money

By the mid-nineteenth century, four interrelated propositions were characteristic of classical economic monetary thought. First, money's existence 'does not interfere with the operation of any laws of value' (J. S. Mill, *Principles of Political Economy* (1871), quoted in Laidler 1991: 9).[6] Second, the value of money is determined by the value of the precious metals it contains, which can be explained under the rubric of the theories of relative prices and costs of production. The value of money 'is determined ... temporarily by supply and demand, permanently and on the average by costs of production' (Mill, quoted in Laidler 1991: 10). Third, variation in the quantity of money causes price movements, and not vice versa. Fourth, the existence of bank liabilities in the form of notes and bills are acknowledged as part of the money supply only if they are convertible into gold and/or silver. Other increasingly important forms of credit – such as bills of exchange and promissory notes – were usually simply left out of the reckoning. This was achieved, as I have already noted, by the evasive, inconsistent and unclear distinction between 'credit' and 'currency' (that is, 'cash in hand', or 'money proper').

Eventually, as we shall see, the incoherence of the efforts to maintain the distinction between money and credit proved to be the most problematic for orthodox analysis. But in the second half of the nineteenth century, concern was focused on tension in classical economics between two explanations of the determination of value – that is, in terms of either the immediate interplay of supply and demand for money, or the ultimate costs of its production. The details need not concern us here, but most mid-nineteenth-century economists were agreed that the values of gold and silver are ultimately governed, like those of all other commodities, by the costs of production (Laidler 1991: 31). By the late nineteenth century, however, there had been a decisive move away from this theorem. As Marshall pointed out in his *Evidence to the Indian Currency Committee* (1899), gold and silver were so durable that a year's supply is never more than a very small part of the total stock of circulating coins (Laidler 1991: 56). That is to say, the 'velocity' of money meant that its value would not conform closely to its costs of production. Increasing emphasis was given to the *individual demand* for money, which, it was argued, ultimately determined its aggregate stock in the economy. The demand for 'cash balances' depended upon the balance between the convenience obtained and the risk avoided (Pigou, quoted in Laidler 1991: 63). That is to say, the demand for money depended on its 'marginal utility' for the individual.[7]

Theoretically, this meant that the questions of what money is and how it actually gets into the economy were subordinated to the question of *how much* of it is *demanded* at any time. The empirical facts of its issue from mints and banks were obvious; but precisely how this happened was not considered to be theoretically relevant. Money was called forth by demand, but the specification of the actual *transmission mechanism* whereby demand induced increases in the quantity of money and, in turn, raised the level of prices remained a matter of *conjecture*. From a strictly theoretical standpoint, late nineteenth-century monetary theory was concerned with the *consequences* and not the causes of variations in the supply of money. These might stem from gold discoveries or unsound inconvertible paper money that was to be avoided, such as the infamous *assignats* of Revolutionary France and the 'greenbacks' of the American Civil War.[8]

'Quantity theory' received its classic exposition in Fisher's *The Purchasing Power of Money* (1911). By defining money as both notes and coins (M) and current account bank deposits (M_1), Fisher moved some way towards taking bank money into account; but in accord with the general approach, the question of the origin of the supply of bank deposits was left indeterminate. He simply asserted that 'under any given conditions of industry and civilisation, deposits tend to hold a *fixed or normal* ratio to money in circulation' (Fisher 1911: 151). Fisher's starting-point was the Cambridge 'equation of exchange', as

formulated by Edgeworth (1887) and others. This expressed, in alge-
braic form, the balance of the quantity of money and the price level as
a result of all individual exchanges of money for goods over the period
of a year. It was one of the first mathematical models of the 'real'
economy in which, as we have seen, money is *not* distinguished from
other goods.

The equation is saved from tautology by the addition of two further
variables which were allowed to *vary independently* of the quantity of
money. These are velocity of circulation (V) and transaction volumes
(T). In his hands the quantity equation was written as follows:

$$MV + M^1V^1 = \Sigma pQ = PT$$

Money is notes and coin (M) and chequable deposits (M^1); Vs are
their velocities of circulation; p is the money price of any good; Q is its
quantity; so P is the general price level. An index of the ps and T, the
volume of the transactions, is an index of the Qs. All Fisher's efforts
were directed to demonstrating that *causation could not run from prices
to money*, and, as the equation was logically true, it had, therefore, to
operate in the opposite direction. In short, MV (money and its velocity) caused the level of PT (prices and transactions). He rejected
outright any explanations of the *autonomy* of rising prices as the result,
for example, of pressure from 'industrial and labour combinations'
(1911: 179). But the transmission mechanism from quantity to price
was not demonstrated, nor was it supported by empirical data. Fisher
simply asserted that 'high prices at any *time* do not cause an increase
in money at that time; for money, so to speak flows *away* from that
time . . . people will seek to avoid paying money at the high prices and
wait until the prices are lower' (1911: 173, original italics). Of course,
the opposite might also occur. One could equally well argue, to
continue with Fisher's metaphor, that money might 'flow' towards
the prices in order to avoid the impact of future price rises, as argued
in later orthodox economic models of hyperinflation, where individual
rationality causes this unwelcome unintended consequence. In his
review, Keynes observed that Fisher paid insufficient attention to
the process that starts prices rising *in the first place* (Keynes 1983:
377). We shall return to this important question.

Despite the inexorable growth of bank credit-money, orthodox
academic economists clung, with increasing desperation, to the anachronistic theory. Their model of money supply was, in effect, an
empirical generalization of a naturally constrained supply of a metallic
monetary base provided by a central authority (the mint) that was

outside the market. That is to say, in the terminology of the late twentieth century, it was 'exogenous'.[9] The retention of the commodity theory and its assumptions was achieved by maintaining a sharp distinction between money-proper and credit. The credit supply was seen as the top of a large inverted pyramid on the narrower base of the gold standard.

The direct question of whether credit was money was studiously avoided in orthodox circles, but given its pivotal importance in capitalist economies, credit was gradually incorporated into orthodox quantity analysis. However, this merely exposed the contradictions and inconsistencies in the commodity theory. For example, most orthodox economists of the early twentieth century got little further than seeing credit as a means of economizing on money-proper. But they all stopped short of the idea that bank loans might *create* credit-*money* in the form of deposits that were relatively autonomous with respect to the stock of precious metal money. Credit could not easily be accommodated in the concept of the 'real' economy as a structure of exchange ratios (object–object relations) based on the preferences of individual utility maximizers (agent–object relations). The creation of money by the creation of the *social relation* of debt (agent–agent relations) was utterly incompatible with the methodology of orthodox neoclassical economics. And the extension of this idea – to be considered in the following chapters – that *all* forms of money, including commodity-money, are constituted by a social relation of credit was anathema.

An Analytical Critique of Commodity Theory

As we shall see in Part II, the historical record does not support the orthodox theory of money's sequential development from barter to commodity-money to 'virtual' money (see also Wray 1998, 2003). Here we are concerned with an internal, or analytical, critique of the theory.

The specificity of money

As I noted in the Introduction, the orthodox theory of money, as a medium of exchange, is unable uniquely to specify money except in terms of a purely *logical description*. Money is specified as the commodity that can be traded for *all* other commodities (Clower 1984 [1967]: 86).[10] In Menger's conjectural history, money evolves from the rational use of the most tradable commodity as a medium of exchange that maximizes trading options. However, he realized that base metal coins and inconvertible paper money broke this link. Why, Menger (1892) asked, should individuals be ready to exchange goods for 'worthless' little metal disks or paper symbols?

Subsequently, neoclassical economics has tried to resolve the problem and establish the 'micro-foundations' of money by showing that holding (non-commodity) money reduces transaction costs for the individual (for example, Jones 1976; Dowd 2000, Klein and Selgin 2000). However, these arguments cannot explain the existence of money, and, moreover, they express the logical circularity of neoclassical economics' methodological individualism. It is only 'advantageous for any given agent to mediate his transactions by money *provided that all other agents do likewise*' (Hahn 1987: 26). To state the sociologically obvious: the advantages of money for the individual presuppose the existence of money as an *institution* in which its 'moneyness' is established.

Despite its absence from the model of the 'real' economy, the obvious fact that money is used as a store of abstract value led to efforts to accommodate this function in orthodox micro-economic analysis. These have been entirely unsuccessful. For example, the very title of Samuelson's classic paper – 'An exact consumption-loan model of interest with or without the social contrivance of money' (1966 [1958]) – betrays the logical problem. This analysis of money as a means for the intergenerational transfer of value was completely unable to specify why money, as opposed to any alternative financial asset, performs this role. Why, he asked, are stocks and bonds not money? Samuelson correctly observed that money could not be uniquely specified as a store of value; but he was unable to explain this function of money within the framework of orthodox microeconomic methodology. The fact that money has proved to be a relatively poor store of value – especially during periods in the twentieth century – merely adds to the difficulties for neoclassical economic analysis. A huge literature has resulted from the efforts to resolve the problem; but it would appear to be incapable of a solution within this school. Micro-economic methodology becomes locked into exactly the same kind of circularity that we saw above in the explanation of money's existence as a medium of exchange. With the tenet that all phenomena must be explained as a result of their utility for the maximizing individual, orthodox economics cannot answer the question it poses. Is money a means of final payment (settlement) because it is a store of value? Or, conversely, is it a store of value because it is accepted as a means of debt settlement? As we shall see, the only way to break the circularity is to move from the analytical confines of the

methodological individualism of micro-economics and the model of
the 'real' economy.

Money of account

The fundamental problem in economic orthodoxy, from which all the
other difficulties stem, is the misunderstanding of *money of account*.
Medium of exchange is the key function, and it is assumed that all the
others follow from it. The market spontaneously produces a transac-
tions-cost-efficient medium of exchange that becomes the standard of
value and numerical money of account. Coins are said to have evolved
from *weighing* pieces of precious metal that were cut from bars and,
after standardization, *counted*. Alternatively, a standard commodity
or 'bundle' of commodities, *with a given value*, acts as the *numéraire*.

   The nub of the issue, as we have noted, is whether money of account
can be convincingly shown to be the spontaneous outcome of 'truck
barter and exchange', as economic orthodoxy implies. In other words,
can money of account be deduced from the existence of a medium of
exchange? This conjecture is illustrated with examples such as the use
of cigarettes in prisons, not merely as media of exchange that maximize trading opportunities, but also as a unit of account, in which
offers of goods are priced. (For the classic participant observation
study of a World War II POW camp, see Radford 1945.) But it is not
clear that cigarettes are actually a unit of account, as opposed to being
the commodity most in demand. The fact that non-smokers were
willing to offer their goods for cigarettes does not make them, in
Keynes's terms, anything more than a 'convenient medium of exchange on the spot' (Keynes 1930: 3). Two points are relevant. First,
it was the atypical conditions of repeated 'spot' exchanges in the small-
scale, closed prison camp economy, with few commodities, that gave
cigarettes their stable exchange ratio. In such a relatively stable population, all the traders' preferences were sufficiently well known for the
non-smoking trader to learn the likely exchange ratios and that he
would not have to hold a stock of cigarettes for long. Second, orthodox analyses argue that the *market exchange-value* of cigarettes produced a stable unit of account, and that precious metallic standards
are analogous (Dowd 2000: 143–4). But unless the exchange-value of
a cigarette was fixed in terms of another linchpin commodity, its
exchange-value would vary from trade to trade for the same commodity. Consequently it would not function as money. For the cigarette to
be a money of account, as opposed to the commodity that could be
traded for all others, its value would have to be stabilized in some
other way in relation to another commodity. (As we shall see, the gold

standard was a *promise*, made in an abstract unit of account, to redeem a note for an amount of the precious metal. The exchange rate between the two was *fixed by an authority*, not determined by the market.)

Complex multilateral indirect exchange – that is, an authentic market – presupposes a money of account. Even with a relatively small number of commodities, barter exchange produces myriad diverse exchange ratios. Without further assumptions, it is difficult to envisage how a money of account could emerge from myriad bilateral barter exchange ratios based upon subjective preferences. One hundred goods could possibly yield 4,950 exchange rates (Davies 1996: 15). How could discrete barter exchange ratios of, say, 3 tins of peaches: 1 cigarette, or 5 tins: 1 cigarette, and so on, produce a single unit of account? The conventional economic answer that a 'cigarette standard' emerges spontaneously involves a circular argument. That is, a *single* 'cigarette standard' cannot be the equilibrium price of cigarettes established by supply and demand because, in the absence of a money of account, cigarettes would continue to have multiple and variable exchange-values. A genuine market which produces a single price for cigarettes requires a money of account – that is, a stable yardstick for measuring value. As opposed to the *commodity* cigarette, the *monetary* cigarette in any cigarette *standard* would be an *abstract* cigarette. The very *idea* of money, which is to say, of abstract accounting for value, is *logically anterior and historically prior to market exchange*. If the process of exchange could not have produced the abstract concept of money of account, how did it originate? The question is actually at the very heart of a problem that distinguishes economics from sociology. Can an *inter*-subjective scale of value (money of account) emerge from myriad subjective preferences? As we noted in the Introduction, the question of money is at the centre of the general question in Parsons's sociological critique of economic theory – although it has not been seen in this light. From its starting-point of individual subjective preferences, utilitarian theory cannot explain social order (Parsons 1937).

Capitalism and credit: the 'real' economy and the 'natural' rate of interest

The model of the natural barter economy with its 'neutral veil' of money is singularly inappropriate for understanding the capitalist monetary system. In the 'real' economy, money exists *only* as a *medium* for the gaining of utility through the *exchange* of commodities (commodity → money → commodity, or C-M-C$_1$). It models the 'village fair' in which capitalist financing of production does not occur (Minsky 1982). In the 'real' economy of continuous spot transactions, there is no investment in Keynes's 'money wage or entrepreneurial economy' (Smithin 2003: 3–4). Capitalism, it will be argued, is distinguished by the entrepreneurial use of credit-money produced by banks to take speculative positions regarding the production of commodities for future sale, or with regard to fluctuations in the value of money itself. Either M (bank credit-money) $\rightarrow$ M-C-M$_1$; or M (bank credit-money) $\rightarrow$ M-M$_1$. (Aristotle and, of course, Marx deplored both forms of exchange.)

The existence of credit was obviously recognized by the early twentieth-century orthodox theorists, but, as we have seen, could not be accommodated readily within the 'real' analysis model of a barter economy. Wicksell's work was the most accomplished attempt to do this, and continues to provide some of mainstream economics' core theoretical assumptions (see Smithin 2003). His analysis is based on a comparison of two abstract models – a 'pure cash economy' and a 'pure credit economy'. In the latter 'there is no need for any money at all . . . neither in the form of coin (except perhaps for small change) nor in the form of notes, but where all domestic payments are effected by means of the Giro system and bookkeeping transfers' (Wicksell 1962 [1898]: 70). He doubted that such a state of affairs would ever occur; but it was a logical possibility with which the commodity theory was unable to cope. (Apart from any other consideration, how, in the hypothetical absence of an actual 'stock' of commodity-based money, were changes in the price level to be explained?)

Most contemporary thinking held that, in a cash economy, the demand for money loans was determined by the supply of a stock of loanable money, mediated by the rate of interest. But in the 'pure credit economy' there could not be a money rate of interest that was determined by the existence of the banks' actual stocks of cash, for none would exist. Consequently, Wicksell argued, in accordance with the underlying meta-theory of the 'real' economy, that in a pure credit economy the interest rate would have to be the 'real' one. This would still be determined by the normal mechanism of supply and demand for loans; but in this case these could not be in money, but rather 'in the form of real capital goods' (1962 [1898]: 102). In the absence of actual stocks of money, the 'natural rate' of interest is that which 'corresponds to the expected yield on the newly created capital' (Wicksell 1935 [1915]: 193), which in turn depends on its marginal productivity (Wicksell 1907; see Laidler 1991: 130).[11]

Wicksell held firmly to the basic 'real' analysis tenet that the rate of interest for money was not an independent force in the economy.

Therefore, as Ricardo had argued, the question of the manipulation of the rate of interest to the advantage of the owners and controllers of money simply did not arise (see Smithin 2003: ch. 6). In Wicksell's 'thought experiment' borrowers and lenders bartered, without the existence of money and banks, to produce a 'natural rate' of interest. He then moved to a closer approximation of actual capitalist economies by introducing four typical roles: entrepreneurs, labour, banks and capitalists (the source of loans to entrepreneurs). Their relations and the economy are set in motion with the *assumption* that the contractual rate of money interest charged by banks is equal to the natural rate. In essence, the natural rate determines the money rate, which in turn determines the quantity of money (both cash and credit-money). But this hypothetical causal sequence is based entirely on the axioms of the theory of the 'real' economy, and is nowhere explained or, more importantly, described empirically. 'The money rate of interest ... is always *tending* to coincide with an ever changing natural rate' (Wicksell 1962 [1898]: 117, emphasis added). However, the tendency is left as an unexplained conjecture.

It should be noted that Wicksell's pure credit economy describes only *one* of the two forms that credit-money might take. He was concerned only with the giro system for the settlement of transactions of debit and credit – that is, book transfer between accounts. But capitalist banks are not merely intermediaries in a giro system; they also produce credit-money through lending and the creation of deposits. As Schumpeter explained, banks are introduced into 'real' analysis only as neutral cost-reducing intermediaries. They place the aggregated savings of many small depositors at the disposal of borrowers of money-capital. In classical theory, 'deposits make loans'. Armed with the common-sense cloakroom analogy, the eminent English economist Cannan defended classical orthodoxy, scornfully dismissing the converse notion that loans make deposits (Cannan, quoted in Schumpeter 1994 [1954]: 1113). The lending of coats left with an attendant for safe keeping, he argued, does not involve the 'creation' of more coats. Before the owners could use them, they would have to be returned. But, as Schumpeter points out, this is precisely what does *not* happen in capitalist banking. Here, depositors and borrowers have simultaneous use of the 'same' money, and, furthermore, new lending creates new money (Schumpeter 1994 [1954]: 1113–14). This notion that 'loans make deposits' (of money) is explored in the next chapter.

In short, for Wicksell, the money rate of interest was a *direct* function of the capacity of productive capital. But, as Schumpeter implied, 'real' analysis is unable to provide an adequate theoretical account of capitalist financing without recourse to considerable intellectual contortion. In this model, 'saving and investment must be interpreted to mean saving of some real factors of production . . . such as buildings, machines, raw materials; and though "in the form of money", it is these physical capital goods that are "really" lent when an industrial borrower arranges for a loan' (Schumpeter 1994 [1954]: 277). As we shall see, it was precisely this impasse that Keynes sought to break with his early heterodox work, *A Treatise on Money* (1930). This alternative view, to be explored later, sees the money rate of interest as influenced in a relatively autonomous way by the operation of the financial system itself. In Keynes's rather obscure phrase, 'the marginal efficiency of capital is determined by forces partly appropriate to itself' (Keynes 1973: 103).

The Persistence of Orthodoxy

Towards the end of the capitalist crises of the 1930s and during the so-called Golden Age after World War II, both theoretical and practical monetary orthodoxy was moved off centre stage – or, at least, had to share it with Keynesian economic theory. Keynes's own *rapprochement* with orthodoxy and the general accommodation of his work within a mainstream 'neoclassical synthesis' need not concern us here (see Rogers and Rymes 2000; Smithin 2003). Some aspects will be considered subsequently; here I shall simply indicate how the 'meta-theory' of the 'real economy' and the axioms of quantity theory continue to inform both academic theory and the practice of monetary policy. (The practical implications of this persistence are discussed in Part II, in chapters 7–9.)

Monetarism

The need to deal with the inflation of the 1970s brought to the fore Friedman's restatement of Fisher's orthodox quantity theory, and his empirical work with Schwartz became the focal point of the 'monetarist' revival (see Smithin 1996). It was conceded that changes in the supply of money could influence the level of economic activity, as they believed events had shown. But monetarists argued in time-honoured fashion that this could only be a *short-run* effect. In the long run, any 'money illusion' would wear off as the 'real' values of the economy reasserted themselves and money resumed its 'natural' neutrality (Friedman 1969). They held to the Wicksellian assumption that in the long run changes in the *money* rate of interest could not affect the *natural* rate. But short-run divergence between the two could create serious economic problems – most notably, inflation.

Without any violation of the 'real' economy model, it could be argued that states, analytically outside the economy, perform a 'public goods' role by providing sound money. It is only when they exceed this function and pursue their own interests that economic dislocation occurs – for example, when sovereigns increase the profits of *seignorage* by debasing precious metal coins, or governments pursue inflationary policies to reduce the burden of state debt. But, most importantly, as the monetarists contended, post-war governments had responded irresponsibly to democratic pressure by increasing the money supply to maintain full employment and provide welfare. This had caused the economy to operate beyond the natural capacity that private economic decision making would have otherwise maintained. The excess money supply and the overheating of the economy had produced the surge in inflation.

Nevertheless, monetarists maintained that the monetary authorities (central banks and treasuries), if they so wished, could control the supply of money, because their debts (liabilities) were held by the banking system as a whole and, by expanding the system's 'fractional' reserves, were a base for the extension of bank credit. (The question is discussed further in Part II, chapters 7 and 8.) Analytically, this government and central bank debt ('high-powered money') had taken the place of the metallic base in the determination of the money supply. It was assumed, at least implicitly, that the monetary authorities could control these reserves with the same precision as a physical commodity. Furthermore, it was asserted that banks were constrained to adapt to the central authority's 'exogenous' creation of money – not vice versa, as argued by the proponents of the theory of 'endogenous' money (see Part II, chapter 7).

Despite the overwhelming preoccupation with the 'over'-supply of money and inflation, monetarists argued, with logical consistency, that monetary authorities and the banking system were equally capable of introducing too little money into the economy. For example, Friedman and Schwartz maintained that the contraction of the money stock between 1929 and 1933 was an important causal factor in the US depression of the 1930s. But even after such a severe contraction, the propensities of the 'real' economy would, in the long run, gradually reassert themselves, and the natural trajectory of economic activity would resume (Friedman and Schwartz 1963). Thus, the key to economic stability was seen to be the control of the supply of money in relation to the *natural rhythms* of the 'real' economy. It followed that if there was a 'natural rate of interest', then there was also a 'natural rate of unemployment'. The aim of economic analysis was to uncover these natural propensities and rhythms in order that the exogenous supply of money could be carefully calibrated to act, as it should, as a 'neutral veil'. If a monetary stimulus reduced unemployment below the natural rate in any particular economy – that is, the rate determined by the marginal productivity of the factors of production ('natural rate of interest') – then inflation would follow.

Monetarist theory was practically applied most vigorously in the UK and the USA from the late 1970s to the mid-1980s; but it proved to be a short-lived experiment. The proximate cause of the abandonment of these attempts directly to control the supply of money was that the theory could not be operationalized. Early applications of the theory referred to a 'narrow money', as some of the early twentieth-century theorists had done, which comprised currency and/or current accounts upon which cheques could be drawn (M_1). But, as we shall see, it is a central characteristic of capitalism that its financial system is able continuously to devise new forms of credit instruments. These may become part of a bank's assets and, consequently, form a base for further lending ('broad money'). Or IOUs such as promissory notes may become a 'near money' means of payment within capitalist business networks. Moreover, when the authorities attempt to regulate and control any particular form of credit instrument or 'near money', the private capitalist financial system creates new ones that are not covered by the regulation.[12] As we shall see in Part II, there is no hard and fast distinction in capitalism between the various forms of increasingly *fungible* credit instruments and the so-called money-proper. This feature of capitalism was intensified, with contradictory effects, by the financial deregulation during the 1980s. Credit instruments proliferated and were rendered more fungible and transferable into cash by the measures. For example, in the both the USA and the UK, the hard and fast regulatory separation of deposit, or savings, accounts and current (cheque) accounts was relaxed, and the money supply was, consequently, augmented and increased. The practical consequences of the well-established, but untenable, distinction between money and credit slowly became more apparent, but not before the myriad forms of credit-money supply had given rise to new measures of the money supply. M_2 led to M_3 and so on to M_{17}. The policy became increasingly inoperable. Later, in the early 1990s, as credit-money continued to expand at annual rates of over 25 per cent per year, but inflation fell quite markedly, the very foundations of quantity theory came under question (Henwood 1997: 201–2; Guttmann 1994).

Monetarism's policy incoherence directly reflected the theoretical incoherence of the revamped orthodox theory of money, which, it must be remembered, was already anachronistic at the time of its refinement by Fisher in the early twentieth century. Monetarist theory was developed, with no significant modification of the assumptions regarding the natural economy. In the hands of the early classical economists, precious metal currency was seen to be an *exogenously* provided 'public good'. Credit-money and bank clearance, which accounted for virtually all the significant transactions of the capitalist economy, were excluded from this category of money-proper. It is, therefore, not too surprising that this analytical framework proved to be totally inadequate for the understanding of the process whereby capitalism's money is created and controlled.

'Rational expectations' and inflation

With the failure of monetarism, orthodox monetary policy has become ever more detached from orthodox monetary theory. The fundamental tenets and assumptions, such as the long-run neutrality of money, survive, but they do not *directly* inform the immediate concerns of practical policy making.[13] Attention is now almost exclusively focused on the means by which 'inflation expectations' might be stabilized (see Part II, chapter 7). 'Rational expectations' theory contends that rational economic agents will wish to avoid inflation. If governments can create a credible commitment to low and stable inflation, then rational agents will not be tempted to engage in a self-defeating round of wage increases in order to try to keep ahead of an anticipated rise in prices.

The forging of 'rational expectations' is seen to be the responsibility of governments, whose fiscal policies are the major determinants of the money supply and, therefore, inflation (Barro and Gordon 1983). To this limited extent, the rational expectations approach to money is consistent with the orthodox ideas that the quantity of money affects prices and that the money supply is exogenously determined (see Part II, chapter 7). It is contended that the expansion of the economy beyond the natural rhythms of the business cycle is largely the result of governments departing from sound monetary principles. The latter may have changed since the days of the gold standard, but the belief remains that such principles exist, and that they are dictated by the natural propensities of the economy. However, we shall pursue an alternative conception of money and monetary policy, in which production of money is seen as the result of a power struggle between the major contending groups and interests in society. The relationships between wages, the level of employment, the 'real' rates of interest, and the exchange rate, as these are represented in macro-economic models, express these struggles (Ingham 1996b; Smithin 2003). In rational expectations models, however, there is no social and political structure from which conflict could result. Rather, the entire analysis is based on the hypothetical responses of rational 'representative agents' to available information.

'New monetary economics'

Towards the end of twentieth century, in a prescient anticipation of the Internet, 'new monetary economics' suggested that computerized bookkeeping could become the basis for gigantic Walrasian 'sophisticated barter systems'. Economic exchange could take place without money, as in the 'real' economy, by the exchange of transferable forms of wealth – that is to say, commodities and financial assets (Fama 1980; Trautwein 1993; see Smithin 2003). Computer technology might be able to eradicate the inconveniences of barter and create markets in which *all* goods are potentially media of exchange and means of payment. Walras had understood that for market clearing prices to develop, there would need to be a *numéraire* in terms of which goods could be priced and their exchange rates established. But there would be no universal form of value outside these goods. That is to say, there would be no good called 'money', which existed as an independent store of value outside the economic 'space' that was constituted by the transactions network of the 'real' economy. With the development of the Internet, this analysis has gained influence. There would be no actual money supply in such a sophisticated barter system, and, consequently, central banks could become redundant (King 1999). They would no longer be required to produce and regulate a supply of money, and, moreover, as quantities of money no longer existed, they could not have an independent distorting effect on prices. The general question of information and communication technology and the debates on the 'end of money' and 'new monetary spaces' will be explored in chapter 9.

Optimum currency area theory

Optimum currency area theory (OCA), first developed by Mundell (1961), has been recently applied to the question of the development of new monetary spaces, such as currency unions, the 'dollarization' of previously independent currencies, and to the question of the economic rationale for the euro. OCA uses the orthodox theory of money to explain the existence and spatial distribution of different currencies. Geographical areas that form internally consistent and coherent economic systems, in terms of structure and costs of production, will tend to evolve a uniform medium of exchange, through a process of transactions-cost minimization. Thus, arguments for and

against joining the euro are couched in terms of the degree of align-
ment of the 'real' characteristics of a potential entrant's economy with
those of the existing participants – that is, interest rates, labour market
flexibility and so on. The criticisms of the orthodox theory of money
outlined above apply to OCA, and will be elaborated in Part II,
chapter 9. From this orthodox viewpoint, monetary space is no more
than a reflection or representation of transactional, or 'market', space,
as this is conceptualized in 'real' analysis. Here we might simply repeat
the basic counter-argument that monetary space is a social and political construction. Moreover, the authoritative imposition of a money
of account over a geographical space can be the *active* element in the
creation of a hitherto fragmented market space. The creation of
monetary space defined by the geographical extent of a money of
account is an act of sovereignty.

Conclusions

By the early twentieth century, academic economic theorists held four
closely interrelated methodological assumptions and theoretical
tenets. Regardless of the institutional changes in monetary systems
and actual forms of money, these have guided all subsequent orthodox
economic analyses of money. First, mainstream economics operates
with a model of a 'real' economy of essentially barter exchange in
which money merely symbolizes the underlying real exchange ratios; it
is a 'neutral veil', and not an economic force *sui generis*. In the long
run, money is unimportant and inessential. Money is able to perform
its fundamental role as a *medium of exchange* because it is itself a
tradable commodity, or the direct representative of a commodity or
commodities. Money is specified as a money-stuff that has an exchange-value. Second, money's functional role in an economy (or its
logical origins) is explained in terms of its elimination of the inefficien-
cies of direct barter – that is, the removal of costly inconveniences
caused by the search for a co-trader with congruent wants. This
explanation of money's existence in terms of its minimization of
transaction costs for the rational individual is consistent with the
canon of economic neoclassicism, and is referred to as the 'micro-
foundations' of money. Third, as it is a commodity (or the direct
symbolic representation of a commodity), money's value may be
explained by general economic theories of value – such as supply
and demand and/or marginal utility. Fourth, it follows, *ceteris paribus*,
from both these theories (supply and demand and marginal utility)
that the price level is a function of the ratio of the *quantity* or *stock* of

money in circulation to the quantity of goods. I have argued that the approach is unable adequately to deal with three fundamental questions that a theory of money should answer. What does money do; or what is money? How is it produced; or how does it get into society? How is the value of money determined?

Most fundamentally, the analytical focus on money's role as a *medium of exchange* fails to identify the quality of 'moneyness', which is to be found, rather, in the abstract measure of value – the unit of account. Economic orthodoxy implies, and sometimes argues, that money of account is directly provided by the commodity standard of value, which consists in, or is represented by, the medium of exchange. Thus media of exchange simply require counting in order to produce a money of account. The notion of the *numéraire* shows that the assertion of the *logical* primacy of money of account is not incompatible with the Walrasian version of neoclassical economic analysis. However, it is significant that this is simply posited as the *arbitrary* assignment of a commodity with an already established value as a standard. The question of the origins of the standard is not addressed. The market model of the spontaneous emergence of a common medium of exchange fails to explain how myriad bilateral exchange ratios of barter trades could produce a stable price for any commodity standard. Rather, it is the money of account, regardless of the existence of any media of exchange or means of payment, which makes an orderly market possible. Money of account is logically anterior to the market (Innes 1913; Hawtrey 1919; Keynes 1930; Einaudi [1953] 1936; Grierson 1977; Hoover 1996; Ingham 1996a). This alternative conception is discussed in the next chapter.

The category error in identifying 'moneyness' with a money-stuff is evident in Adam Smith's 'classical' misinterpretation of two examples of commodity-money which he thought to be vestiges of the primitive stage of monetary evolution (Smith 1986 [1776]: ch. 4). Media of exchange, such as nails in Scotland and dried cod in Newfoundland in the eighteenth century, are not, as Smith argued, examples of primitive 'money'. They were, rather, *payment in kind* of debts that were calculated with *an abstract money of account*. The fishermen and traders in Newfoundland calculated in pounds, shillings and pence. It is absurd, as Mitchell Innes explained nearly a century ago, to conclude that the staple commodity (dried cod) was money, because 'if the fishers paid for their supplies in cod, the traders would equally have to pay for their cod in cod' (Innes 1913: 387).[14] To repeat: it was the unit of account that conferred the quality of 'moneyness' on the nails and cod, and not the converse. Divergences between the money of account in which prices are reckoned and the commodities by which debts are discharged is historically commonplace. However, when the value of a commodity is 'fixed by law or custom' – for example, when 1 pound weight of the best tobacco became the legal equivalent of 3 shillings – then it becomes money (Grierson 1977: 17).

Answers to the second question of how money gets into the economy expose further ambiguities within economic orthodoxy. From a purely theoretical standpoint, the answer is that the supply of money in circulation, and its consequent value, is most efficiently resolved by being left to the market. In other words, the needs of the 'real' economy will dictate the money supply. Indeed, the ultra-orthodox 'free banking' school argues along these lines. 'Free bankers' argue that provision of money is best left entirely to the market, which is understood as comprising rational, perfectly informed individuals who are able to discriminate amongst a range of competing moneys. This school contends that central banks, regardless of their structure or policy, have always distorted the market in money, and hence economic processes in general (L. White 1990). In this account, the history of money is seen as the history of the misuse of political power to further special monopoly and rent-seeking interests. States are tempted to defraud the public by expanding the money supply, inducing inflation, and thereby reducing the value of their indebtedness. Or, in the case of democratic states, they 'print money' in order to finance spending to appease mass electorates. Most other branches of orthodox economics, however, would favour a 'public goods' explanation of the state's role in producing an efficient medium of exchange. Thus, for example, monetary authorities should follow non-inflationary policies and strive to provide transparent information on their operations in order to cultivate 'rational expectations'. None the less, the analytical presuppositions of the extreme free banking school and the economic mainstream are essentially the same.

Mainstream economics' answer to the third question is that the value of money is determined by the ratio of its quantity to that of other commodities. Again, it should be noted that regardless of the nature of modern forms of money, this position is an elaboration of the theory of the origins of money as the most tradable commodity. It is also consistent with the more general axiom of 'marginalist', or neoclassical, economics, that value can be established only in exchange. We have seen that this part of the theory is also beset by considerable logical problems.

Modern macro-economics retains the orthodox idea that it is, in principle, possible, by means of an *a*political search for the most technically efficient means, to arrive at an *optimum* supply of *neutral* money – that is to say, a supply of money that does no more than express the values of the 'real' economy. It is held that this long-run equilibrium of both goods and goods and money and goods is a theoretical possibility. Beyond this, however, the question of precisely how money gets into the economy has not, from a strictly *analytical* standpoint, engaged economic *theory* to any significant degree. Monetary institutions are relevant only in so far as they aid or impede the attainment of the theoretical monetary optimum. Some institutional arrangements are to be preferred in so far as they are believed to stabilize inflation expectations and thereby facilitate the movement to an equation of the quantities of money and goods. To be sure, expectations are important, but they are not formed rationally simply on the basis of economic information about the propensities of the 'real' economy. As we shall see when we return to the question in chapters 7 and 8, the institutional structure of the monetary system comprises relations of power.

Finally, an obvious question arises from this preliminary assessment. How can such inadequate intellectual underpinnings remain the basis for conduct of monetary affairs? (As we shall see, this is asked, if not quite so brusquely, even by mainstream economists who are concerned directly with monetary policy.) The most obvious answer is that this is to be expected in 'normal science'; 'paradigms' can be sustained by the social organization of the scientific community beyond the point that they cease to provide clear understanding (Kuhn 1970). The mainstream conception of money outlined here is an integral part of the dominant paradigm in modern economics. If it were to be seriously challenged from within orthodoxy, it would have equally serious consequences for accepted methodology in general.

However, academic entrenchment can be only part of the explanation for the persistence of this intellectually inadequate meta-theory. For a time, it was reasonable to think that the economics of 'reals', and its associated theory of money, had been superseded. Writing in the middle of the twentieth century, Schumpeter asked a similar question in his magisterial history of economic analysis. He gave a rather unconvincing explanation of the failure of seventeenth- and eighteenth-century credit theory to displace the Aristotelian legacy (Schumpeter 1994 [1954]: 287), but assumed that with the rise of Keynesian economics, what he referred to as 'monetary', as opposed orthodox 'real', analysis, would prevail (p. 278). No doubt he would have been surprised by the revival of nineteenth-century orthodoxy in the analysis of the 'real' economy after the 1970s, but it adds force to our original question.

The analytical reduction of money to a natural commodity, to the mere symbol of a commodity, or to nothing more than the neutral representation of existing values, is a powerful ideological tool. However, money is not merely a useful technique, comparable to weights and measures; it also consists in social relations that are inherently relations of inequality and power. We shall see that in the actual process of the social production of money, promises to pay are ranked hierarchically in a way that expresses and reproduces these inequalities. Money is not naturally robust like gold, but even in the age of dematerialized money, ideological naturalization in economic theory helps to disguise the reality of its fragile social nature. (See Douglas 1986: 48).

2

Abstract Value, Credit and the State

The eye has never seen, nor the hand touched a dollar.

Innes 1914: 155

[M]oney is only a claim upon society. Money appears, so to speak, as a bill of exchange from which the name of the drawee is lacking.

Simmel 1978 [1907]: 177

[M]oney is peculiarly a creation of the State.

Keynes 1930: 4

Alternative conceptions to the Aristotelian commodity-exchange theory of money have existed at least since the time of the early development of capitalism and the modern state in Europe.[1] They flourished in the late seventeenth century and again briefly in the early twentieth century, but subsequently they have been disregarded by the economic mainstream and are little known in the other social sciences. In broad terms, there are two distinct strands in the heterodox analysis of money. On the one hand, efforts to understand the new dematerialized bank credit of early capitalism led to a more general reappraisal of the commodity and metallist theories of money. The new forms of money were not simply *credit* in the sense of *deferred payment*. Rather, these credits were money, in that mere promises to pay (IOUs), issued outside the sovereign mints, began to circulate as *means of payment*. Only later were they backed by bullion in a hybrid bank credit/gold standard. Credit networks denominated in a money of account were used as early as 2000 BC in Babylon, but the *general* use of *transferable* debt is specific to capitalism. Debt is used as means of payment to an anonymous third party: A's IOU held by B is used to pay C. After more than 2,000 years during which coin and money were synonymous, this new money-form posed intellectual puzzles. Some of the answers led to a departure from the Aristotelian theories of commodity-money, and led to the idea that *all* money was credit. They entailed a 'credit theory of money', rather than the 'monetary theory of credit' (Schumpeter 1994 [1954]: 717). These ideas gained a wider acceptance particularly at those times when monetary systems appeared to function effectively in the absence of a metallic standard. In England, for example, the suspension of the gold standard in 1797 and its resumption in 1819 triggered a protracted and rigorous debate on the nature of money. It culminated in the dispute between the Banking and Currency Schools in the 1830s and 1840s, which continues to inform today's monetary analysis and is frequently cited as a precursor of the post-Keynesian theories of endogenous money and the monetary circuit (see Smithin 2003; Wray 1990; Parguez and Seccareccia 2000). A similar debate took place in the USA in the wake of the greenback era of purely paper money during and after the Civil War (Carruthers and Babb 1996; Greider 1987). For Keynes, the credit theorists belonged in the ranks of the 'brave army of heretics' (1973 [1936]: 371); but for the academic mainstream they became the 'monetary cranks' who inhabited the 'underworld' of economic analysis (Schumpeter 1994 [1954]: 282).[2]

A second strand of heterodoxy comes from the 'state theory' of money that was developed by the German Historical School of economics throughout the nineteenth and early twentieth centuries (Ellis 1934; Schumpeter 1994 [1954]; Barkai 1989). These theories influenced Weber and Simmel, and, later, Keynes incorporated their general conclusions in his *A Treatise on Money* (1930). More recently, heterodox economists have revived Knapp's theory in 'neo-chartalism' (Wray 1998; Bell 2000).

Early Claim and Credit Theory

Intellectual efforts to understand the emergence and spread of new forms of credit-money, issued by banks and states across Europe during the seventeenth century, produced the first systematic challenges to commodity-exchange theories of money. The changes will be examined in Part II, chapter 6; here we should note the importance of the *de-linking* of moneys of account and actual forms of money. The two attributes of money had been integrated in the form of the coin for almost 2,000 years, but in the political and monetary anarchy of the post-Roman and early medieval period they became separated. Purely abstract moneys of account, in the sense that they were never incorporated in minted coin, existed as accounting devices – 'ghost money' (Wood 2002: 76; see also Sherman 1997). As Hewitt noted in his eighteenth-century *Treatise upon Money*, the English pound and the French livre were 'Imaginary Money... because there is no Species current, in this or that Kingdom, precisely of the Value of either of those Sums'. They were used to used 'to express a Sum of Money' (quoted in Jackson 1995: 10).[3] Myriad coinages circulated promiscuously within and across the constantly shifting geopolitical boundaries of the fragile jurisdictions that tried to impose their own abstract, or 'ghost', money of account in order to establish sovereignty. In Keynes's terms, many different 'things' (coin) could answer many different 'descriptions' (money of account) of money. The complexity provided fertile ground for reflection on the nature of money.

In seventeenth-century England, for example, Nicholas Barbon and Bishop Berkeley advanced a 'nominalist' conception of money as a 'ticket' or 'counter'; but Sir James Steuart, in the eighteenth century, produced the most extensive and penetrating analysis along these lines. He not only distinguished 'money-coin' from 'money of accompt', but inverted the commodity theory and argued that the latter was *essentially* money. Money is that 'which purely in itself is of no material use to man but which acquires such an estimation from his opinion of it as to become the universal measure of what is called value' (quoted in Schumpeter 1994 [1954]: 297). For Steuart money of account was not the *notation* that merely represented the value of commodity forms of money, or their surrogates. Rather, money was, generically, an abstract value of which metallic coinage was a *special case*. As such, money was no more than a claim against goods; it was purely purchasing power.

However, Steuart had little influence – being scorned eventually by *both* Marx and Ricardo! Rather, the history of monetary analysis in the sixteenth and seventeenth centuries was dominated by the technical and, above all, political problems of establishing a stable precious metals standard. The advocacy of a precious metal monetary system had a practical as well as a theoretical basis; that is to say, many of the proponents of a metallic standard did not necessarily believe in the *intrinsic* value of gold and silver (Schumpeter 1994 [1954]: 288–9). The two architects of British 'monetary orthodoxy' – Locke and Newton – were primarily concerned with securing a strong currency, as the basis for a strong but liberal state.[4]

By the end of the eighteenth century, the English gold standard had become the monetary model for all modern states, and the commodity theory of money seemed to provide a satisfactory explanation for its operation. However, intellectual problems remained. What was the basis for the circulating credit that fuelled the expanding capitalist economy? Until the practice and theory of 'fractional reserves' of bullion in a centralized banking system, credit could not be subsumed under the commodity theory of money. Defoe's bemusement was typical.

> [Credit] gives Motion, yet it self cannot be said to Exist; it creates Forms, yet has no Form; it is neither Quantity nor Quality; it has no Whereness, or Whenness, Scite, or Habit. I should say that it is the essential Shadow of Something that is Not. (Daniel Defoe, *An Essay on Publick Credit* (London, 1710), cited in Sherman 1997: 327)

By the early nineteenth century, metallic currency had fallen to below 50 per cent of the money supply. Furthermore, the Bank of England's suspension of the convertibility of its paper notes into gold during the Napoleonic Wars was not accompanied by the monetary instability and inflation which classical commodity or 'metallist' theories would have predicted. A theoretical reappraisal of the nature of money followed.

The Nineteenth-Century Debates: Gold and Credit

Banking and currency in England

Two related debates on the English monetary system in the early nineteenth century followed the suspension of convertibility after 1797. The Bullionist Controversy preceded the resumption of convertibility in 1821, and this was followed by the Banking versus Currency School debates which prepared the way for the Bank Charter Acts of 1844.

The central issue concerned the role of credit (promissory notes, bills of exchange) in the determination of inflation and exchange rates (see Wray 1990 and Smithin 2003). Following Ricardo, the Currency School argued that the quantity of bank notes should correspond to the quantity of bullion which, in accordance with the early quantity theory of money, would stabilize prices and provide a mechanism for regulating the exchange rate. In classical mode, they maintained that if the supply of money were increased, inflation would follow, and a balance of trade deficit would be the effect of high domestic prices. High prices would reduce exports and stimulate imports; but the imbalance would be self-correcting with a relatively inelastic supply of precious metal money. The 'specie-flow' mechanism formulated by Hume in the mid-eighteenth century posited that the outflow of gold to pay for the deficit would contract the money supply and automatically lead to the reduction of domestic prices – as if by an 'invisible hand'.

Banking School theorists argued that private credit instruments, such as bills of exchange and including bank notes, were issued in response to a real demand for the facilitation of production and trade. Therefore, they insisted, like post-Keynesians over a century later, that the creation of credit could never be 'excessive' and the cause of inflation. The debates became increasingly complex. Some Banking School theorists actually used their opponent's arguments to make their own case. For example, it was argued that trade credit should be seen not as money, but rather as private debt. As it was a money substitute and did not add to the quantity of money in circulation, it could not cause inflation. In short, the debate created conceptual uncertainty:

> The real question then to be considered is not whether this or that particular form of credit be entitled to the designation of 'money', but whether, without a perversion of terms and an outrage of principle, that denomination can be applied to credit in any shape. (John Fullarton, *On the Regulation of Currencies* (London, 1844), quoted in Wray 1990: 105)

The Banking and Currency School debates, like the earlier one in the seventeenth century between Barbon and Locke, show how theories of money were an integral part of the struggle between different interests for the production and control of money. In broad terms, the two sides represented the two agencies which, in a capitalist system, share the creation of money – the state and the banks. Behind these lay the two 'money classes' in capitalism: on the one hand, the entrepreneurial debtors and, on the other, the rentiers and creditors. By and large, the Banking School had the support of provincial bankers and industrialists. The latter wanted 'soft credit' from the bankers, who in turn resisted the Bank of England's growing domination of the monetary system. The bankers and industrialists believed that the Bank exercised its increasingly centralized power in its own particular interests, based on control of gold bullion reserves. A distinctive proto-Keynesian school of economics centred on Birmingham advocated the creation of credit to the point at which 'the general demand for labour, in all the great departments of industry, becomes permanently greater than its supply' (Thomas Attwood, quoted in Ingham 1984: 108).

The Birmingham School also insisted that a 'hard currency', in which all notes were backed by gold under strict convertibility rules, would not only be deflationary but would also enrich the creditors, who would take advantage of the shortage of money-capital to raise interest rates. 'Sound money' increased inequality – it was not 'neutral'. 'Half the circulation of the Kingdom is determined in stagnant masses into what is called the money market, in order to gorge the money interest' (Thomas Attwood, quoted in Ingham 1984: 108). Against this, the Currency School's arguments found favour with creditors, who feared inflation. Above all, the aristocratic governing class saw gold as the best foundation for a strong state. As Lord Melbourne informed Attwood, 'Birmingham is not England' (quoted in Ingham 1984: 109).

The Currency School's case for a strict gold standard was also based on the consideration that it would remove the currency from control by particular economic interests. The danger associated with inconvertible bank notes was not simply an issue over credit to producers and traders by provincial banks. Ricardo feared that the Bank of England itself would be tempted to make profits by manipulating the issue of notes and, thereby, the price of gold. '[T]he only use of a standard is to regulate the quantity, and by the quantity, the value of the currency – and that without a standard it would be exposed to all the fluctuations to which the ignorance and interests of the issuers might subject it' (Ricardo, quoted in Sraffa 1951: 58–9).

Although the Currency School's analysis formed the basis for the reform of the monetary system, the Bank Charter Acts of 1844–5 were something of a compromise, in that they combined both a gold-backed and a fiduciary issue of notes. The gold base was intended to produce a self-regulating system that would reduce the discretionary power of the Bank of England to that of an independent and neutral management.[5] But, in effect, it succeeded in further increasing the centralization of the monetary and banking system through the Bank's rate of interest, as the Banking School critics had warned. However, despite the continued growth of bank credit-money, the legislation had officially defined money as precious metal. And as we saw in the previous chapter, 'economic science' proceeded to refine the ancient theory that was held to explain it.

Greenbacks and gold in post-bellum America

The greenback era, which followed the suspension of the convertibility of bank notes into gold and silver in the Civil War, lasted until the resumption of the gold standard in 1879.[6] During this period, the relative merits of precious metallic and inconvertible paper money were vigorously contested. It was less theoretically sophisticated than the English Banking and Currency School debate, but the American controversy shows a more explicit consideration of the fundamental nature of money and value. In this regard it more closely resembled the first English debates on credit and money in the seventeenth and early eighteenth centuries.

As in the seventeenth-century English polemic, one side accepted 'theoretical metallism'. '[T]he yardstick becomes the measure of length by having length within itself... So metallic money having intrinsic value is made a measure of value by its coinage based on its metallic value' (Bartley, quoted in Carruthers and Babb 1996: 1567).[7] Again, the association between land and precious metal, as *natural* phenomena, played a central role in their arguments. As the Honest Money League explained: 'There is all the difference between true money, real money and paper money, that there is between your land and a deed for it. Money is a reality, a weight, of a certain metal of a certain fineness. But a paper dollar is simply a deed' (quoted in Carruthers and Babb 1996: 1568).

Greenbackers exposed the illogical confusion: 'it matters not whether the yardstick and the pound weight be of wood, iron or gold; length and weight are the only properties necessary to be expressed by them' (Campbell, quoted in Carruthers and Babb 1996: 1569). Implicitly, at least, they understood that money was a social construction. Political authority was responsible for establishing the unit and the standard, and the objects that carried these abstract values were essentially only the *claims* to goods of the same value. In late nineteenth-century American democracy, this had far-reaching political implications. If the people make the government and, in turn, the government makes money, then, the greenbackers argued, we 'make our own money, we issue it, we control it' (Wolcott, quoted in Carruthers and Babb 1996: 1572).

As in all other disputes, the complex struggle between creditors and debtors, on the one hand, and the state, on the other, determined the outcome. Basing their arguments on the quantity theory, 'metallists' and creditor interests feared that inflation would be the inevitable consequence of an inconvertible paper currency.[8] But they were not all necessarily convinced by the commodity theory of money. Many did not trust a democratic government to maintain control of a non-metallic currency – that is, they were 'practical metallists' (Schumpeter 1994 [1954]: 288–9). In the same manner as some of the English Currency School, they argued that an inconvertible credit-money system would be destabilized by the struggle between economic classes and interests. Anchored in a natural substance, commodity-money would transcend this conflict. The greenbackers dismissed this appeal to a common good and argued that, on the contrary, a fixed metallic standard outside democratic control actually ceded too much power to the bankers and creditors. In effect, the greenbackers were attempting to demystify the ideological identification of the social relation of money with the supposedly natural form of precious metal coinage. Money was a social product, and they believed that its identification with gold masked the bankers' private control of the public good that should be under popular control.

The greenbackers lost the struggle and, with the establishment of the Federal Reserve Bank in 1913, the United States completed the construction of a sovereign monetary space that was defined by a dollar money of account based on a gold standard. As we saw in the previous chapter, Fisher's *The Purchasing Power of Money* was published in 1911, and whilst it did not advocate a gold standard, it claimed to present a mathematical proof of the direct relationship between the quantity of money and the price level. Apart from any other consideration, control of a quantity of gold, upon which the rules of the monetary system could be based, was an easier proposition than regulation of the lending policy of the thousands of local state banks that comprised the highly decentralized US system. At this precise moment, two remarkably iconoclastic articles appeared in the influential New York monthly, *The Banking Law Journal* (Innes 1913, 1914). In a succinct critique of the commodity theory of money, Innes found it deeply puzzling that 'it may be said without exaggeration that no scientific theory has ever been put forward which was more completely lacking in foundation' (1914: 383).[9] At the apogee of the gold standard, he confidently stated that 'there was never such a thing as a metallic standard of value' (1914: 379). Innes acknowledges that some of the earlier credit theorists – such as Steuart, Mun, Boisguillebert and, in particular, Macleod – had seen the essential nature of money as an *abstract* measure of debt. 'All that we can touch or see is a promise to pay or satisfy a debt due for an amount called a dollar [which is] intangible, immaterial, abstract' (1914: 159; 1913: 399).

His critique of the metallist theory of money has two main parts. First, he shows that the history of the weight and fineness of coinage could not be explained by the theory of a metallic standard. The earliest known coins in Greece and Asia Minor, during the first millennium BC, were of such irregularity that they could not have been the basis for a metallic standard. But, more importantly, they did not possess any numerical indication of their value. Later, in Rome for example, coins were marked with their value, but 'the most striking thing about them is the extreme irregularity of their weight and/or the composition of the alloys' (Innes 1913: 380). Marks of value were defined by the money of account, and 'we thus get the remarkable fact that for many hundreds of years the unit of account remained unaltered independently of the coinage which passed through many vicissitudes' (Innes 1914: 381). Commodity theorists maintain that these 'lags' show how people may be successfully duped, but that eventually the gradual debasement causes a depreciation of the coinage and price inflation. We shall look at this issue again in Part II; but here we may simply note the implausibility of this hypothesis in light of the very long periods of time it took for changes in the price level to occur – several centuries in Rome, for example.

Innes had no doubt that all the coins were tokens, and that the weight and composition were not regarded as matters of importance. What was important was 'the name or distinguishing mark of the issuer, which was never absent' (Innes 1914: 382). As we shall see in the discussion of the state theory of money, the issuer's mark did not necessarily guarantee a metallic standard, but simply that the issuer would accept the token in payment of a tax debt. (That is to say, the money was issued as a token of indebtedness.) Coins were, like all forms of money, credit instruments that represented abstract value or purchasing power. 'Credit and credit alone is money' (Innes 1913: 392).

The second part of Innes's argument points out that debtor–creditor relations denominated in a money of account pre-date the first coins by more than 2,000 years. Babylonian clay tablets (*shubati*) from around 2500 BC represented the acknowledgement of indebtedness measured in a money of account (Innes 1913: 396). Innes also maintains that such commercial instruments continued to be the major forms of money throughout the coinage era. In other words, his analysis does not support the idea of a progressive dematerialization or abstraction of money that is found in many heterodox theories (see, for example, Simmel 1978 [1907]; Aglietta 2002). According to Innes, clay tablets, brittle metal objects and tally sticks that could be broken in two to signify credit and debt were followed by bills of exchange, and permitted the clearance of debts without recourse to any circulating medium.[10]

After such a long period of debate and political struggle in which a metallic standard and a central bank had been established in the USA, Innes's ideas could not expect to find favour. In fact, they caused short-lived outrage and a dismissive response from the established economic orthodoxy that consigned his views to oblivion.[11] However, Innes was, fundamentally, correct. And during the recent revival of

interest in heterodox theories of money, his work has been re-
discovered along with some of the work of the late nineteenth-century
German Historical School of Economics (Smithin 2000; Wray 2000;
Bell 2000; Wray 2004).

The German Historical Schools and the
State Theory of Money

As we have noted, the analysis of money occupied centre stage in the
Methodenstreit (Barkai 1989; Ellis 1934). In general, the Historical
School opposed the explanation of money's origins and development
as a commodity in market exchange.[12] Some went much further and
maintained, in utter contradiction to Anglo-American economic
orthodoxy, that 'the quantity of money is a determinand and not a
determinant of the price level' (Barkai 1989: 197).

State theory may be traced to the early nineteenth century and
to Muller's *New Theory of Money*, which attempted to explain
money value as an expression of communal trust and national will
(Schumpeter 1994 [1954]: 421–2), and culminated in Knapp's *State
Theory of Money*, first published in German in 1905. Knapp considered it absurd to attempt to understand money 'without the idea
of the state' (Knapp 1973 [1924]: vii–viii). Money is not a medium that
emerges from exchange. It is rather a means for accounting for and
settling *debts*, the most important of which are tax debts. The value
of debts is expressed in money of account – 'the unit in which the
amount of the payment is expressed'; and the actual means of payment
of debts is a '*bearer* of units of value' (Knapp 1973 [1924]: 7–8,
emphasis added). The material form of the money-stuff, which *bears*
the abstraction, is of secondary importance because it is 'moveable'
(Knapp 1973 [1924]: 8–25). That is to say, what is accepted in payment
of debts, denominated in the unit of account, can be, and frequently is,
subject to change. A whole range of means of payment – precious or
base metal coin, inanimate or animate organic matter such as leather,
tobacco, cattle, etc. – may be accepted as representing the abstract
value of the unit of account.

By declaring what it will accept for the discharge of tax debt,
assessed in the unit of account at the public pay offices, the state
creates money. The state establishes the nominal unit of account
and, in a metallic monetary system, fixes the conversion rates – for
example, so many ounces of silver or gold for the nominal money of
dollars, pounds, etc. In this way the state establishes the 'validity'
(*Geltung*) of money. It is important to note that Knapp does not say

that the state is the *only* issuer of money; rather, it is the state's 'acceptation,...which is decisive' (Knapp 1973 [1924]: 95). Credit notes and bills, issued by banks and denominated in the state's money of account, therefore, become 'money' (or 'valuata' money in his terminology) when they are accepted as payment of tax debts owed to the state and reissued in payment to the state's creditors (Knapp 1973 [1924]: 143; 196). In other words, the structural relationship between banks and the state confers 'moneyness' on bank credit. All money, regardless of its particular material form, is a token that bears or carries the units of abstract value. Using the Latin word *charta* ('token'), Knapp defined money as 'a Chartal means of payment' (Knapp 1973 [1924]: 38).

This was anathema to economic 'theorists' such as Menger and von Mises (see von Mises 1934 [1912]: 413–18). They poured scorn on the notion that states could establish the purchasing power of money; value, they insisted, could be established only in exchange. But, as we have seen, the same economic theories were unable to explain why all goods with value did not become money, or why certain 'goods' without exchange value (paper, for example) had purchasing power. In their indignation, the economic theorists failed to notice Knapp's important distinction between valuableness and value. Money possesses a specific quality of valuableness, or validity, as opposed to its particular value, or purchasing power. States confer the quality of valuableness by accepting the tokens as payment for taxes and using them to make their own purchases. The substantive value of money is a closely related, but, none the less, distinct question.

Most importantly, money's valuableness can be established *only* in relation to a nominal money of account. Knapp insisted that money is the measure and not the thing measured – that is say, money is abstract value. This is the only way to make sense of the fact that twenty shillings equal one pound – regardless of the enormous variations in the actual silver content of the shilling, or the fact that the pound was never minted as silver coin (Einaudi 1953 [1936]; Innes 1913).

The implications of state theory struck at the very core of the underlying meta-theory of modern economics – that is, the idea of a real or natural economic substratum and the axiom that value can be established only in free exchange based on individual preferences. Historically, the state's role in fixing and manipulating the standard of value and in issuing money-stuff is incontrovertible. As we have noted, orthodox economics can accommodate the state's role within a 'public goods' theory of money. But the implication of

Knapp's theory is that an authority is a necessary or *logical* condition for money's existence. As I argued in chapter 1, 'moneyness' is conferred by money of account, which cannot be produced by the free interplay of economic interests in the market; it must be introduced by an 'authority'. In this way, the state theory of money raises the further question of the *political* nature of the relationship (or contract) between the guarantor of the validity of money and its users. Money, in this conception, inevitably involves the question of *sovereignty*.

The quantity theory explanation of money's value was also disregarded by some of the Historical School. In the midst of the German hyperinflation in July 1922, the president of the Reichsbank apologized for not being able to print money fast enough. He did not for a moment think that his actions would exacerbate an already dire situation. The quantity of money in the form of a huge issue of notes, Haverstein averred, was not the cause, but the *consequence* of the fall in the value of the mark. Haverstein was expressing the widely held belief of economists and the political elite that prices determined the quantity of money, and not vice versa, as in Anglo-American economic theory. The view, noted above, that the amount of money does not determine, but is a *determinand* of, prices had been propounded by two leading figures in the nineteenth-century Historical School: Roscher in his *Principles of Political Economy* and Knies in *Gold and Credit* (Barkai 1989). This intellectual case for a repudiation of classic quantity theory disappeared along with the Weimar Republic in the aftermath of the hyperinflation. However, the unquestioned assumption that heterodox monetary theories played a causal role in these disastrous events is very much open to doubt.

Essentially the same questions about money linger on, as we shall see, in disputes about money and monetary policy. Can the market produce and sustain its own money? Would a purely market money be more economically efficient? Or, in relation to some current questions, will electronic money and massive computing power bring about the 'end of money' and the actualization of the 'real' economy as envisaged in Walras's and Wicksell's models? The persistence of these models owes more to their origins in the arbitrary separation of mainstream academic economics from the other social sciences after the *Methodenstreit* than it does to their intellectual merit. These issues are more compelling than at any time since the publication of Knapp's *Staatliche Theorie des Geldes*, and we shall return to them in Part II. At present, we need to examine the book's short-lived influence on the work of Keynes.

The Influence on Keynes

In the early twentieth century, those English economists trying to understand the nature of dematerialized money were quick to see the relevance of the nominalist, state and credit theories.[13] Inconsistency and eventual equivocation aside, Hawtrey and, more importantly in the long run, Keynes dropped the assumptions of (neo)classical 'real' analysis. They sought to develop theories in which money was given autonomy or independence as a factor in the process of production and, in particular, in the booms and slumps of the business cycle.[14]

State and credit theories removed money from its analytical anchorage in commodities and the 'real' economy. However, I would argue that a satisfactory answer to the question of what money was actually anchored in – if not the 'real' economy, or precious metal – required a decisive break with (neo)classical economics. Keynes and other establishment economists were ultimately unable to make it. By the 1930s, they had reverted – or perhaps one should say regressed – towards the orthodox economics of the 'real' and had abandoned the radical conception of money.[15]

A Treatise on Money (Keynes 1930) presented a challenge to the commodity-exchange theories of both the Cambridge tradition of Jevons, Marshall and Pigou and the Austrian theorists such as Menger and von Mises. It combined nineteenth-century English credit theory with German monetary nominalism and state theory. An awareness of the latter had inspired Keynes's self-confessed 'Babylonian madness'. In the mid-1920s, Keynes studied metrology and numismatics in a search for the historical and logical origins of money in ancient Near East civilizations.[16] As a result, *A Treatise on Money* opens with an unequivocal repudiation of orthodoxy: 'Money-of-Account, namely that in which Debts and Prices and General Purchasing Power are expressed, is the *primary concept* of a Theory of Money' (Keynes 1930: 3, emphasis added). Nominal money is primary in so far as actual money, or 'that by delivery of which debt-contracts and price-contracts are discharged . . . derives its character from its relationship to the Money-of-Account, *since debts and prices must first have been expressed in terms of the latter*' (Keynes 1930: 3, emphasis added). In short, 'The Age of Money had succeeded the Age of Barter as soon as men had adopted a money-of-account' (Keynes 1930: 5).[17]

Moreover, it is the 'State or Community', not the market, which decides the description of the thing (money of account) and declares what thing (money-proper) corresponds to the name (Keynes 1930: 4). Referring to Babylon, he makes the fundamental nominalist case that it was not necessary for the talents and shekels to be minted as coin for them to be money. Rather, the state need only define what weight and fineness of silver would constitute a payment expressed in the money of account of talents or shekels (Keynes 1930: 12).

Chapter 2, 'The "Creation" of Bank-Money', almost, but not quite, advances a pure credit theory of money. Keynes notes that transferable claims (cheques, bills and notes) to 'money-proper' may be accepted as a more convenient method of payment than handling cash (Keynes 1930: 23). By issuing such claims against itself in the form of loans or advances, a bank creates deposits and, thereby, creates money (Keynes 1930: 24–30). Then, as Wicksell had done, he pushes the argument to its limit by way of a thought experiment. However, without Wicksell's commitment to the idea of a natural rate of interest, which expresses the natural productive propensities of the real economy, Keynes reaches quite different conclusions. He imagines a closed banking system in which all payments are by cheque or by an inter-bank giro or book transfer – that is to say, it is without cash or money-proper. In these circumstances, he concluded:

> it is evident that there is no limit to the amount of bank money which the banks can safely create *provided that they move forward in step*. The words italicised are clue to the behaviour of the system . . . Each Bank Chairman sitting in his parlour may regard himself as the passive instrument of outside forces over which he has no control; yet the 'outside forces' may be nothing but himself and his fellow-chairmen, and certainly not his depositors. (Keynes 1930: 26–7)

Here, Keynes realizes that money in the form of deposits is being socially constructed by discretionary bank lending, according to norms and conventions which render them relatively autonomous from savers' deposits. This line of reasoning, that the banks 'manufacture' money, caused consternation in orthodox economic ranks.[18]

From what was in the 1920s still a hypothetical case, Keynes then moves on to discuss the orthodox understanding of bank credit as being anchored, to some significant degree at least, in the cash reserves of money-proper – that is, the 'monetary theory of credit'. But his analysis remained thoroughly heterodox in the emphasis given to the social and political determination of the supply of bank credit-money, rather than to the cash reserves' supposed representation of 'real' factors of production. On the one hand, he argues that the level of reserves that it will be prudent for banks to aim at will depend on the *conventions* and practices of the banks and their clients (Keynes 1930: 28–9). On the other hand, the central bank 'is the conductor of the orchestra and sets the tempo' by virtue of its *power* to issue notes and to set the interest rate at which it will lend to the banking system as a whole (Keynes 1930: 30, 189).

Keynes pursued the theoretical implications of the analytical detachment of the money-creating process from the underlying 'real' economy in an early draft of *The General Theory of Employment, Interest and Money*. Here he contrasted the (neo)classical barter-exchange model of the 'real' economy, or 'a co-operative economy', with the capitalist 'money wage or entrepreneurial economy' based on bank-created credit-money (Asimakopoulos 1988: 74–6). However, the published version represents a significant compromise with orthodoxy. The more radical import of nominalism and claim theory, that money is more than an expression of the 'real' economy, was modified by the analytical device of *ex post* savings. Investment must equal savings, but these need not be *ex ante* as in orthodox classical theory. Thus, Keynes's position could be construed, to the satisfaction of influential academic opponents and detractors, as being consistent with the axiom that money was neutral in the long run. During the post-World War II period, Keynesian macro-economics was gradually further refashioned into a shape that was even more acceptable to neoclassical orthodoxy (Rochon 1999). However, his earlier more heterodox sketch of capitalist banking has resurfaced to influence post-Keynesian theories of endogenous money and the French and Italian circuit theory of credit money.

Post-Keynesian Theory: Endogenous Money and the Monetary Circuit

Endogenous money

The persistent antinomy between the commodity-exchange theory and alternative conceptions of credit-money have found more recent expression in the endogenous versus exogenous money debate. As we saw in the previous chapter, the theory of exogenous money was associated with monetarism, and sought to establish that the supply of money, conceptualized as a 'stock', is controllable by the monetary authority. Guided by the correct theory, the monetary authority may then exogenously introduce money, in the appropriate quantities, into the economy.

The opposing theory of endogenous money was originally developed as a theory of capitalist bank credit-money, and its intellectual pedigree is frequently traced to the writings of the nineteenth-century

Banking School, as outlined above. Money is produced endogenously by banks in the *normal* course of financing of capitalist production (for an account of the early views, see Rochon 1999; Smithin 2003). In short, there are three related essential propositions in the theory: '[f]irst, loans make deposits, second, deposits make reserves, and third, money demand induces money supply' (Wray 1990: 73–4). Because the demand for money is the demand for productive investment or consumption that will stimulate production, the monetarist idea of an excessive money supply that creates inflation does not make sense. Endogenous money theorists imply, at least, a reversal of the direction of causation in the classical quantity theory of money – that is, from prices to the quantity of money. Many favour a 'cost-push' theory, in which inflation is primarily the result of the wage demands that were made in the period of full employment when a 'labour standard' had replaced the gold standard (Hicks 1982 [1955]).

Orthodox exogenous money theorists acknowledge that the banking system creates credit-money, but insist that the central bank is able to exercise *control* over this process by its power to create the 'high power'-base money reserves for the system. We shall return to empirical details of this process in chapter 7; here we need only make note of the post-Keynesian counter-arguments.[19] The issue is complicated, however, by the disputes within this camp – for example, between the 'horizontalists' and the 'structuralists' on the rate of interest and the determination of the supply of credit-money (see Smithin 2003: 122–3, 202–3). Structuralists hold to a more orthodox supply and demand model. But the horizontalists maintain that central banks are presented with a *fait accompli* by the commercial banks, which meet any level of demand for loans that satisfies their creditworthiness criteria (Thus, at a given rate of interest, the supply curve for credit-money is horizontal.) In order not to lose control of the banking system, a central bank has little or no choice but to provide the reserves of its own money to accommodate any level of endogenous demand for money.[20] Rather, as we shall see, it is suggested that the central bank can, at best, influence the creation of money only indirectly, through its discount rate. I would argue that the post-Keynesians – particularly, the horizontalists – imply an empirical sociological generalization about the production of credit-money, based on a hypothesis which can be explained only with reference to the social structure of the power relations in typical capitalist banking systems.[21] This is made more explicit in a continental European version of post-Keynesianism, known as 'theory of the monetary circuit'.

The theory of the monetary circuit

The French and Italian 'circuitists' hold to a more radical and, arguably, more faithful interpretation of Keynes's 'long struggle of escape... from the habitual modes of thought and expression' (Keynes 1973 [1936]: xxiii). They are the most heterodox troop under the post-Keynesian banner, and differ in important respects from many of the British and American post-Keynesians (see Graziani 1990; Parguez and Seccareccia 2000). Circuitists tend to reject the treatment of money in *The General Theory* in favour of that in *A Treatise on Money* and Keynes's articles of the late 1930s (Rochon 1999: 9). They are more consistent in their endorsement of the credit theory of money: 'money is a debt which circulates freely' (Schmitt 1975: 106). And, most importantly, this conception of money has led to a focus on the *actual structure* of relationships that constitutes the capitalist monetary circuit. Indeed, a number of these French and Italian writers entirely reject the analytical framework of the supply and demand for money.

The structure of the monetary circuit that they have in mind is based on the interpretation of bank lending that is found, for example, in the nineteenth-century Banking School and, in particular, the writing of Thomas Tooke. Money moves, according to Tooke, in two phases. In the first, 'efflux' phase, debts are issued by bank credit to allow private firms to start production. In the 'reflux phase' the debts are extinguished when firms reimburse the banks with the circulating debt that they have acquired through the sale of production. Money is *created* by bank credit and *destroyed* by the repayment of the debt from the profits of production at the end of the circuit.

This approach lies quite outside the orthodox economic methodology that also informs a good deal of post-Keynesian theory – for example, the attention the structuralists give to the individual demand for money ('liquidity preference') or its 'velocity' (Rochon 1999; Smithin 2003). In contrast, circuit analysis is more explicitly sociological: money is a 'social reality within the system: a non-commodity in a universe of commodities' (de Vroey 1984: 383). Other formulations have begun to move further away from the traditional metaphors of 'things' that 'flow', or even move in a 'circuit'. As Cencini, argues, following Tooke, credit-money does not flow; rather, it is an emission that 'appears' and 'disappears' in the credits and debits of double-entry bookkeeping.[22] Rather, the specific network of the (social) relations of the circuit *constitutes* money. This network may be seen as a three-way balance sheet relation between the issuers of credit, the borrowers and those employed by the borrowers who spend it as money (Parguez and Seccareccia 2000: 101). Graziani (1990), for example, has outlined this social structure in more detail. Macro-groups in the economy are linked in the three relationships that constitute the monetary circuit – banks and firms, firms and workers, and banks and the central bank. Most importantly, 'banks and firms must be considered as *two distinct kinds of agents* [which] cannot be aggregated into one single sector' (Graziani 1990: 11, emphasis added). In other words, following the early Keynes, Schumpeter and Minsky, the money and production sides of the capitalist economy must be seen as institutionally distinct and relatively autonomous in their contributions to the economic process (Minsky 1982).

Modern Neo-Chartalism

Any influence that Knapp's *State Theory of Money* might have had on even heterodox economic theories of money has been almost entirely, and indirectly, through Keynes. However, a post-Keynesian econo-mist has recently moved on from the analysis of endogenous credit-money (Wray 1990) and produced a bold application of the state theory of money to the problem of securing non-inflationary full employment (Wray 1998, 2000; Bell 2000, 2001).[23]

We shall have to return to some of the historical and substantive details of neo-chartalism; but here we need only outline the basic structure of the argument. It is very closely based on Knapp, and also makes use of Keynes and Innes. To repeat: money is peculiarly a creation of the state, which declares the abstract money of account and the means of payment that is authorized to represent it. Money's validity is secured by its acceptance by the state as payment of taxes and in payment by the state for the goods and services of its citizens. Wray presents further examples of how colonial rulers were able to establish wage labour by enforcing the payment of taxation. Tax levels were set high enough to ensure that the indigenous population had to work continuously to meet their obligations. In a refreshing counter to the increasing emphasis on the role of 'trust' as the basis for the use of money, Wray's analysis points to the more fundamental role of coer-cion (Wray 1998). Flogging, imprisonment and branding with red-hot coins were the penalties for not paying taxes in the money issued and accepted by the state.

With regard to monetary policy, Wray integrates the fundamental state theory propositions concerning taxation with Lerner's theory of 'functional finance' (Lerner 1943, 1947). Writing at the beginning of the 'Keynesian' phase of fiscal policy in the USA, Lerner argued that the traditional doctrines of 'sound' government finance should be replaced by a level of spending in the economy that was 'neither greater nor less than that rate which at the current prices would buy all the goods that it is possible to produce' (Lerner 1943: 39). As Thomas Attwood and the Birmingham School argued in the 1820s, the state should act as the employer of last resort (Mosler 1997). Neo-chartalists correctly identify the state's role in the social and economic structure of monetary creation. However, like most economists of any persuasion, they tend to overlook the fact that monetary policy is not simply a matter of functionality; it is also the result of social and political struggle in which economic theory informs, and gives meaning to, the conflicting interests. In contradiction of the positivist implications of mainstream economics' naturalistic conception, theories of money are an essential part of the social process of producing money. They are 'performative' (see the discussions in chapters 3 and 7).

Conclusions

Four themes are to be found in these heterodox traditions: that money is essentially an abstract measure of value; that money consists in a claim or a credit; that the state, or an authority, is an essential basis for money; that money is not neutral in the economic process. They are rarely integrated in any one work, and, of course, there is considerable ambiguity and, at times, contradiction. For example, there is no consistent distinctively heterodox answer to the question of how money gets its value. Indeed, many economists in the post-Keynesian tradition hold quite conventional views on the supply and demand for money and the impact on prices. But all four themes are antithetical to orthodox economic analysis and give different answers to the questions of what money does, how it is produced and how its value is determined. These elements will be drawn together and elaborated in the following chapter.

In contrast to its neglect in the economic mainstream, the unit of account function of money is given primacy in credit theories of money. Money of account confers the quality of 'moneyness' (Hoover 1996; Einaudi 1953 [1936]). Money is uniquely specified as an abstract measure of value, and thereby distinguished from other commodities. As Keynes argued, money of account is the 'primary concept'; that is, the description of money which various things may answer (Keynes 1930: 3). A commodity could not answer to the description of money, as it does in the commodity theory, simply by having an exchange-value in relation to other commodities. As a result of the focus on money of account, this approach is sometimes referred to as monetary nominalism (Ellis 1934; Schumpeter 1994 [1954]).[24]

Second, the value of money does not derive either directly or indirectly, as a symbol, from the commodity that comprises the money-stuff, or from a commodity standard that money expresses. Rather, money is held to be a claim against goods; it is *abstract* purchasing power. The form of money-stuff is of secondary importance, because all monetary instruments are 'tokens' or 'tickets'. The holder of money is owed goods, and therefore the creation of money entails the creation of debt. Money is issued as payment for goods – that is to say, for the discharge of a debt incurred by the state, for example. Or, money is issued as a loan which may be repaid in the same money. Regardless of the particular form and substance it has as a medium of exchange and/or payment, the value of *all* money is its value as credit denominated in an abstract money of account.[25]

An insistence that the market alone cannot make and sustain a viable money is a third characteristic of heterodox thinking on money. The conjecture that money evolves to overcome the inefficiency of barter is rejected. Both the logical and the historical origins of money are to be found in the state. Only an authority can overcome the anarchy of barter and impose a uniform money of account measure of value. Monetary space is sovereign space; it does not consist simply in the symbolic representation of market transactions, as it does in orthodox economic theory.[26]

A rejection of the axiom of money's neutrality in the barter-exchange model of the 'real' economy is a fourth distinguishing feature of the heterodox tradition. It is for this reason that the approach is referred to as 'monetary' economic analysis (Schumpeter 1994 [1954]: 277–8; Rogers 1989). Prices, rates of interest and so on are considered to be independent forces in the economy, and not merely symbols of the actual substructure of the 'real' (see Smithin 2003: ch. 6). It should be noted that there is no logical connection between credit theory and the rejection of the model of the 'real' economy. As Wicksell's work and the 'new monetary economics' show, tickets, tokens or simply a credit giro clearance of debits and credits could be seen as 'neutral veils' that merely signify 'real' exchange ratios. But there is an important *implicit* interconnection between the two positions – that is to say, between claim/credit theory and monetary analysis. Keynes and others argued that the theoretically unlimited elasticity of production of credit-money could be a catalyst for stimulating and creating new economic activity.[27] In sharp contrast to Wicksell, the rate of interest is not merely a measure of the 'real' economy's propensities; rather, it 'enters as a real determinant in the economic scheme' (Keynes 1973

[1936]: 191). In short, heterodox theories see money as a non-neutral 'force of production' (Minksy 1986). One way or another, the heterodox analysis of money points implicitly to the fact that money is socially and politically constructed *and* constituted – that is, to say, money *is* a social relation. This has not been fully developed within economic heterodoxy and, as I have suggested, it has been largely ignored within sociology.

3

Money in Sociological Theory

When barter is replaced by money transactions a third factor is introduced between the two parties... the direct line of contact between them... moves to the relationship which each of them... has with the economic community that accepts the money.

Simmel 1978 [1907]: 177

In the Introduction, I suggested that the analysis of money had suffered as a result of the division of intellectual labour after the *Methodenstreit*.[1] Economics abandoned any theoretical interest in the ontology of money, and sociology appeared to shun those very sociological and historical questions about money that were an essential part of the methodological battles. Outside the Marxian schools, sociology began to redefine its interest in the economic realm in terms of the social and cultural field that economics had allowed it to retain.[2] This one-sided emphasis on the 'cultural' and the narrowly 'social' would not matter if economics had provided an adequate explanation of money's existence and functions; but it did not. The question of the nature of money somehow got lost.

A thorough intellectual history of the neglect of the sociology of money would have little intrinsic interest, nor would it advance the understanding of money. However, some ground clearing is necessary. I shall be concerned only with money in sociological *theory*. The chapter has two aims. The first is briefly to outline how the conception of money in two major twentieth-century sociological traditions has

resulted in its existence being taken for granted. Second, in a short
reinterpretation of Weber's and Simmel's analysis of money, I wish to
draw out the important elements of their work, inherited from the
Historical School, which were subsequently ignored by the sociological mainstream.

Money as a Symbolic Medium

Parsons's early work played a part in confirming the terms of the
division of intellectual labour between economics and sociology. They
are distinct, but complementary, as he was assured of 'the essential
soundness, from a sociological view, of the main core tradition in
economics' (Parsons 1991 [1953]). From a sociological standpoint,
money is a symbolic generalized medium of communication and interaction (Parsons 1950; Parsons and Smelser 1956). It facilitates the
integration of the functionally differentiated parts of the social system
– in an analogous way to integration through prices in economic
theory. But as a 'symbol', money is 'neutral' in so far as it does not
affect the underlying constitution of either the 'real' economy or the
social system. Parsons followed economics' axiom that value is realiz-
able only in exchange, and that money is only a symbol of value – that
is, money, as *symbolic medium*, is without value (Ganssmann 1988:
308). Like its economic counterpart, this notion does not fully grasp
the obvious fact of money's duality as a socially constructed store of
abstract value that is also privately appropriated. Furthermore,
Parsonian sociology failed to take into account not only that domination derives from the *possession* of money, but also that it derives
from control of the actual process of money's *production* by states and
banks. Apart from a description of money's integrative functions, all
other questions could be left to economics.
   This general orientation has persisted in sociology. Habermas,
Luhmann and Giddens, for example, have all followed this concept
of money as a 'symbolic token' or 'media of interchange' [sic]
(Giddens 1990: 22; see Dodd's (1994) secondary analysis of Habermas
and Luhmann). Money promotes 'systemic complexity' and the 'time
space distanciation' of modernity; but its existence is taken for
granted. The importance of trust is repeated, but this has 'as much
explanatory value as saying that credit comes from *credere*'
(Ganssmann 1988: 293). Rather, explaining money involves the historical analysis of a specific form of social technology that accounts
for abstract value and transports it through time. To be sure, money
has the *consequences* that Giddens and others outline – but only if the

social relations of its production remain intact. In the absence of this analysis, modern mainstream sociology implies a functionalist explanation of money's existence that parallels the teleological theorems to be found in mainstream economics. Like economics, much modern sociology has lost sight of the obvious. Money is not merely a symbolic token that integrates 'disembedded' social systems (Giddens 1990); it is also *value* in itself. Control of money's production is a pivotal social institution.

Marx and Marxian Analysis

Parsons's dismissal of Marx as a minor classical economist is a gross exaggeration, but it contains a grain of truth. The labour theory of value committed Marx, and his successors, to a version of the commodity theory of money, with all its attendant errors. To this extent, Marx's general theory of money was mistaken. He could not have been more wrong, and the error could not have been more unequivocally stated. 'The principal difficulty in the analysis of money is surmounted as soon as it is understood that the commodity is the origin of money' (Marx 1970: 64). Most importantly, this attachment to the labour theory of value of commodity-money prevented Marx from realizing that his theory of *capital* as a *social relation* applied also to money. Furthermore, the preoccupation with the labour theory of value and commodity-money prevented a clear understanding of capitalist credit-money (Cutler et al. 1978: 24–6). Later Marxian and sociological analyses of finance capital have perpetuated the misunderstanding (for example, Scott 1997; on Hilferding's errors, see Henwood 1997).[3]

Like Adam Smith, Marx held that '[g]old confronts other commodities as money only because it previously confronted them as a commodity ... It acts as a universal measure of value, and only through performing this function does gold ... become money' (Marx 1976: 162, 188). Precious metal can become a measure of value because mining and minting embody labour, which can be expressed in 'the quantity of any other commodity in which the same amount of labour-time is congealed' (Marx 1976: 186). Forms of credit are derivative: bank notes and bills of exchange are money in so far as they directly *represent* both precious metals and/or commodities in exchange.

But Marx's distinctive departure from classical economics is to show that monetary relationships do not merely represent a *natural economic* reality, but also mask the latter's underlying reality of the *social relations* of production. These constitute the reality that appears in a monetized alienated form. For Marx there are *two* 'veils'. Behind money lie 'real' economic forces, as they do in a somewhat different manner in orthodox economics. In turn, behind these economic forces lie the 'real' social relations, which also appear as monetary relations. Tearing away these monetary masks or veils will demystify capitalism and its money, which will become 'visible and dazzling to our eyes' (Marx 1976: 187).

This kind of reasoning is why Marx is considered a classical sociologist; but it also implies that money can be analytically 'bracketed'. Notwithstanding the *two* veils, Marx's *analytical* position is similar to that of classical economics. Emphasis on the social relations of production of commodities and the labour theory of value prevented Marx (and almost all his contemporaries) from recognizing the *relative autonomy* of the production of abstract value in the form of credit-money, or the more radical position that all money is token credit. Marx dismissed as 'professorial twaddle' Roscher's perfectly aimed complaint that economists 'do not bear sufficiently in mind the peculiarities that distinguish money from other commodities' (Marx 1976: 187, n. 13). In company with all commodity theorists, Marx failed to consider money as abstract value, defined by a money of account and sustained by its own social relations of production.

At times, Marx appeared to have grasped that capitalist credit-money can be created autonomously outside the sphere of the production and circulation of commodities; but then he thinks that it plays an essentially *dysfunctional* role. Bank credit could expand beyond 'its necessary proportions' and become 'the most potent means of driving capitalist production beyond its own limits, and this has become one of the most effective vehicles of crises and swindle' (Marx 1981: 735–9). Marx held the conventional contemporary Currency School view that credit instruments (bills of exchange, promissory notes, etc.) were, or rather should be, in a rationally organized system, no more than functional substitutes for hard cash.

The anachronistic and misleading commodity-exchange theory of money is evident in Hilferding's *Finance Capital* (1981 [1910]), which, despite the ostensible critique, was entirely consistent with the orthodox economic theory of the time. He dismissed Knapp's state theory for 'eschewing all economic explanation'. Rather, 'money... originates in the exchange process and requires no other condition' (Hilferding 1981 [1910]: 36; see also p. 376). Credit creation is anchored in the 'real' economy of production, and therefore 'the quantity of credit money is limited by the level of production and circulation' (Hilferding 1981 [1910]: 64–5). Banks aid the capitalist process by garnering the bourgeoisie's 'idle capital' together with the 'idle money of all other classes for use in production' (Hilferding 1981 [1910]: 90). All this is perfectly true. But, as Schumpeter and Keynes argued, the *differentia specifica* of capitalism lies in banks' endogenous creation of new deposits of credit-money *ex nihilo* – or, more accurately, out of the *social relation* of debt. This lending is *new* money, and not merely the collection of pre-existing 'little pools' into larger reservoirs (Schumpeter 1994 [1954]: 1113). In failing to see this essentially capitalist process, Hilferding and generations of Marxists and sociologists have actually underestimated the power of finance capital!

Like orthodox economics, the Marxian analysis of money has been disabled by the search for the value of money in the commodity (Fine and Lapavitsas 2000 and the critique in Ingham 2001). It has been unable to consider the proposition that *all* money consists in symbolic tokens of *abstract* value that signify, and are constituted by, their own social relations of credit-debt. From a sociological standpoint, these social relations must be considered as the reality of money. We may now turn to those aspects of Simmel's and Weber's work which contain similar arguments that were taken from the Historical School.

Simmel's *The Philosophy of Money*

Unfortunately, sociology has taken Simmel at his misleading word that *The Philosophy of Money* is not really about money, but rather about how money expresses the essence of modern life (Dodd 1994: 175). The modern spirit of discontinuous, fragmented, increasingly abstract impersonal relations finds its most perfect expression in money. 'The more the life of society becomes dominated by monetary relationships, the more the relativistic character of existence finds its expression in conscious life' (Simmel 1978 [1907]: 512). This form of 'sociation' generates individuality, personal freedom and intellectualism (Dodd 1994; B. Turner 1999). However, in addition to the analysis of the effects of money, *The Philosophy of Money* contains important, but fragmented, accounts of money's nature – its origins, its essential qualities and how these are produced. Two aspects of *The Philosophy of Money* have received less attention than they deserve: the analysis of money as *abstract* value, and as a form of *sociation* in itself – that is to say, as *constituted* by social relations.

Simmel rejects all economic theory, including Marxian theory, which locates money's value in the specific substance or content of the money-stuff. The value of money does not derive from the costs of its production, or supply and demand, or labour value. Rather, money is the representative of *abstract* value (Simmel 1978 [1907]: 120); it is 'the value of things without the things themselves' (Simmel 1978 [1907]: 121). Money is the 'distilled exchangeability of objects... the *relation* between things, a relation that persists in spite of the changes in the things themselves' (Simmel 1978 [1907]: 124, emphasis original). Simmel's critique of commodity theories of money is developed with a dismissal of their argument that measures must have the same quality as the object to be measured – for example, measures of length are long, and therefore a measure of value must be valuable (Simmel 1978 [1907]: 131). Some measures of length are long; but, as Simmel argued, this is because measure and measured object *share the same quality* of length. 'To establish a proportion between two quantities, not by direct comparison, but in terms of the fact that each of them relates to a third quantity and that these relations are equal or unequal' is one of society's great accomplishments (Simmel 1978 [1907]: 146). Thus, following the nominalists of the Historical School, Simmel asserts the logical primacy of the abstraction of money of account. Money is 'one of those normative ideas that obey the norms that they themselves represent' (Simmel 1978 [1907]: 122; see Orlean 1998: money is *auto-référentielle*; see also Searle 1995).

Writing at the apogee of the gold standard, Simmel conceded that '[m]oney performs its services best when it is not simply money, that is when it does not merely represent the value of things in pure abstraction' (Simmel 1978 [1907]: 165). But he does not lose sight of his essential and prescient point. 'It is not technically feasible', Simmel continues, 'to accomplish what is technically correct, namely to transform the money function into a pure token money, and to detach it completely from every substantial value that limits the quantity of money, *even though the actual development of money suggests that this will be the final outcome*' (Simmel 1978 [1907]: 165, emphasis added). Indeed, with the breaking of the link between gold and the dollar in 1971, commodity-money ceased to exist as even a standard of value.

In contrast to orthodox economists, Simmel understands that exchange by money is structurally different from barter, in that it is constituted by the social relation of credit. Money is a form of sociation, and not a 'thing'; 'money is only a claim upon society' (Simmel 1978 [1907]: 177). Indeed, '[m]etallic money, which is usually regarded as the absolute opposite of credit money, contains in fact two presuppositions of credit which are particularly intertwined' (Simmel 1978 [1907]: 178). First, the metallic substance cannot normally be tested in cash transactions and is, rather, verified by the secondary characteristics stamped on coins by the issuing authority. Second, people must *trust* that the tokens of value will retain their value. This may be based on objective probabilities; but this 'kind of trust is only a weak form of inductive knowledge' (Simmel 1978 [1907]: 179). There can never be sufficient information for it to be the only basis for holding money. Additionally, money requires an element of 'supra-theoretical belief' or 'social-psychological quasi-religious faith' (Simmel 1978 [1907]: 179). 'Money is the purest reification of means, a concrete instrument which is absolutely identical with its abstract concept; it is a pure instrument' (Simmel 1978 [1907]: 211). And the qualities of this pure abstract value reside in 'social organisation and ... supra-subjective norms' (Simmel 1978 [1907]: 210).

Modern sociology's exclusive emphasis on trust tends to trivialize Simmel's analysis. Like Weber, he saw that the development of modern state and non-metallic, dematerialized money were intimately connected. Modern states were built, in large part, on the basis of credible metallic standards and coinage. Money led to the dissolution of the personalized bonds of feudal relations, and the '*enforcement* of money transactions meant an extension of royal power into areas in which private and personal modes of exchange had existed' (Simmel 1978 [1907]: 185, emphasis added). However, in a dialectical process, the 'value of money is based on a guarantee represented by the central political power, which eventually replaces the significance of the metal' (Simmel 1978 [1907]: 184). In this historical process, coercion, as always, preceded any 'trust' in the establishment of a currency. Again it should be noted that modern sociological analysis tends to forget that monetary sovereignty was established to a large extent by extreme physical coercion – such as branding on the forehead with coins and execution for counterfeiting.

However, having rejected essentialist theories of intrinsic precious metallic value and the classical labour theory of value, Simmel is left with the very same problem that the marginalist and Austrian subjectivist economic theorists had to face – how can myriad individual preferences produce a scale of inter-subjective value? 'Money as abstract value expresses nothing but the relativity of things that constitute value' (Simmel 1978 [1907]: 121); but, *at the same time*, it transcends the relativity of exchangeable values and 'as the stable pole, contrasts with the eternal movements, fluctuations of the objects with all others' (Simmel 1978 [1907]: 121, emphasis added). But how does it do it?

Simmel answers the question with a historical analysis of money's transformation from substance to pure abstraction (chapter 2, section III). It is full of insights gleaned from the Historical School, but is no more than a *description* of the process of becoming the non-material abstraction he correctly identified as money. Moreover, it is confused. For example, he failed to see that if all money is credit, then

Hildebrand's 'barter → commodity-money → credit' evolutionary scheme is contradictory.

Two fundamental questions remained unanswered in *The Philosophy of Money*. First, what are the origins of the *concept* of money as value? Simmel agrees with the Austrian economists that money expresses exchangeability, but sees that it cannot have been the *result of the process of exchange*. Rather, it 'can have developed only out of *previously existing values*' (Simmel 1978 [1907]: 119, emphasis added). But what might these have been? Simmel left no more than scattered clues. Second, how is the abstract value of modern dematerialized money established and maintained? Precious metal is a means of maintaining confidence, but in an 'ideal world' money would be no more than 'its essential function', as a symbol of abstract value. Here, Simmel reverts to a thoroughly positivist economic conception of money. '[M]oney would then reach a *neutral* position which would be as little affected by the fluctuations in commodities as is the yardstick by the different lengths that it measures' (Simmel 1978 [1907]: 191, emphasis added). In other words, Simmel accepts the economists' 'ideal world' in which the value of commodities is the result of the interplay of subjective preferences, mediated by the *neutral symbol* of money. But this 'ideal world' is not explained; it does not have a *social structure*. We need to turn to Weber for a sociological formulation in which the value of money expresses the social conflict that lies behind subjective preferences.

Weber on Money

The enormous secondary sociological literature on Weber's analysis of capitalism scarcely refers to his analysis of money. The chapters on money and banking in *General Economic History* have been almost completely ignored (Weber 1981 [1927]). The emphasis on religion has led to a distorted view of his work.[4] For example, he argued that the underdevelopment of capitalism in China was as much the result of the fact that its money was 'scarcely as developed as Ptolemaic Egypt' as it was of its religious ethic (Weber 1951: 3). This neglect is more puzzling in light of his lavish praise for Knapp's *State Theory of Money*. One would have expected scholars to have followed Weber's lead in exploring the 'permanently fundamental importance' of this 'magnificent work' (Weber 1978: 184, 169; also 78–9).

Money expands market, or 'indirect', exchange by which it is 'possible to obtain goods which are separated from those offered in exchange for them in space, in time, in respect of the persons involved, and, what is very important, in respect to the quantity in each side of the transaction' (Weber 1978: 80). As we noted in the Introduction, the most important element is not the existence of a commodity-money as a medium of exchange, but the possibility of monetary calculation – 'assigning money values to all goods and services' (Weber 1978: 81). *Money of account* – the 'continuity of the nominal unit of money, even though the monetary material may have changed' – makes this calculation possible. It is as an *abstraction* that 'the individual values the nominal unit of money as a certain proportional part of his income, and not as a chartal piece of metal or note' (Weber 1978: 168). Following Knapp, Weber refers to the state's definition of money in terms of a unit of account for the legal payment of debts, as its *formal validity* (1978: 169).

Weber upheld Knapp's distinction between valuableness and value (Weber 1978: 193; see also 78–9). But, in addition to money's formal validity (valuableness), there must also exist 'the probability that it will be at some future time acceptable in exchange for specified or unspecified goods in price relationships which are capable of approximate estimate' (Weber 1978: 169). In this emendation of state theory, Weber followed economic orthodoxy, and his critique of Knapp's analysis of inflation is based, to some extent, upon the commodity and quantity theories of money (Weber 1978: 192, also 180–4). Weber deplored the kind of disciplinary segregation that eventually came about after the *Methodenstreit*, but he believed that the analysis of the price of goods – including the purchasing power of money – was more properly part of economics (Weber 1978: 79). None the less, he was unable to resist making incisive comments, mainly in footnotes, on the nature of economic theorizing. *Economy and Society* contains the germs of a sociological recasting of a substantive theory of money (Weber 1978: 190), which implies a further departure from orthodox economic thought.

Typically, Weber confronts *both* economic orthodoxy and its socialist critics (Weber 1978: 78–80, 107–9). Prices, which in conventional theory are the result of the interplay of supply and demand, are seen as the 'product of conflicts of interest [that] result from power constellations' in 'the struggle for economic existence'. Consequently, money is not economic theory's 'neutral veil' draped over exchange ratios of commodities. Rather, money 'is primarily a weapon in this struggle, and prices are expressions of this struggle; they are instruments in this struggle only as estimated quantifications of relative chances in this struggle' (Weber 1978: 108).

The market may be a power struggle; but Weber offers no comfort to the socialists, who, following Marx, wished to remedy the inequality by 'issuing vouchers for an agreed quantity of socially useful labour'. But, in order to produce rational calculability, money has to be a weapon in the struggle for economic existence between 'the play of interests oriented only to profitability' (Weber 1978: 183). The exchange of a socially agreed quantity of labour for specific goods would 'follow the rules of barter' (Weber 1978: 80), and could not produce a measure of abstract value. Weber agreed with the Austrian theoretical economists in the 'socialist calculation' debate, that money can never be a 'harmless voucher', as its valuation is 'always in very complex ways dependent on its scarcity' (Weber 1978: 79). Any equilibrium or price stability in equations of quantities of money and goods, in particular the interest rate, will be the expression of a *predictable balance of power*. Conversely, in this admittedly incomplete formulation, price instability in general is as much the result of the 'economic struggle for existence' as it is the product of an overabundance (inflation) or scarcity (deflation) of money. In short, socialism could not produce rational monetary calculation. Bureaucratic administration could never produce the ' "right" volume or the "right" type of money' because state bureaucracies are 'primarily oriented to the creation of purchasing power for certain interest groups' (including the state itself) – which would cause inflation (Weber 1978: 183).

Simmel and Weber saw clearly the merits of the nominalist, state and credit theories of money. These provide some of the foundations for a more comprehensive sociological theory of money as a social institution.

4

Fundamentals of a Theory of Money

There is no denying that views on money are as difficult to describe as shifting clouds.

Schumpeter 1994 [1954]: 289

We may now draw together those elements from the critiques that will form the general framework to be used and elaborated in the analysis of some empirical and historical questions in Part II. The three inter-related questions posed in the Introduction are addressed: What is money? How is money produced? How does money obtain, retain or lose its value?

What is Money?

Taken no further, the textbook list of money's functions does not provide a satisfactory specification of money's properties. Apart from the unresolved questions regarding the relationships between the different functions and their relative importance, other 'things' can perform some of them. Many commodities act as media of exchange – for example, cigarettes – and there are many better stores of value than even the most stable money. Moreover, the focus on money, as a *medium of exchange*, results in a category error in which specific forms of money are mistaken for the generic quality of 'moneyness'. This has produced confusion *vis-à-vis* a number of closely related issues – for example, the distinction between money and credit; the so-called dematerialization of money; the advent of electronic money and the supposed 'end of money'; and the debate on new monetary spaces, such as the eurozone (see the discussions in Part II, chapter 9). In particular, the orthodox conception of money as a medium of exchange, as it appears in optimum currency area theory, has confused the debate on the problem of establishing viable money in the 'transition' economies of the former Soviet bloc, especially Russia.[1]

Furthermore, this approach strongly implies a teleological, functionalist explanation of both money's origins and its continued existence. It is held that money evolved to overcome costly inefficiency in market exchange for both individuals and the system as a whole. Money clearly does have efficient consequences, but unless they can be shown to have been in the minds of the earliest users of money, they cannot be taken to be causes of origin. As we shall see, the historical record does not support these conjectures. Moreover, it is also obvious that mere knowledge of money's advantages is not sufficient to bring about a viable monetary system or to guarantee its persistence. Money has definite social and political conditions of existence; it is an 'institutional fact' with 'constitutive rules' (Searle 1995: 13). How money is able to perform its functions is to be explained as the result of social and political processes.

The test of 'moneyness' depends on the satisfaction of both of two conditions. These describe the specific functions that are assigned socially and politically in a process whereby money becomes an 'institutional fact' (Searle 1995). Money is uniquely specified as a *measure of abstract value* (money of account) (Keynes 1930; Grierson 1977; Hicks 1989; Hoover 1996); and as a *means of storing* and *transporting* this abstract value (for means of final payment or settlement of debt) (Knapp 1973 [1924]). All the other functions – medium of exchange, for example – may be subsumed under these two attributes (Hicks 1989). (Convenient media of exchange, such as cigarettes in prison, can exist quite independently without becoming money.) Money of account is logically anterior to any form of money that bears the abstract value (Keynes 1930; Grierson 1977; Hoover 1996). 'Moneyness' is *assigned* by the money of account, not by the form of money. 'Materiality' and the 'tangibility' or 'portability' of forms should not be confused with the abstract quality of money. 'Forms' need not be tangible, but may exist 'materially' merely as book entries or magnetic traces in the computer networks that represent the credit relations that comprise the monetary system (see Searle 1995).

Money has a purchasing power that exists independently of the goods it can buy – 'the value of things in *pure abstraction*' (Simmel 1978 [1907]: 165). *Ultimately*, the consumers' good is the only final means of payment of the 'claim' that is stored in money's purchasing power (Schumpeter 1994 [1954]: 321). But this is not to say that money is *reducible* to the value of goods in any but the hypothetical circumstances described by mainstream economic theory's long-run 'end state'. This formulation omits all that is important in the actual routine operation of money economies. The *prospective* value of money is a *means* for producing price lists for goods that would otherwise have myriad barter exchange ratios. In Weber's terms, the 'substantive' value of money (purchasing power) at any moment in time is the result of the economic 'battle of man with man' in which money is a weapon (Weber 1978: 92–3). It is not a 'neutral veil', or a 'harmless voucher' (Weber 1978: 79). Any balance of money and goods is an expression of a temporary balance of economic power; it does not represent the achievement of the long-run equilibrium described by economic theory.

The fact that 'moneyness' is conferred by money of account becomes clearer with consideration of both the *multiplicity* and *dissociation* of money 'things'. The measure (money of account), means of payment for the unilateral discharge of debt, and any media of exchange need not be integrated in a single form – as in coinage. Even as late as the nineteenth century, the pound sterling was represented by a range of media – gold sovereigns, myriad bank notes, inland bills of exchange, local copper coinage. '[T]he pound as an abstraction was constituted precisely by its capacity to assume these heterogeneous forms' (Rowlinson 1999: 64–5). Today many media coexist: cash, plastic cards, cheques, magnetic traces in computer disks and so on.

'Monetary space' is defined by money of account in terms of which debts are contracted and discharged and all transactions are conducted. Monetary space need not be 'national space', but unless it is located in something other than economic transactions, monetary space tends to be unstable. Monetary space is not reducible to the actual transactional or market space as it is in, say, optimum currency area theory (see chapter 1). Rather, monetary space is the site, or field, of *potential* transactions that may be conducted under specific monetary conditions – that is to say, monetary space is sovereign space (on economic fields, see Fligstein 2001: 15–16).

The *means of storing* and *transporting* this *abstract value* consist in the *social organization* of the monetary system. It is only by these means that money is able to embody the abstraction of value, by lifting it not only out of any particular material object or commodity, but also out of any anchorage in the particular time and space of any actual transaction. A money transaction differs from barter in that the burden of trust is removed from the participants in the actual transaction and placed on a third party – the issuer of money.[2] How this institutional fact is accomplished involves our second question of how money is produced (see next section). Here we need note only how this emphasis differs from the orthodox economic *theoretical* understanding of money, which has difficulty in accounting for the movement of abstract value through real time. By contrast, Keynes saw clearly the importance of money as a social technology for connecting present and future. '[O]ur desire to hold money as a store of wealth is a barometer of the degree of our distrust of our own calculations and conventions concerning the future ... The possession of actual money lulls our disquietude' (Keynes 1973: 116–17).

Furthermore, it is this property of money that creates the ironic contradiction that was at the centre of Keynes's economic analysis. Money makes the 'monetary production economy' (capitalism) possible; but if everyone were to lull their disquietude in this way, investment and demand in the monetary production economy would disappear – that is to say, liquidity is not an option for 'the community as a whole' (Keynes 1973 [1936]: 155). Conversely, when 'animal spirits' revive, the need to hold wealth in the form of money diminishes, and consumers and investors spend. Money can never be neutral (see the discussion of debt deflation in Part II, chapter 9).

All money is constituted by credit–debt relations – that is, social relations. First, as Schumpeter noted, the holder of money is owed goods; money is a claim on the social product. Second, as we shall see in the following section, money is a credit for the user because it is a debt (liability) for the issuer. (Issuers promise to accept back their own money in payment of a debt.) Thus, the holder of money is both owed goods and has the means of discharging any debt contracted in money of account that exists to be discharged in that monetary space. Money cannot be created without the simultaneous creation of debt. For money to *be* money presupposes the existence of a debt measured in money of account elsewhere in the social system and, most importantly, in the debt created by the issuer's promises to accept back its money in settlement. In other words, the money debt is *assignable* – or transferable, or negotiable. Whilst all money is credit, it is not true to say that all credit is money, as some credit-money theorists imply (see the discussion of Minsky in Bell 2000).

The origins of modern capitalism may be traced to the expansion of assignable privately issued debts from the sixteenth century onwards (Part II, chapter 6). But it must be stressed that in the beginning the assignability of these private debts was limited to commercial networks and remained based in personal trust – as it had been in second-century BC Babylon (see Part II, chapter 5). As we shall see, general assignability is produced by monetary space that is not reducible to such market networks. Conceptualization of money in terms of generalized credit relations moves attention away from money and goods to the social relations between debtors and creditors in the process of price formation (that is to say, to our third question – the value of money).

Exchange with money is structurally different from barter, not only in the relation between user and issuer, but also in that transactions with money have *two* levels, as opposed to the one-dimensional exchange of goods. Money is exchanged *for* goods; it is also the abstract value *by* which goods are priced and exchanged. Goods and money 'change hands', but the money is also cancelling the *debt* incurred for the goods priced in the money of account in abstract value. A sale does not involve an exchange for 'some intermediate commodity called the "medium of exchange"', as it would do if money were no more than 'efficient' barter. Rather, a sale is the exchange of a commodity for a 'credit' which, in accordance with the 'primitive law of commerce', represents the 'debt' in the next purchase (Innes 1913: 393).

In advancing their argument, some credit theorists have referred to money as 'circulating debt' (on Schumpeter's formulation, see Earley 1994: 337).[3] However, this traditional metaphor, taken from the commonly used seventeenth-century analogy with blood, is inappropriate (Cencini 1988: 74). Rather, money consists in vast dense networks of overlapping and interconnected multilateral credit–debit relationships which are mediated by the issuers in a process referred to by Tooke in the early nineteenth century as 'efflux and reflux'. This is more obvious in the case of the 'clearing' of debits and credits in a bank giro, where money-stuff does not actually 'flow' around or through the accounts. The conception is even clearer in the case of credit cards. On one level, they are media of exchange, but on another they are the means of contracting a three-cornered relation of credit and debt between the buyer, seller and card-issuing bank. Coins and notes should also be seen in this light, and might be referred to as 'portable debt' (Gardiner 1993: 224). Coins were never simply distributed by the monarch as a 'public good', as is sometimes implied in economic explanations. They were issued in payment of a specific royal debt. Their acceptability was guaranteed by their assignability, which was, in turn, conferred by re-acceptance in payment of a (tax) debt owed to the monarch. The coin is simply reusable credit in myriad credit and debit relations. This reusability has been conceptualized as 'velocity' in orthodox economic theory, but this is misleading. It is not so much a matter of the same 'money' circulating serially, as the creation of credit–debit relations denominated in a money of account for which there is an ultimate means of final settlement. Schumpeter's quip bears repetition: unlike a commodity, money can have 'a velocity so great that it enables a thing to be in different places at the same time' (Schumpeter 1994 [1954]: 320).[4]

How is Money Produced?

Money is 'one of those normative ideas that obey the norms that they themselves represent' (Simmel 1978 [1907]: 122). Unlike economic theory's functionalist account, this conception is saved from tautology by the fact that money is seen to obey its own norms because the functions have to be continuously assigned in a social process of 'collective intentionality' (Searle 1995: 32–4, 52–4). Money is a promise, and the production of a promise involves trust. The importance of trust is increasingly recognized in orthodox economic theory (Dasgupta 1988). Significantly, however, it is treated here in exactly the same way as money itself, and, consequently, the logical circularities, noted in chapter 1, are compounded. Trust is seen as a lubricant that reduces friction in economic transactions that would none the less take place without it. But typically, trust is explained in these accounts as the result of a *knowledge* of trustworthiness – that is to say, trust is reduced to confidence, based on probability, that a known behaviour will continue (see Dasgupta 1988). In other words, in this conflation, trust is held to be based on the very thing it is supposed to replace – objective knowledge. Furthermore, as I have stressed, the question of trust in money is not a matter of co-traders' *personal* trust, as it is understood in micro-economics' dyadic exchange models. On the contrary, money's significance lies in the fact that it resolves this problem precisely in large anonymous markets where interpersonal trust *cannot* be generated. Money is *assignable* trust. In the face of real-world radical uncertainty, self-fulfilling long-term trust is rooted in a social and political legitimacy whereby potentially personally untrustworthy strangers are able to participate in complex multilateral relationships. Historically, this has been the work of states.

However, the social relations that constitute money are not based entirely on the existence of some overarching trust, as many sociological treatments imply. The assignability of the monetary promise also involves a more transparent guarantee in the *three-cornered interdependence* between the issuer of money and the users of money, and between the users. Fundamentally, as we have noted, this takes the form of a promise that the money, or 'credit', will be accepted back by the issuer in settlement of its own debt. 'The holder of a coin ... has the absolute right to pay any debt due to the government by tendering that coin ..., and it is this right and nothing else which gives them their value' (Innes 1914: 161). Furthermore, even under a gold standard, it is not the *commodity* but the government's *obligation* that produces the *money*. In the first place, the price of gold is fixed by the government, 'but redemption of paper issues in gold coin is not redemption at all, but merely the exchange of one form of obligation for another of *an identical nature*' (Innes 1914: 165, emphasis added).

The monarch's coin will pay taxes, and the return of the bank's note will repay a loan to that bank. Money is always issued as a debt, or liability, which conversely creates a credit, simultaneously granted to buyers of goods and services. As we shall see in Part II, different modes for producing money entail different additional or complementary kinds of promises – fixing the prices and exchange rates of the different precious metals to the money of account, or accomplished delivery of a credible promise to observe an inflation target. Ultimately, however, it is the *existence of a debt that gives the money value*. The complementary promise embodied in the precious metal is related to the existence of either a promise that the gold will be 'bought' by the monetary authorities, or by the market price. In the first instance, as Innes pointed out in the above quotation, it is the promise itself that confers the value. In the case of market price, the bullion is weighed and becomes a commodity whose price is separated from its denominated value as coin.

This distinction is typically conflated in the commodity and metallist theories of money. To be sure, there is a connection; but it is less direct than assumed, and does not follow the 'law' of commodity exchange. In the metallist theory, it is argued that the purchasing power of money is related to the metallic content of the coins – hence the insistence on a direct link between debasement and inflation. With less metallic content, more coins will be demanded for any commodity. However, there is little evidence of a *direct linear relationship*. In the first place, it is difficult routinely accurately to assess the fineness and weight of precious metal coinage. This is precisely the role of states (Goodhart 1998), and precisely the role that they have been able to exploit. Second, the tax rate is the major determinant of the use of the coins. If it is acceptable as a means of tax payment, the metallic content is irrelevant (Knapp 1973 [1924]; Innes 1913). Rather, it is in the use of coins as *stores of value* that the reduction of the metallic content causes a problem. First, if the market price of the metal exceeds the nominal value of the coins by a significant amount over a lengthy period of time, they are consequently melted down for bullion (Gresham's Law). Second, this problem is exacerbated in a bimetallic standard in which one coin becomes seriously undervalued as money, ceases to be a good store of value, and is effectively demonetized in a break with the nominal money of account. It is at this juncture that confidence in the monetary system breaks down and there is a rush out of money, as a store of value, and into other commodities, usually with an inflationary result. This would appear to have occurred, for example, in fourth-century AD Rome and again in mid-sixteenth-century England (see Part II, chapters 5 and 6).

Establishing the promise requires 'authority', which ultimately rests on coercion. Crimes and offences against the institution of money constitute a subversion of the assignment of its functions. Default, especially on tax debts, counterfeiting and so on elicit punishment. In short, the monopolistic imposition of a money of account, and a refusal to accept any other than the approved credit tokens of the issuer, go hand in hand with monopolization of physical force. In nineteenth-century colonial Africa, taxation backed by severe punishment for non-payment was used to coerce subjugated populations into wage labour. Tax would be pitched at a level that elicited the required amount of work. In Kenya during the 1920s, average taxation was almost 75 per cent of annual wages (Wray 1998: 57–61). It is significant that the Belgian Congo was one of the few countries not to introduce colonial money and, rather, to continue to rely on forced rather than 'free' wage labour (Helleiner 2003: 174).

But monetary sovereignty is rarely complete. As we shall see, coinages circulated promiscuously across ill-defined and insecure jurisdictions in late medieval Europe; local money was issued as late as the mid-nineteenth century in Europe; and capitalist networks have always developed their own 'private' media and means of payment – 'near money' such as 'certificates of deposit'. In many societies, 'local exchange trading schemes' (LETS) have recently produced their own media to facilitate exchange within those groups that through unemployment do not have access to the dominant money. Furthermore, not all common media of exchange are fully acceptable throughout the space that is defined by a dominant money of account – for example, cheques or credit cards, bankers' drafts and so on. Typically, however, these restricted monetary networks and circuits are organized in *hierarchy* that is structured by the degree of acceptability in terms of the fungibility of these restricted 'moneys' with those of the most powerful and legitimate issuer. This is almost always the state's money, which 'answers the description' given by its declared money of account. Again, it must be stressed that this is a question of sovereignty. For example, all attempts to create a modern currency under central bank control in early twenty-first-century Afghanistan are compromised by the ability of local warlords to print their own money for the payment of their soldiers and the collection of local tribute.

Money consists in vast networks of debtor–creditor relationships between issuers and users, and the seemingly obvious point that monetary systems involve the continuous contracting and discharging of debts must not be overlooked. Routinely, money is produced by the maintenance of the integrity of systems of payment. These vary according to the different modes of monetary production, as outlined below. Three elements are important. Debtors must be, first, willing and, second, able to pay. Third, there needs to be effective organization for the transfer of debts and credits. As we shall see, this is especially important in a 'pure' credit system in which money consists exclusively in the promise to pay. Confidence is required on both sides of the money relation. First, the supply and demand of credit-money creation is mediated by the norms of creditworthiness and morality of indebtedness. Money creation is founded on the bank's assessment of the debtor's ability to repay. Credit is 'rationed' according to socially constructed criteria, and the normative framing of bankruptcy attempts to distinguish between rogues and genuine losers in the competitive process (see Part II, chapters 6 and 7). Second, the issuers' creditors (depositors) – that is, the holders' of the issuers' liability – must have confidence in the issuers' viability. Consideration of this aspect draws attention to the fact that in a pure credit system, it is the actual operation of the payments system – 'efflux and reflux' – that constitutes money. For example, it would appear that electronic book-keeping and transfers have significantly increased the incidence of fraudulent withdrawals from deposits. Efforts to deal with the problem are inhibited by the banks' unwillingness fully to acknowledge that one exists. To do so would lead to a loss of confidence. Banks are unwilling to disclose evidence to the authorities, and prefer simply to write off such losses as bad loans (*Financial Times*, 3 March, 2003, p. 21). In some economies fraudulent disruption of the payments system in this way virtually paralyses the monetary system and seriously affects the functioning of the economy – for example, in Nigeria and Russia. These considerations draw attention to the fact that the economic ties that are constituted by the vast network of credits and debts fundamentally comprise a 'moral' network that depends on the keeping of promises.

Different *modes of the production of money* may be identified. These consist in *social relations* between issuers, between issuer and users and

between users and in the *technological means* available for the storage
and transportation of abstract value – from clay tablets to coins, pen
and paper, magnetic traces and so on. The following ideal types
identify four successive, but overlapping, modes of monetary production. The question of the social origins of the 'concept' of money
(money of account) and the debate on 'primitive money' will be
dealt with in Part II, chapter 5, together with a more detailed examination of significant changes in these 'modes':

1   Money accounting according to a standard of value, without transferable
    tokens (earliest known case: Mesopotamia, third millennium BC)
2   Precious metal coinage systems (Asia Minor, *c.* 700 BC to early twentieth
    century AD)
3   Dual system of precious metal coinage and credit-money (fifteenth to
    early twentieth century)
4   The pure capitalist credit-money system (mid-twentieth century onwards)

The different modes for the production of money entail, as we shall
see, typical struggles which are also involved in establishing the value
of money. For example, in capitalism, a central conflict is between the
debtor classes, who demand 'soft credit', and the creditors, who want
safe 'hard money'.

Finally, we must address the question of what *kind* of social and
political relationships the various agencies of issuers and users are
involved in when they produce the money. Are they the result of
mutual co-operation intentionally designed to bring about greater
efficiency and individual cost reduction, as outlined by orthodox
economic theory? Obviously, the recognition of collective advantage
plays a part in the creation of money. But, as Weber remarked, the
public treasury 'does not simply apply the rules of a monetary system
which somehow seem to it ideal, but its acts are determined by its own
financial interests and those of important economic groups' (Weber
1978: 172). Money is produced in a struggle for power, and I shall
argue that the *value* of money is also a direct result of struggle.

In anticipation of the more detailed analysis in Part II, we may
briefly consider two illustrations of the general approach. First, medieval coinage systems were based on precious metals standards in which
precious metals, denominated in the sovereign's money of account,
were accepted as final payment. These were the result of a struggle
over control of the mines and the supply of bullion, the actual manufacturing process of striking and minting by 'moneyers', and the
sovereign's control of the money of account through the power to
tax. A further significant struggle developed between the merchants,

who used private credit for their wholesale transactions, and kings, who considered this to be a breach of their monetary sovereignty. As we shall see in Part II, different outcomes of this conflict had far-reaching effects on capitalist development, whereby the production of money was eventually shared between two agencies – banks and the state.

Second, the production of money in modern capitalism involves a struggle between the state and its creditors (buyers of government stock) and (debtors) taxpayers. As shall see in Part II, chapter 6, this was a central political struggle in eighteenth-century England, and its outcome had a fundamentally important effect on the money supply (Ingham 1999; Ferguson 2001). In their investigation of the possibilities for non-inflationary full employment, modern neo-chartalist economists have addressed the questions of which *actually* finances state expenditure – taxes or bonds; and, as it is the ultimate source of all money, whether the state needs its citizens' tax money at all (Wray 1998, 2000; Bell 2000).[5] However, this narrow concern with the economic or accountancy question of what actually pays for what misses the *sociological* significance of the struggles between debtors, creditors, taxpayers and government bond-holders. In Weberian terms, the question of sound and unsound finance in relation to any normatively defined ratios of taxation and borrowing cannot be separated from the economic 'battle of man with man' (Weber 1978: 93; see also p. 79). On one level, the neo-chartalists are correct to say that the state doesn't actually need the taxpayers' money and that it is the taxpayers who need the state's money to meet their tax debt. However, the tax question cannot be seen only in these bookkeeping terms. Bookkeeping, like money, is not neutral. In capitalism, taxation is also a part of the settlement with the state's creditors – the rentiers, whose dividends are *believed* to be secured by taxes. Concepts of 'sound finance' comprise the 'fiscal norms' that govern struggles surrounding this exchange of goods, services and money between the state and the major economic interest groups. And, fundamentally, these settlements in capitalist societies consist in relations of credit and debt. It is precisely this kind of fiscal settlement that has proved so difficult to establish, as we shall see, in some otherwise economically advantaged states – such as Argentina.

Finally, it should be noted that the production of money is accompanied by an attempt ideologically to 'naturalize' the social relation of money. Social institutions and conventions based on no more than either an equilibrium of competing interests or a consensual agreement are fragile; they require a stronger foundation (Douglas 1986). 'There needs to be an analogy by which the formal structure of a crucial set of social relations is found in the physical world, or in the super-natural world, or in eternity, anywhere, so long as it is not seen as a socially contrived arrangement' (Douglas 1986: 48). Until the twentieth century, the ideological naturalization of money was achieved, and its social construction concealed, by the commodity form of money in the gold standard and the commodity-exchange theory of orthodox economics. With the abandonment of gold, however, the fiction of universal, immutable, natural money became increasingly difficult to sustain. None the less, as we shall see, the rhetoric of a natural economic process persists in the modern economic theory that underpins current monetary policy's efforts to maintain a working fiction of a monetary invariant through time so that 'debt contracts (the ultimate locus of value creation ...) may be written in terms of the unit at different dates' (Mirowski 1991: 579). These questions will be pursued in Part II.

The Value of Money

This is the quintessential economic question. Since separating from the other social and historical sciences in the early twentieth century, theoretical economics has insisted that the only acceptable explanation of value must be in terms of value in exchange. The intensity of the disputes and the extreme positions taken during the *Methodenstreit* were an indication of just how important the question was for economics' explanatory framework.[6] If the methodology of supply and demand, marginal utility, etc. could not explain the value of money, what could it explain? It was argued in chapter 1 that these narrow economic answers to the question are illogical and incomplete. If, as I have contended, money is more than either a commodity with exchange-value or a mere symbolic representation of existing commodity values, then, the answer to the question of its value must be sought, at least in part, from outside orthodox economic theory. Once constructed as an institutional fact, money is, of course, traded as a commodity; but, as we shall see, the creation of its 'valuableness' cannot be entirely divorced from its substantive value. In various ways, the uncertain prospective value of money influences its present value.

What follows does not claim to do any more than present elements of an alternative approach that departs from orthodox economics in two fundamental ways. First, at the most general level, the idea that there exists an optimum supply and value of money that is ultimately determined by the propensities of the 'real' economy is rejected.

Rather, as the social relations for the production of money and of commodities must be seen as comprising two distinct, relatively autonomous sectors, the value of money is the enacted outcome of social and political conflicts between the main interests in the economy. As argued above, money's value is the result of the struggle for economic existence – that is to say, for example, stable money expresses a stable balance of power. '[S]o long as it *is* money' (Weber 1978: 79), its value will depend on a conflict of interests; it is these, 'rather than the "ideas" of the economic administration that will rule the world' (Weber 1978: 184). Secondly, money's value is in part determined by its own conditions of existence in the relatively autonomous monetary system – that is, how it is produced. Its quality and quantity of pure abstraction reside in its 'social organization and . . . supra-subjective norms' (Simmel 1978 [1907]: 210).

As we have seen, the Keynesian and post-Keynesian 'cost-push' and 'demand-pull' theory of inflation implies a reversal of the quantity theory equation's causal sequence. That is to say, groups struggle to monetize their positions of power by raising their prices (see Fischer 1996: 200–3, 232–4, especially the reference to Slawson's work in the 1930s). These claims may then be met, as the post-Keynesian 'horizontalists' argue, by the endogenous creation of credit-money in the banking system. The role of the distribution of power in the generation and control of inflation is seen clearly in wartime. Exigencies in general, and the level of state demand in particular, shift the balance of power between the state and various economic groups. Notwithstanding appeals to patriotism, this presents an opportunity to exploit 'bottle-necks' by means of an inflationary 'mark-up' of the price of goods, services and labour. During World War II, the control of inflation in Britain was, arguably, as much the result of the politically negotiated 'industrial concordat' on incomes and profits, and the direct control of key prices, as it was of the economic and administrative skills of Keynes and the Treasury (Skidelsky 2000: ch. 8). The hyperinflation of the 1970s produced a promising sociology of inflation along these lines, based on the theory of 'distributional conflicts', but it waned with its subject-matter (Hirsch and Goldthorpe 1978; see especially Maier 1978; for a more recent general non-economic model, see Fischer 1996). As yet, the growing deflationary pressures in the early twenty-first century have not elicited a similar response. But I would suggest, for example, that an answer to the economic puzzle of Japan's protracted recession and deflation since 1990 requires an approach that goes beyond mainstream economic analysis and policy prescription (see Part II, chapter 8).

Changes in the balance of power between capital and labour, and between producers and consumers, affects the purchasing power of money; but arguably the pivotal struggle is between creditors and debtors. Historically, the struggle between creditors and debtors may be the most significant class struggle (Ferguson 2001). Late twentieth-century capitalism saw a significant conflict over the 'real' rate of interest (nominal rate minus the rate of inflation) which was expressed at the ideological level between Keynesianism and monetarism (Smithin 1996; see also Part II, chapter 8). Creditors seek to safeguard their positions by the minimization of risk through default or the erosion of the value of the debt through inflation. Schumpeter rightly designated the money market as the headquarters of capitalism, and as we shall see in Part II, chapter 7, the market for state securities represents its inner sanctum. Here the offers of long-term rates of interest on government bonds are weighed against the likelihood of inflation to produce a key rate of interest that affects investment behaviour in general, and the central bank's prime rate in particular. In addition to the central bank's linchpin rate of interest, the supply and demand of credit-money creation is also mediated by norms of creditworthiness and indebtedness, as we have noted. First, credit is rationed by lenders according to socially constructed criteria. Secondly, willingness to incur debt, and thereby to create credit-money, increased considerably during the twentieth century, after early capitalism's emphasis on thrift. Successful capitalist economies, such as the USA, have largely abandoned the strict moral condemnation of debt and bankruptcy, and have relaxed the law accordingly. Since the rulers of fourth-century BC Sumer periodically employed a 'clean slate' policy, to restart the economy after it had ground to halt under a burden of debt (Hudson 2003), it has been a prime aim of monetary policy to steer a course between such debt deflation and inflation.

The idea that money comprises a distinct and autonomous sector of the economy – that is to say, one which is constituted by its own social structure of norms, rules and power relations – is empirically obvious. As we shall see, this is now implicitly recognized, to some extent, in the economic analysis of the way in which central banks are involved in the creation and management of inflation expectations. However, this is not incorporated *systematically* into the basic tenets of economic theory, because it is not considered relevant to the question of money's fundamental value, which, it is held, resides in the long-run equilibrium between quantities of money and goods. But this somewhat contradictory position cannot be sustained. In the first place, all money has a fiduciary character. In the absence of the perfect information that is assumed in the economic model, the monetary authority's legitimacy and credibility will influence the value of money, because willingness to hold money, which in part determines its value, is in part based on estimations of its *future* value. Under a metallic standard, credibility was founded on the government's promise to maintain the fixed price of precious metal. In the era of pure credit-money, the credibility resides in governments' and central banks' transparent maintenance of sound money practice (see chapter 7).

More obviously, within a sovereign monetary space, issuers of money have the authority to change the value of money by manipulating the money of account. Indeed, as we shall see in Part II, this has been one of the main means by which money's value has changed. Altering the exchange rate between the coinage and the nominal money of account and standard of value was a common way of increasing taxation in medieval Europe and adjusting the relations between debtors and creditors. By 'crying down' the coinage, more coins would have to be paid to meet the demand (Innes 1913: 399; Wray 2003). In open capitalist economies under a floating exchange regime, the attempt to manipulate a currency's external exchange rate is a more prevalent means of altering the domestic value (purchasing power) of money. This may be pursued by the central banks' buying and selling on the foreign exchange markets, or by base interest rate changes to attract or deter buyers of currency. In this regard, the value of money is affected by its status as a commodity, and, consequently, it can largely be explained in terms of supply and demand. However, even here the explanation of the levels of supply and demand clearly has to go outside the orthodox framework, because the process of the production of money has an impact on estimations of its future value. Foreign exchange markets speculate on the basis of interpretations of the impact of government and central bank macro-economic policy on the value of money (on exchange rate politics, see Kirshner 1995).

The conception of money as a social relation, rather than a thing that circulates with velocity, also directs attention to the fact that its value depends on a fundamental core, or 'critical mass', of continuous (re)payments – that is, an efflux-reflux of debits and credits. Money is created and destroyed through indebtedness and repayment, as in the double-entry balance sheet. Counter-intuitively, it has been frequently observed, money would disappear if everyone repaid his or her debts (see Part II, chapter 7, n. 6). The production of 'new' money involves the creation of new debt that is as yet unmatched by a credit reflux. Thus, the scarcity (or abundance) of money is a function of the willingness to contract new debt – in particular, the willingness of the issuers of the ultimate means of payment. It is widely acknowledged that a faster growth on one side of the overall complex balance sheet that comprises the monetary system is associated with changes in the value of money. For example, money appreciates in value in debt deflation when economic agents stop borrowing (creating money) and spending in order to restore manageable balance sheets – as in the 1930s depression and in Japan today. Conversely, the expansion of debt is widely held to lead to a depreciation of the purchasing power of money (inflation); but, as we shall see, this need not be the case (see Part II, chapter 8).

From an empirical standpoint, the role of the state as an economic agent is central to the maintenance of this critical mass of the efflux and reflux of money. When economic theorists railed against the idea that a state's 'legal tender' laws could establish the value of money, they misunderstood the consequences of the 'factual' existence of the state as the single largest economic agency.[7] The state not only establishes the valuableness of money by its declaration of what it will accept in payment of taxation; it also determines its substantive value by influencing what must be done in the economy in order to earn the income to pay the tax. 'A dollar of money is a dollar ... because of the dollar of tax imposed to redeem it' (Innes 1914: 152). On the other hand, the state's purchases further circumscribe what is to be done to acquire the state's credits to pay the tax debt. As modern states are by far the biggest creditors and debtors within their own monetary spaces, it is inevitable that they will continue to exert the most important influence on the supply and substantive value of money. (Ultra-liberal economic orthodoxy might advocate a drastic reduction of the state's role, but it is impossible to see how this might be brought about.) This is recognized, of course, in orthodox macro-economic theory and policy making in the form of counter cyclical taxation and spending measures to stabilize the economy. Again, however, this should not be seen as a matter of mechanical relationships between levels of state expenditure, revenue and inflation/deflation as expressed in orthodox monetary theory. The balance of power and the *theoretical* understanding of the hypothetical impact of fiscal and monetary policy always *mediate* the impact of a given level of expenditure.[8] In this regard, economic theory plays a performative role – that is to say, it is part of the process whereby the balance of power in any monetary regime is established (as the doctrinal shift to monetarism during the late twentieth century demonstrated so clearly). And, as we have noted, this 'performativity' is also ideological, in its attempt to produce the working fiction of stable money (see Mirowski 1991 above).

A coherent and comprehensive answer to this question of the determination of the purchasing power of money scarcely exists. As we saw in chapter 1, monetarism's attempt to establish determinate quantitative short-run relations between money and goods failed utterly. None the less, orthodox economics persists with its theory of the 'real' economy, and, by focusing on the long-run neutrality of money, it is disabled from making any theoretical advances. As we shall see in Part II, chapter 7, the practice of modern monetary policy is increasingly divorced from any foundation in economic theory. Building on earlier developments that were arrested by economics' hegemony, I have sketched the tentative outline of an alternative conception of the problem and the means for its solution.

Part II

History and Analysis

5

The Historical Origins of Money and its Pre-capitalist Forms

One of the greatest advances made by mankind – the discovery of a new world out of the old – is to establish a proportion between two quantities, not by direct comparison, but in terms of the fact that each of them relates to a third quantity and that these two relations are either equal or unequal.

Simmel 1978 [1907]: 146

Money lies behind coinage.

Grierson 1977: 12

As the logical foundation of money is to be found in money of account, it is here that we should attempt to locate its historical origins, not in the excavation and dating of money-stuff (Grierson 1977: 12). The paucity of the archaeological record poses difficulties, but the evidence does not lend support to economic orthodoxy's theory of the transition from barter to money (see, for example, Davies 1996; Goodhart 1998; Wray 1998, 2004).[1] However, there are two closely linked alternative accounts. One attempts to locate the beginning of money's evolution in the more inclusive social category of debt. The other has looked for the origins of the very idea of money – that is, the concept of a measure of the value, or money of account.[2]

Origins of Money: Debt and Measure of Value

Debt and sacrifice

The historical importance of tax debts is, as we have seen, the basis for
state theory; but it is also argued that money originated in more
elementary social obligations that constitute one of the fundamental
social bonds between the individual and society (Aglietta and Orlean
1998). The level of payment for such debts is specified by a 'hierarchy
of value' by which an individual's position and status in society were
established (Aglietta and Orlean 1998: 21; see Andreau's analysis of
the Roman census, 213–52). Such hierarchies are historically prior to
the market, considered as a mechanism for producing prices. It is only
with the separation of the economic sphere from the rest of society in
the modern era that money takes on its historically exceptional role in
representing private property and private contracts (Aglietta and
Orlean 1998: 15).[3] Money became a general medium of exchange
only when the economy became detached from the rest of society.

The primordial debt is that owed by the living to the continuity and
durability of the society that secures their individual existence. The
ultimate discharge of this fundamental debt is sacrifice of the living to
appease and express gratitude to the ancestors and deities of the
cosmos (Aglietta and Orlean 1982).[4] In addition to human sacrifice,
'debt payment' also took the form of sacrificial privation. Scarce and
valuable materials or food would be given up to a 'brotherhood' of
priests who mediated between the society and the cosmos.[5] Such
hypotheses must remain conjectural, but there is considerable indirect
etymological evidence. In all Indo-European languages, words for
'debt' are synonymous with those for 'sin' or 'guilt', illustrating the
links between religion, payment and the mediation of the sacred and
profane realms by 'money'. For example, there is a connection between money (German *Geld*), indemnity or sacrifice (Old English
Geild), tax (Gothic *Gild*) and, of course, guilt (Hudson 2004). Value
at this stage of social development is the value of society to its
members, as measured by sacrifices of various kinds. But we are still
a considerable distance from the identification of an abstraction of
these values as a scale, later represented in universally equivalent
money. The problem involves attempting to fill in the intermediate
stages in the process of the progressive abstraction of money from a
substantive fixed 'payment', in the form of an offering of an institutionally specific sacred debt, to decontextualized symbolic tokens
denominated in money of account.

Measures of value and money of account

Unilateral debt, unlike the neutral medium of exchange in commodity theory, is inherently a relation of social inequality. Members of early human society were subordinated by their debt to ancestors, deities and, eventually, their earthly representatives in the priesthood. But it is impossible to say whether the debts of human and material sacrifice were borne equally by all members of society. Were children of all statuses potential sacrificial victims? Did all members have to give the same amount of food sacrifice? In those societies with little or no surplus, where the distribution of the subsistence resources was governed by norms of hospitality and reciprocity, no scale for measuring differential payments would have been needed.[6] In other words, a fairly well-developed division of labour and systematic inequality would seem to have been the necessary basis for a scaled measure of value by which to calculate differential debts to society. 'Primitive communism' would have had no use for 'money' – either as a precise measure of value or as a generalized abstract means of payment. (See the account of the transition from egalitarian tribal to stratified Pharaonic Egypt from 4000 to 2500 BC and the development of money in Henry 2004).

Broadly speaking, there are two theories of the origin of measures of value that confer 'moneyness' on the various forms. The first may be subsumed under a general of theory of public debts to society, as outlined above. Here measures of value are traced to the *Wergeld* institutions by which penalties were calculated for the expiation of the transgression of society's values. The second approach locates the use of money of account in the need to calculate economic equivalencies of goods in the agrarian command economies of the ancient Mesopotamian and Egyptian empires. The inadequacy of the historical written record again creates a significant problem. The best evidence for *Wergeld* comes from the European tribes of the fifth and sixth centuries AD – that is, several millennia after the use of money of account recorded on clay tablets in ancient Mesopotamia. However, there is also some evidence for *Wergeld* payments at this earlier time (Hudson 2004). It would seem reasonable to conclude that the codification of public debts in *Wergeld* institutions was typical of human societies before the ancient Near Eastern empires. Here, with the development of number and writing, the calculation of social obligations was transformed into a means of measuring the equivalencies between commodities.

Wergeld and money of account

'Behind the phenomenon of coin is the phenomenon of money, the origins of which are not to be sought in the market but in a much earlier stage of communal development, when worth and *Wergeld* were interchangeable terms' (Grierson 1977: 33). *Wergeld*, or 'worth payment', was a means of compensating for injuries and damage in communal or tribal societies as an alternative to socially and economically debilitating blood feuds (Grierson 1977: 28). As argued in chapter 1, the concept of 'money's worth' could not have originated directly from the exchange of commodities.[7]

'The conditions under which these laws were put together would appear to satisfy much better than the market mechanism, the prerequisites for the establishment of a monetary system. The tariffs for damages were established in public assemblies....Since what is laid down consists of evaluations of injuries, not evaluation of commodities, the conceptual difficulty of devising a common measure for appraising unrelated objects is avoided' (Grierson 1977: 20–1).

This analysis lends itself to a Durkheimian interpretation whereby *Wergeld* may be seen as a 'collective representation' for which the analogue is the structure of society, as implied in the above discussion of primordial debt and sacrifice. *Wergeld* expressed the two meanings of 'worth' that derive from the two basic elements of social structure: the utilitarian and the moral. Again, there is compelling etymological support for this interpretation. For example, *Geld* originated from *Vergeltung*, which implies the settling of scores and revenge (Einzig 1966: 379); and *shilling* from *skillan*, which means killing or wounding (Simmel 1978 [1907]: 357). The construction and imposition of indemnity schemes for functional impairment caused by damage, injury and loss to individuals, groups and even society at large could be imposed despotically, but would be more effective if accorded legitimacy based on a value consensus. Moreover, society's moral order is inextricably bound up with the evaluation of functional or utilitarian 'worth'. In the absence of unequivocally objective measures, a hierarchy of status is required to rank the functional contributions to the operation of society. Consequently, *Wergeld* was inevitably a matter of injury and insult. For example, it 'cost four times as much to deprive a Russian of his moustache or beard as to cut off one of his fingers' (Grierson 1977: 20). Loss of face was literally more important than some small loss of function. Moreover, it is quite clear that the expiation of the culprit was not intended to compensate precisely for destroyed functional value, but also involved punishment for the transgression of the values of the symbolic and sacred realms.

Of course, these arguments are simply a restatement of the familiar sociological critique of Adam Smith's primordial market of truck and barter – that is, the theory in which society's basic foundation is the advantaged interdependence of utility-maximizing individuals. However, ontologically, society is a moral community before it is a market.[8] *Wergeld* symbolically represented society's two faces. On the one hand, it attempted to quantify the functional contribution of social roles by the imposition of payments for the loss or impairment of the individual incumbents. On the other hand, these scales were informed by a codification of the values without which the attribution of functional worth to society would have remained anomic and anarchic. There would have been no means of resolving claims, counter-claims and 'blood feuds'. In other words, money has its origins in law.

Wergeld codified elements of social structure into a hierarchy of value, and thereby transformed them into elementary moneys of account. Payment would originally have been in terms of valued objects that could be standardized by being counted. This might be 'countable-usable (slaves, cattle, furs, fruit) or countable ornamental (teeth, shells, beads)' (Grierson 1977: 33), but it is the countability that transforms the valuable object into money of account. A next stage involved the measurement of the equivalencies between the objects that were the basis of the measure of 'worth' in the 'worth payment' (cattle, grain, etc.) and other objects and resources in the society.

Standards of value and equivalencies

Three ideal types for allocation of economic resources may be identified: reciprocity, redistribution and market price (Polanyi 1957).[9] The Mesopotamian and Egyptian empires (*c.*3000 to 500 BC) occupy the significant transition in human history when the organization of agriculture, based on the control of irrigation, secured freedom from subsistence. Sharing meagre resources according to norms of reciprocity and hospitality gave way to the taxation and redistribution of a surplus.[10] These were the first 'economies' in the sense that material life was now produced by a distinct sector of society with a division of labour – but it was not a 'market' economy. Almost the entire means of production were held by the palaces and temples, which developed money accounting to organize and manage agricultural production and its redistribution. The basic link between society and the sacred was mediated by obligation and taxation (debt) and controlled by the temple priesthood. Political, economic and ideological control was centralized and exercised through the money of account.

The money accounting system combined the various elements of social technology (means) and social practice (social relations) that had been slowly developing. First, a scale for measuring value, based on the counting of debt payments in hierarchically organized society, was already available. Second, clay tokens were used to represent items of agricultural surplus (grain, oil) and units of work (time or production). This elementary bookkeeping was the likely basis for writing. The use of clay tokens as representations of goods involved a conceptual leap in which each token was endowed with a specific meaning that could be understood independently of the context to which it originally referred (Schmandt-Besserat 1992: 161). For example, notches on tally sticks could not be used to distinguish different objects, and were consequently specific to each transaction. As the sign-tokens could each represent a different object in the abstract, it was possible to manipulate the data. The total production of dates, for example, could be calculated with a single sign that could refer to ten or more date sign-tokens in the abstract. Third, these tokens could also replace the payment in actual kind of tribal obligations and debts to the ruling class of priests and chiefs.

It is probably at this juncture that the link was made between token measures of material values (goods) and precious metals. Gold and silver and an accumulation of tokens of indebtedness were all symbols of sovereign and priestly power and status. The integration of the two – that is, precious metal and debt tokens – was probably a step in the development of forms of money that culminated in coinage. The metals were perfectly durable, and in the case of gold did not even tarnish with age; they were, therefore, excellent representations of the eternity of the cosmos. Precious metal tokens are to be found among the funerary goods in graves of the ruling classes in these early hierarchical societies (Schmandt-Besserat 1992: 171). Thus, by 3000 BC in the agrarian command economies, counting and writing were integrated in a system of money accounting to represent goods, debts, symbols of status and, most importantly, the mediating link between the sacred and profane. It is of the utmost importance to note that the value of precious metals derives, in the first place, from their use as symbols of power and prestige. Even when coinage was eventually introduced in the seventh century BC, pure gold coins were primarily status symbols and stores of value for the elite, rather than means of payment and media of exchange.

Mesopotamia's monetary accounting system was based on the value equivalence of the shekel weight of silver (240 barley grains, or 8 g) and the monthly consumption unit of a gur (about 1.2 hectolitres) of barley. It seems probable that this equivalence was based on the redistributed barley ration necessary to sustain a labourer and his family. The developmental sequence begins with *counting* grains of barley, not weighing either barley or silver; neither was it necessary for the talent and shekel to be minted. Rather, 'it was sufficient that these units should be state-created in the sense that it was the state which defined ... what weight and fineness of silver would ... satisfy a debt or customary payment in talents or in shekels of silver' (Keynes 1930: 12–13). In short, these command economies had moved from simple counting with, say, beads, teeth or head of cattle to counting an authoritatively declared standard of value measured by weight. The units referred to the weights that were used to make calculations. The magnitude of these measures of value should also be noted; the smallest – a single shekel – was the equivalent of a month's barley ration. These denominations of the money of account were designed for the calculation of large quantities of goods and debts, not as media of exchange in the market. Actual payment in silver by weight was not commonplace, especially in early Babylon; that is to say, silver bullion was not a proto-currency in the modern sense. Rents and taxes owed to the secular and religious authorities were calculated in the money of account and standard of value, but were paid in commodities and labour services (Goldsmith 1987: 10). The pivot of the system was the crop rental relationship between the temples and palaces and the farmers. Rents could be paid, at the official silver rate, in barley, which was then redistributed by the central temple and palace authorities to other workers. All other prices were similarly fixed, which served to stabilize the public–private leasing arrangements and the distribution and sale of goods to the rest of the economy (Hudson 2004; Polanyi 1957: 20–1, 264–5).[11] The development of coinage did not occur for a further 2,000 years.

The economic systems of the ancient Near Eastern empires (Mesopotamia, Egypt and the Indus plain, from the third to the middle of the first millennium BC) were not organized and integrated by the price mechanism of the market (Polanyi 1957; Weber 1981 [1927]; Mann 1986). However, despite the absence of freely circulating media of exchange, it is misleading to conclude, as do all conventional accounts, that 'these countries and millennia were essentially non-monetised' (Goldsmith 1987: 10). On the contrary, money was the very means by which society was organized and managed by a hierarchy of value (money of account) which measured the flows and allocation of resources and the pivotal temple–farmer, creditor–debtor relation. Poor or failed harvests prevented the repayment of rent debts in barley, and its subsequent redistribution could trigger crises. These were overcome by simply writing off the debts (Hudson 2004). The

network of debts was a social bond structured by the money of
account and standard of value. However, the debts were not generally
transferable as they are in modern capitalism's banking system.

Ancient banking

The question of ancient banking occupied an important place in
the primitivist–modernist debate that followed the *Methodenstreit*
in the social sciences (see n. 9). Valuable commodities, such as grain
and precious metals, were stored in the temples and palaces of the
ancient empires, and receipts for these deposits were used in the
transfer and clearing of debts within the state elite. Also the temples,
palaces and, exceptionally, independent families were able to lend at a
rate of interest. The economic theorists and their modernist and
formalist followers argue that these financial operations were no
different from modern practices and represent the 'invention' of
banking (see Heichelheim 1958 [1938]; Baskin and Miranti 1997).
On the other hand, the primitivists and substantivist historians and
anthropologists have maintained that these financial practices were
pre-modern, and could be understood only in the context of social
structure in which they were 'embedded' (Polanyi et al. 1957). The
equivocal nature of the archaeological evidence permits quite free and
fanciful interpretations. As if to demonstrate the timeless and almost
natural character of capitalism, many guides and commentaries on
modern sophisticated financial techniques make the implausible claim
that they can be traced directly to Babylon (see, for example, Dunbar
2001: 24–6).[12]

In the absence of coinage, most financial transactions in Babylon
were based on the 'transfer and assignments of credits' organized by the
temples and palaces, and were based on their control of the stores of
grain (Weber 1981 [1927]: 254; Innes 1913, 1914). The extent to which
the clay tablet records refer to private transfers between individual
depositors or merely to budgetary redistribution by the bureaucracy is
not at all clear. But all the evidence leads to the conclusion that private
transfers outside the command economy comprised an insignificant
part of total financial transactions. However, more extensive evidence
does exist for a sophisticated giro system, based on the deposits in the
granaries of Ptolemaic Egypt, for making transfers of value in writing
denominated in money of account (Davies 1996: 51–4). But money's
main role was in tax collection, bureaucratic auditing and accounting
control, and the distribution of ration tokens.

Furthermore, the credit transactions differed from modern capitalist banking. First, lending was controlled at very high rates of interest

by modern standards (20–33 per cent), and was only rarely private (Goldsmith 1987: 14; Weber 1981 [1927]: 256). The few firms operating in the middle of the first millennium BC in Babylon (the Egibi family) or Nineveh (the Murasu family) were not banks in the modern capitalist sense – although they have been frequently described as such. They did not receive deposits, and they combined money lending with many other activities (Goldsmith 1987: 14). As Weber warns in his analysis of pre-capitalist banking, 'one must guard against thinking in terms too modern . . . [and] one must not think in this connection of bank notes in our sense, for the modern bank note circulates independently of any deposit by a particular individual. In contrast, the Babylonian bank notes or tickets were merely a means for the more rapid and secure transmission of payments between depositor-customers' (Weber 1981 [1927]: 254–5). As we noted in Part I, and will examine in more detail later, the issue and circulation of bank notes independently of any particular individual's deposit or, indeed, of particular aggregate level of deposits requires the impersonal or universalistic transferability of debt as a means of payment. This social relation was entirely absent from both the ancient and, as we shall see, classical economies.

Giro clearance of mutual indebtedness did occur on a small scale within the merchant classes (Innes 1913, 1914; Hudson 2003; Henry 2004). But the main temple–farmer debts were personalized and could not be freely transferred to third parties for the payment of debt. Moreover, the standard of value (silver by weight) was not embodied in a transferable and portable form that was independent of a particular debt. This is precisely what coinage was to do. The issuers' token of debt – payment for goods and services – became detached from a particular transaction and furthered the progressive universalization and abstraction of money.

The Early Development of Coinage

For two millennia after the seventh century BC, 'money' was identified with coin, and the intellectual confusion over the nature of money began. In the commodity theory of money the exchange-value of the money-stuff (precious metal) determines its purchasing power. Coins embodied a measure of value within a conveniently portable medium of exchange and acceptable means of payment (settlement). However, Keynes (1930: 11) did not 'think that the act of coinage effected so significant a change as is commonly attributed to it'. To be sure, coin is not the origin of money, but it was undoubtedly significant.

The first true coins date from *c.* 640 BC in the Near Eastern kingdom of Lydia (western Turkey) (Davies 1996: 63). However, they were extremely irregular in weight and in the composition of the alloys, and did not possess any numerical indication of their value (Innes 1913: 380). That is to say, there could have been no stable relationship between the metallic content and the purchasing power value. Within half a century these lumps had been developed into rounded pieces, or 'coins', stamped with the lion's head symbol of the Lydian dynasty. From here, coinage spread to Ionia and the Greek mainland.

How is this development to be explained? Coinage did of course ease some of the 'inconveniences' of trade, as commodity-exchange theory argues; but it cannot be explained in this way. In the first place, barter continued to be a convenient and efficient means of conducting large-scale trade of the kind that occurred between the command economies of the ancient Near East.[13] Second, the small commercial sectors within these states recorded credit relations on clay tablets, which were periodically settled with various means of payment – barley, silver by weight, etc. Arguably, this was a more efficient means of reducing transaction costs. (It was much safer, as the symbols of credit were specific to the transactions and were not in danger of being stolen.) Despite the presence of all the technical means for its development – money of account, standard of value and payment in bullion – coinage did not come about. In fact, it is difficult to see how Mesopotamia and Egypt might have benefited by the integration of the functions of money in coinage. The opposite effect would have been more likely; economic co-ordination by coinage might have eroded the bureaucratic control of the redistributive system, as indeed it did later in the city-states of classical Greece (Kurke 1999). Coined wealth can be more readily appropriated and stored as a means of evading a central authority. It is difficult to discern the conditions within the ancient empires that might have favoured its emergence. To this extent, at least, the Polanyi school was correct in arguing that the money of the ancient empires was 'embedded' in their social structures.

The decisive factor in the evolution of coinage was the result of changes in the geopolitical structure of the ancient Near East. In the wake of the disintegration of the empires towards the end of the first millennium BC, myriad smaller kingdoms and city-states emerged. It seems probable that two subsequent developments culminated in the emergence of the earliest coins. First, unlike the later collapse of the Roman Empire, the political changes were not sufficient to seriously inhibit trade. (Indeed, continued economic growth and trade might well have increased with the loosening of the command and redistribution systems.) One response was the increased use of convenient and useful media of exchange in the form of peasant 'tool money' (Grierson 1977). Metal tools and stamped bars of useful metals, as highly liquid tradable goods, were used extensively around the eastern Mediterranean from about 1000 BC. It is easy to see how they could be taken to be to 'proto-coinage' (Mann 1986: 194), as outlined in the Mengerian account of money's origins. And it is possible that the exchange of useful and valuable metal outside the command economies played a role in the evolution of coinage. But it must be borne in mind that without attachment to a money of account, these media remained part of barter exchange. The exchange ratios of tools, metals and other commodities would have varied by transaction, and not in relation to the common denominator of a monetary unit. None the less, it would seem likely that such trading practices increased the use of liquid stores of value, and were a direct result of the needs of an emerging market system.

The critical step in the integration of value by weight – as in the shekel weight of silver – with countability and portability came with the world's first large-scale wage labour – mercenary soldiers (Cook 1958; Kraay 1964). The same peasant-farmers who were part of the increasingly dense trading networks after the disintegration of the empires were also the mercenary 'hoplite' troops whose new tactics and organization led to a demand for their services throughout the Mediterranean and the Near East. Large mercenary armies required a steady supply of a portable means of payment that could be used, in the process of expansion and conquest, outside its jurisdiction of origin. However, as sovereign monetary spaces were unstable, and the fineness and weight of the metal uncertain, a coin's value in exchange could vary quite considerably. Consequently, there would be little point in assigning and stamping coins with numerical symbols. In other words, early coins represented a transition between money (fixed by money of account) and a convenient medium of exchange with a variable exchange rate.[14]

It would be no exaggeration to refer to a 'military–coinage complex' in the second half of the first millennium BC. After his accession to the Macedonian throne in 336 BC, 'Alexander had need of a prolific and stable coinage' when he embarked on the creation of a vast empire that stretched from the eastern Mediterranean across Asia Minor to India (Hammond, quoted in Davies 1996: 80). In the early stages, his coins came from Macedonia and Greece, but captured booty, foreign mints and mines eventually were needed to meet the enormous costs of paying his soldiers. At the peak of its activity in Asia Minor, Alexander's army received about 120,000 drachmas per day, which required over half a ton of silver. In addition, the troops' outstanding debts to civilians were also met, and on one occasion this required 200 talents – that is, over one million drachmas (Davies 1996: 81).

The 'multiplier' effect of these incomes and the stimulus to economic growth of military activity in general have been noted frequently (Davies 1996: 83; see also Mann's (1986: 150) reference to 'military Keynesianism'). But the consequences of the connection between conquest, the consolidation of states through taxation, and the creation of sovereign monetary spaces should also be noted. With the imposition of taxation after conquest, the coins that the defeated people had received from the soldiers, in exchange for goods, would find their way back to the issuer. Now, states could indirectly influence labour towards preferred activities by setting a tax rate and paying for goods and services in the coin acceptable for tax payment. In many circumstances this was far more cost-effective than the use of slavery or forced labour, as European colonial powers rediscovered in the nineteenth century (Wray 1998). The creation of taxation-based imperial monetary spaces had a further impact on traditional non-market economic relations such as local barter and customary and gift transactions using a commodity such as grain. This would have had the effect of breaking down the ethical dualism of reciprocity, charity and hospitality inside the community and the distrust, exploitation and cheating of outsiders which had prevented the growth of large spheres of impersonal market exchange (Weber 1981 [1927]: 356).

Although coinage was a jealously guarded instrument of state, it inevitably enabled economic power to escape from state control through the massive injection of portable abstract value into the relatively loosely integrated Greek and, later, Roman empires. The possession of liquid economic power enabled the control of economic activity outside both traditional households and command states, and, consequently, economic classes made their appearance (see the general discussion in Mann 1986, especially 216–28).[15] However, in comparison with the modern capitalist world, this escape of economic power by means of coined money was limited; it was restricted to the simple accumulation of value in the form of coin, the supply of which remained under state control. Such accumulation was the basis for money lending, which appeared from the late fifth century BC in Athens. Again, this has raised the question of the existence of early banking. The arguments presented above in relation to Babylon apply equally to Greece and Rome. Modern capitalist banking, as opposed to money lending and the giro clearance of debts, involves the creation of deposits through the act of lending, and there is no evidence to suggest that this occurred. In any case, the business of accepting deposits for safe keeping and extending loans was negligible (Goldsmith 1987: 28; for an alternative, modernist view of classical Greek banking based on orthodox economic theory, see E. Cohen 1992).

The Roman Monetary System

At the death of Augustus in AD 14, Rome's ' "sound money" was accepted over an area larger than any before or after until the nineteenth century' (Goldsmith 1987: 36). Half the national product was monetized, and all imperial trade 'was conducted entirely on a cash basis' (Goldsmith 1987: 47). The Roman economy was driven by the state's activity; but, because it owned a far smaller proportion of resources than the earlier Mesopotamian and Egyptian empires, direct control was much weaker. On the other hand, coinage coupled with enough coercion and administrative organization to collect taxes helped considerably in extending the empire. 'Money taxes were exacted in the core provinces (such as Gaul, Spain and Asia) and were mostly spent in Italy or on army pay in the frontier provinces; core provinces had to export goods to the centre in order *to buy back the money with which to pay the taxes*' (Hopkins 1978: 94, emphasis added). But this was not simply a fiscal relation, as some have argued (Crawford 1970: 46). Rome had to buy its supplies privately, and, consequently, its issue of coinage also had an important economic multiplier effect. There is evidence to suggest that more coins were issued than were needed for immediate purposes, in order to stimulate production and exchange, in a proto-Keynesian fashion. During the first phase of imperial expansion, expenditure released far more coins into the provinces, via the superb network of roads, canals and sea routes, than were collected back in taxation.[16]

Unlike the early capitalist states of sixteenth- and seventeenth-century Europe, Rome did not sell bonds to its wealthy citizens to finance expenditure; that is to say, there was no 'national debt'. The Roman state's 'debt', so to speak, consisted in liabilities issued in the form of coin for payment for goods and services. Consequently, any disruption of the credit–debt relations of the 'coinage multiplier' could produce a crisis. The system depended on the maintenance of three interdependent elements: the control and inflow of bullion, an effective system for tax collection and sufficient economic activity (mainly the state's) for the generation of income in coin to meet tax debts. Eventually each was disrupted to an extent that threatened the continued reproduction of reciprocal money relations. Imperial 'over-reach' affected both the supply of precious metals and the collection of taxation. The inability fully to impose money taxation in the imperial hinterland inhibited the extension of relations between the fiscal and economic elements of the 'coinage multiplier' (see Weber 1981 [1927]: 60). Outside the coastal trading regions of early imperial expansion, manorial and feudal relations persisted, and were resistant to production for the market that elsewhere was driven by the need to acquire Roman coins for payment of taxes. Over several centuries, the balance between, on the one hand, the returns to Rome of both marketed goods and services and, on the other hand, taxes and the expenditure on military expansion gradually shifted from positive to negative. Other factors, such as bad harvest and slave revolts, were involved, but the difficulty of reproducing the relations of the monetary system had an independent effect on the eventual fall of the Roman Empire. With a dwindling income, the state was unable to finance the defence of the unproductive outposts against the barbarian invasions.

Since it was advanced by Gibbon in the eighteenth century, the idea that the 'decline and fall' of the Roman Empire was at least acceler-ated by inflation produced by the debasement of the coinage has been widely accepted. Both occurred, but they were not the direct cause of gradual imperial decline and fall; they were, rather, symptoms of a more fundamental disturbance of monetary relations, as outlined above. Despite its inability fully to extend fiscal relations to the hinterland, first-century AD Rome nevertheless found it difficult to secure an adequate supply of precious metal to maintain the required increases in coinage to meet its expenditure and tax demands. It became necessary to spread the metal, especially silver, more thinly, and this set in train a slow but progressive dislocation of the money of account and standard of value.[17]

First, there was a partial dissociation of the means of payment from media of exchange. Rome used two precious metal means of payment. The gold aureus was used mainly as a store of value, and for very large purchases such as land. The silver denarius coins were for taxation and other significant purchases. These were supplemented by base metal media of exchange – the sestertius of copper, zinc or tin and the quadrans of copper – for the routine purchase of small items.[18] The latter were not accepted in payment of taxes, and were not good stores of value.

Secondly, from the second century AD onwards, the state decreed, by fiat, the rates between the gold and silver coins, and began continu-ously to debase the silver denarius. (Unlike the capitalist states of modern Europe, Rome did not practise 'hylophantism' – that is, it did not promise to redeem coins for bullion at a fixed rate.) Eventually, the gold aureus became undervalued in relation to silver, and an increasingly poor store of value in its money form. Money and its value had become determined, in part, by a struggle between, on the one hand, the state bureaucracy and military commanders and, on the other, the landowners. The conflict was rooted in the opposition between the state's fiscal need of sufficient means of payment for taxation and military expenses in silver denarii and the agrarian ruling class's use of gold, either bullion or coined, as a symbol and store of wealth. At the time of Diocletian's attempt to stabilize prices in his Edict of AD 301, a pound of silver produced over 130 times more denarii than it had at the death of Augustus, almost three centuries earlier (Goldsmith 1987: 37).

However, from the standpoint of the orthodox commodity theory of money, the effects of debasement were very slow to appear, and prices did not rise significantly for some time. 'Silver "money illusion" seems to have persisted for over a century' (Goldsmith 1987: 37). But, of course, a reduction of metallic content will not necessarily affect prices if the coins continue to be accepted, at their face value, in payment of taxes. In commercial transactions, it would also be difficult to assess accurately the fineness and weight of precious metal coinage and adjust prices accordingly (Goodhart 1998; Innes 1913). However, with the progressive devaluation of gold, *in the form of money*, because of changes in the aureus/denarius exchange rate, it was gradually demonetized. Gold was hoarded in bullion form, and used in 'barter' transaction for land or 'gifts' to advance political careers. The withdrawal of gold from circulation caused shortages that disrupted large payments and transactions (Aglietta 2002), but, most importantly, it began to break the trust in the entire monetary system.

The heavy demands of state expenditure on dwindling resources, the slowing down in the supply of slaves and the effect of the rising demand for land were the real underlying causes of the rise in prices. It is significant that Diocletian combined his monetary policy of restoring confidence in money with full-weight gold coins with an attempt to control prices and wages (Davies 1996: 101–2). Neither had any lasting effect on inflation. Eventually, however, the continuation of inflation and debasement, in conjunction with increasing political and military problems, completely undermined trust in the coinage. At this juncture, in the fourth century AD, general trust in the monetary system broke down, and there was a rush out of money, as a store of value, into other commodities, which further fuelled inflation. The coinage broke its link with the money of account. Not only gold, but also silver coins, ceased to be 'money' and became speculative commodities that were valued in private transactions, conducted in the money of account (Aglietta 2002). This demonetization further impaired the already weakened taxation system, and undoubtedly contributed significantly to the disintegration of the empire.

'Banking' and 'capitalism' in Rome

Studies employing orthodox economic methodology view classical Greek and Roman finance either as essentially the same as that of the modern world, or as a proto-capitalist early stage of development (for example, Baskin and Miranti 1997; see the discussion in Davies 1996).[19] Greek and Roman merchants, like ancient Babylonians, kept credit accounts of their transactions, which could be settled by being periodically 'netted out'. But these activities were only marginal to the operation of the monetary system. Secondly, modernist interpretations of the classical economies also refer to money changing and lending coin as banking. But neither entailed the endogenous deposit creation of modern banking and the transferability of financial claims (see Part I, chapter 2).

As we shall see in the following chapter, transferable private 'credit' became 'money' as a result of changes in the social structure of early modern Europe. At present, we need only note that early modern Europe differed from Rome and the ancient world in general in two important, related respects. The first was the existence of a powerful class of capitalist bankers who produced their own private money, based on the bill of exchange, and from whom the city-states borrowed (Boyer-Xambeu et al. 1994). The second step in the creation of capitalist credit-money occurred when these private promises to pay became generally transferable to third parties as an accepted means of payment. But Roman social structure was inimical to such a development. As 'a result of the highly personalised character of the debt relationship, instruments payable to the order of the payee or to the bearer, which served for the transfer of claims, especially monetary claims, and of powers of disposition over commercial goods and membership rights in commercial enterprises ... had been utterly unknown in Roman law' (Weber 1978: 681–3).[20] A plutocracy did develop in Rome (Mann 1986: 267–72). Tax-farmers, who purchased the rights to collection, were conspicuous members of this class; but they were dependent upon the fiscal arrangements and were subservient to the state that controlled them. This privatization of tax collection did not constitute capitalism and the rise of a 'capitalist' class, unless this is simply identified with profit making – as it is in most modernist accounts based on orthodox economic theory.

The aftermath of Rome's fall further illustrates the significance of the relative autonomy of money – or, rather, the social relations that constitute money. In 'real' terms, the material resources of the Roman Empire did not vanish; but, as a consequence of the disintegration of money, they atrophied. Most importantly, the former Roman monetary space was eventually utterly destroyed by the inability of the barbarian chiefs to impose taxation that might bring about the acceptability of their coinages. Furthermore, contrary to ultra-orthodox economic monetary theory, competition between the chiefs' issues of coinage did not eventually produce more efficient money. Rather, it led to monetary anarchy, which, in turn, accelerated the economic disintegration. Issuers and mints and coinages multiplied. Significantly, coercion and terror fuelled the anarchy as the warlords attempted to impose and enforce their own issues. The severity of the punishment for the use of non-acceptable coins was a measure of the disintegration of sovereign monetary space (see MacDonald's description, cited in Goodhart 1998: 428–9).

As they penetrated each other's territories, competing chiefs collected their adversaries' coins for melting down and reissue as their own. But as the new states were too weak to impose a stable tax system, minting slowed almost to a standstill, causing further economic dislocation, and in large areas of the former empire barter was resumed. However, monetary relations did not entirely disappear, and the Roman abstract money of account continued to be used to calculate credits and debts that were settled with a wide range of different means of payment. This radical de-linking of the money of account and means of payment was to have, as we shall see, far-reaching effects on the next stage of money's historical development.

Conclusions

All evidence points to the historical origins of money as a means of calculating obligations and debts in pre-market tribal and clan society. Early settled agricultural societies developed a more complex division of labour than the hunters and gatherers, generating a surplus that was distributed unequally. Measures for the assessment of differential social and political obligations were developed. These varied by the nature of the transgression and the status of the injured party, and formed the conceptual basis for money of account. The first money-calculating societies for which records exist are the command economies of the ancient Near East. Here the measure of value was not integrated into a circulating material form. The main function of money of account was in assessing rents and taxes and calculating economic equivalencies between stocks and flows of different commodities. Payment was typically in the basic staple of barley, but could be in a silver equivalent – denominated by the money of account. The value of the Mesopotamian shekel did not derive from its silver weight, but from the monetary equivalency between silver and barley established by the state.

The integration of money of account and means of payment occurred in the wake of the disintegration of the agrarian empires. The widespread use of mercenaries in the ensuing warfare required a reasonably standardized and convenient form of payment that would be widely acceptable across different jurisdictions. These looser relationships between the state, military force and economic exchange weakened the monetary circuit between state and taxation. Mercenaries did not necessarily owe a tax debt to their employers, whilst, on the other hand, they had need of an acceptable medium of exchange. The connection between the mercenary's political freedom, economic autonomy and the extension of market exchange should be noted.

Paradoxically, this loosening of the links between money and political and administrative control eventually led to a greater extension of territorial control in a 'taxation–coinage multiplier'. Mercenary armies developed into Greek city-states with citizen-soldiers and their own sovereign coinage. From these the empires of Alexander and Rome arose. Between 150 and 50 BC, during a century of great Roman imperial expansion, silver coinage increased tenfold, and 'money percolated into a myriad of transactions which had previously been embedded in the subsistence economy' (Hopkins 1980: 110).

Despite the hitherto unparalleled sophistication of the coinage and the extension of market exchange, it should not be forgotten that Rome's overall level of monetization was relatively low by modern capitalist standards (Goldsmith 1987: 58). Aside from the military, there was no wage labour, and money was used mainly for the exchange between taxation and the acquisition of the means of payment through the sale of commodities to the imperial state. The private commercial sector was no greater than it had been in Egypt or Greece, and 'did not in general represent progress' (Goldsmith 1987: 58). Like the emergence of coinage after the fall of Babylon, it was the disintegration of the Roman Empire that created the conditions for developments in monetary practice that became the basis for modern capitalism.

6

The Development of Capitalist Credit-Money

'Credit' operations of whatever shape and kind do affect the working of the monetary system; more important, they do affect the working of the capitalist engine – so much so as to become a central part of it without which the rest cannot be understood at all.

Schumpeter 1994 [1954]: 318

The Banque does not solely belong to its shareholders; it also belongs to the state which granted it the privilege of creating money.

Napoleon Bonaparte (1806), quoted in Crouzet 1999: 76

Accounts of the rise of capitalism influenced by neoclassical economics and classical Marxism have focused, respectively, on the exchange and production of commodities. Money is seen to play a passive role. Changes in its forms and functions are explained as responses to the need for more efficient transactions and to developments that occurred elsewhere in the economy.[1] However, notwithstanding the importance of the free market, machine technology, factory organization and labour–capital relations, the historical specificity of capitalism is also to be found in its distinctive credit-money system.

The idea that the development of credit-money was a force in capitalist development is to be found in the work of writers who were influenced by the German Historical School of economics and, to a lesser degree, in the French *Annales* school of history.[2] '[T]he financial complement of capitalist production and trade', Schumpeter also wrote, was so important that the 'development of the law and practice of negotiable paper and of "created" deposits afford the best indication we have for dating the rise of capitalism' (Schumpeter 1994 [1954]: 78). The crucial element is that the production of credit-money in a banking *system* is a self-generating, relatively autonomous process in so far as the 'banks can always grant further loans, since the larger amounts going out are then matched by larger amounts coming in' (Schumpeter 1917: 207, quoted in Arena and Festre 1999: 119). Moreover, Schumpeter believed that the distinctiveness of capitalism was, in part, to be found in the entrepreneur's role as debtor. Although accumulated wealth 'constitutes a practical advantage', usually someone 'can only become an entrepreneur by previously becoming a debtor'. Furthermore, in capitalism 'no one else is a debtor by the nature of his economic function' (Schumpeter 1934: 101–3, quoted in Arena and Festre 1999: 119). From the French School, Bloch captured this same essential element of capitalism with the observation that it is 'a regime that would collapse if everyone paid his debts' (Bloch 1954 [1936]: 77). The essence of capitalism lies in the elastic creation of money by means of readily transferable debt.

As we shall see, capitalist credit-money was the result of two related changes in the social relations of monetary production in medieval and early modern Europe. First, the private media of exchange (bills of exchange), used in merchant networks, became detached from the existence of any particular commodities in exchange and transit, and were used as pure credit between traders. Later, in a crucial further stage of dislocation, bills became detachable from the particular individuals named in the creditor–debtor relation. Signifiers of debt became transferable to third parties, and could circulate as private money within commercial networks (Kindleberger 1984; Boyer-Xambeu et al. 1994). For the very first time, the *extensive* production of a form of money took place outside the state's monopoly of currency issue. Eventually, such signifiers of debt became completely *depersonalized* (that is, payable to 'X' or 'bearer') and were issued as *bank money*; that is to say, the promises to pay drawn on banks became a widely accepted means of payment. With this change, the *private* capitalistic financing of enterprise on a large scale became a possibility. In a second, and related, major structural change, some states began to finance their activities by borrowing from their wealthy merchant classes. Their promises to repay these national debts became the basis for public credit-money, which existed in an uneasy and uncertain relationship with the coinage.

Orthodox economic explanations imply that the development of credit and modern forms of finance result from economizing on mining and minting and/or as a response to the insufficiently elastic supply of commodity-money to meet the needs of the expansion of commerce and industrial production in capitalism (North 1981). Of course, economic interest was a spur to the development of advantageous monetary practices; but these were made possible by changes in social and political structure that were, in the first instance, only indirectly related to the pursuit of cost efficiency. In the first place, monetary practice, as ever, evolved with regard to the demands made by states in pursuit of their own interests. Second, the particular character of these changes cannot be understood outside the circumstances that were presented by the unique configuration of medieval Europe's social and political structure. The disintegration of Rome left the cultural shell of a civilization coextensive with Christendom, but comprising multiple, insecure, acephalous political jurisdictions (Mann 1986). The evolution of capitalist credit-money was, arguably, one of the most important consequences of these circumstances

The De-linking of the Money of Account and the Means of Payment

After the fall of Rome in the middle of the fourth century AD, money almost disappeared. As imperial trade and production diminished, and mercenary soldiers' wages no longer needed to be paid, the demand for media of exchange and payment fell considerably. But, most importantly, as we have seen, the *fiscal flows* of the Roman Empire dried up. This situation held particularly on the Celtic margins of the former empire, where coinage became redundant for two centuries, after having been in continuous use for more than 500 years (Spufford 1988: 9). As the archaeological finds of large 'hoards' of money imply, it was no longer routinely needed. Given the very small silver content of late Roman coins, it is likely that they were simply dumped (Davies 1996: 116–17). The two basic functions of money as a unit of account and a means of payment were unable to operate. The social and political system that was 'accounted for' by the abstract money of account no longer existed.

The resumption of minting on a large scale in the eleventh and twelfth centuries was an expression of the growth of kingdoms, principalities, duchies and local ecclesiastical jurisdictions, which began to emerge from the feudal networks of personal allegiances (Bloch 1962). The silver penny (from the Roman denarius) was the basic coin, but it was produced in a vast proliferation of different weights and fineness by the myriad jurisdictions (Spufford 1986: xix–xx; Boyer-Xambeu et al. 1994: chs 3 and 5). However, the fragmentation was partially overcome by the use of a common money of account, which the framework of Latin Christianity was able to sustain. In order to establish a degree of fiscal coherence across the loosely integrated Holy Roman Empire, Charlemagne (768–814) imposed a money of account, derived from the Roman system. There were 240 pence (denarii) to the pound (libra) of silver, which, in turn, was divided into 20 shillings (solidii). Only the silver pennies were extensively minted, and these, as we have noted, were of differing weight and fineness. The money of account, based on pounds, shillings and pence, did not necessarily correspond to any of the actual minted coins in use (Einaudi 1953 [1936]; Innes 1913). The two primary functions of money, integrated by Roman coinage in a single object, had become de-linked – 'le décrochement de la monnaie de compte' (Bloch 1954 [1936]: 46). The measure of value was a pure *abstraction* for monetary calculation. Payment could be made in kind, or in the freely circulating coins from the different jurisdictions that were given value by the abstract money of account – not by their metallic content (Bloch 1962: 66). This state of affairs prevailed across the whole of medieval Europe, and persisted in some parts until the late eighteenth century. The dislocation of money of account and precious metal coinage means of payment fostered a consciousness of money as dematerialized or 'imaginary' in which 'people acquired the habit of counting in pounds of 20 shillings with each shilling divided into 12 pence' (Einaudi 1953 [1936]: 230; see also Bloch 1954 [1936]).

It is essential to understand that the 'imaginary money' was *invariable*, in that people continued to count in these ratios regardless of the debasement, clipping or deterioration of the actual coinage (Innes 1913; Einaudi 1953 [1936]). By the late seventeenth century, minted pound coins weighed only 7 pennyweights of silver, not the 240 of the money of account; that is to say, 3 per cent of its abstract ratio. None the less, its purchasing power, in relation to the other coins, was the same as it had been at the time of Charlemagne's decree. Thus, by the late Middle Ages, when people priced things, they had in mind not coins, but commodities and obligations denominated in money of account (Einaudi 1953 [1936]: 230).[3] The *décrochement* of the money of account from the means of payment firmly re-established the abstract monetary calculation that had been practised in ancient Babylon.

Contrary to orthodox economic histories of money, Charlemagne did not intend to provide a standard measure of value as a 'public good', in order to facilitate market exchange. Rather, as in all previous monetary developments, the fiscal needs of church and state were most important – especially ecclesiastical transfers across European Christendom. But the use of a standard money of account across the Christian ecumene did of course eventually provide the foundation for a trans-European market. In response to the quickening of trade and fiscal demands, scores of authorities in many hundreds of mints produced coins – again, it must be stressed, with countless variations in weight and fineness.[4] These circulated freely across European Christendom, and all were evaluated against a benchmark money of account. A list of coins used as means of payment in a large transaction in Normandy in 1473 illustrates the diversity. Nine kinds of coin were itemized: French gold *écus*, English gold nobles, English groats, various French silver coins, Flemish and German silver, and some silver struck by the duke of Britanny. All were rated in terms of the money of account – *livre tournois* – and the total was rounded by adding 7s. 2d. of 'white money now current' (Lane and Mueller 1985: 12; see also Einaudi 1953 [1936]: 236; Day 1999).[5]

From time to time, the original Carolingian unit of account of pounds, shillings and pence and coinage were integrated by a standard of value coin that was struck by one of the more powerful kingdoms. In 1226, Louis of France struck the *livre*, or *gros*, *tournois*, which had the weight and fineness of the 'imaginary' *sou* (shilling). For a time, the 'real' and the 'imaginary' were reunited, at least in the French provinces. But eventually, minting stopped, and the *livre tournois* itself existed only as a unit of account, as in the above example of the fifteenth-century transaction in Normandy.

From the thirteenth century, the most powerful of the emerging states asserted their sovereignty, as Louis of France had done, by proclaiming their own moneys of account, most of which were variants of the Carolingian pounds, shillings and pence (Bloch 1954 [1936]; Spufford 1988; Boyer-Xambeu et al. 1994; Day 1999: 59–109). These were used not only to denominate local coins, but also to impose an exchange-value on the foreign coins that circulated freely across the imprecise and permeable territorial boundaries. Now, as *both* moneys of account and coinages varied, monetary relations became extremely complex. Any coins had multiple values, one of which was declared in the state of issue, but also others, expressed in the money of account of the zone of sovereignty in which it happened to be circulating at the time. The exchange relations between the values were *purely abstract monetary* relations, in the sense that the money of account, not their metallic content, determined the relative values of coined money. In other words, coins and, as we shall see, credit instruments such as bills of exchange were all established, as *money*, by moneys of account. In short, the various media of exchange and payment became money by being *counted* – not weighed, or otherwise assayed as a valuable *commodity* (Boyer-Xambeu et al. 1994: 6).[6]

Under these circumstances, monetary policy involved manipulation of one or both of the two elements: the weight and fineness standard in an actual coin, and the valuation of the myriad coinages in existence in relation to the money of account. In the first instance, policy was driven by two contradictory aims. On the one hand, monarchs gained extra seignorage profit by reducing the metallic content of coins. (Some of their debts could be paid in bullion rather than coinage.) However, given the promiscuous circulation of coins, monarchs also had an interest, on the other hand, in extending the issue of their own coins. This could be achieved by the imposition and effective collection of taxes, but in the typical conditions of the weaker states this also required the maintenance of an acceptable metallic content – especially for the large-value gold coins that were used as stores of value.

It must be stressed again that variations in metallic content did not have any obvious and direct impact on prices, as orthodox economic theory maintains (see Fischer 1996).[7] Even if states had direct control of sources of precious metal, it was much easier to impose and manipulate a sovereign money of account – that is to say, to declare a value of existing coins in relation to an 'imaginary' standard coin that need not be minted. The devaluation and revaluation of money was achieved by 'crying down' and 'crying up' the money of account (Innes 1913). Depreciating the nominal value of the coins – that is, 'crying down' the coinage – was an alternative to increasing the tax rate as a means of increasing the monarch's purchasing power. It would be declared, for example, that an increased number of pennies were equal to the money of account of, say, a florin. However, this strategy was a short-lived expedient, as other prices were soon adjusted upwards in order to gain sufficient devalued coins to pay for the increased taxation.[8]

In short, medieval money was produced in a struggle for control of bullion, coinage and the money of account; it was anarchic and chaotic, but the turmoil provided the conditions for a significant monetary development (for a graphic description of the confusing complexity, see Day 1999: 59–110).

The De-linking of the Money of Account and the Evolution of Capitalist Credit-Money

The separation of moneys of account from means of payment and the free circulation of coins with multiple territorially determined values had two important implications for the development of modern capitalist banking and its distinctive forms of money. First, the circulation of coins outside their jurisdiction of issue increased the need for money-changers, whose activities provided the basis for the re-emergence of *deposit banking* (Usher 1953 [1934]; Mueller 1997). Second, and more importantly, these particular circumstances of anarchic coinage and increasingly long-range trade provided the stimulus for the development of the *bill of exchange* into a form of transnational private money denominated in an agreed money of account. Eventually, when the advantages of these new forms of money had become obvious, and where states were strong enough to enforce the transferability of debt, capitalist credit-money came into being. Again, it should be stressed that this was not a straightforward process dictated simply by a growing awareness of the efficiency of the new forms of money. The actual outcome was produced by particular circumstances, which were always accompanied by conflicts of economic and political interest.

By firmly establishing the practice of abstract money accounting, the fortuitous separation of money of account from means of payment laid the foundations for these innovations. The conceptual distinction between, on the one hand, money as money of account (*'description* or *title'*) and, on the other, money as means of payment ('the *thing* which answers to the description') would be of no practical significance if the thing always answered to the description, or if the description referred only to one thing (Keynes 1930: 4, emphasis original). However, the de-linking opened up the possibility that a range of 'things' might be taken as answering to the 'description' and could, therefore, be used as means of payment. By the late fifteenth century, Pacioli, in his treatise on double-entry bookkeeping, listed *nine* ways by which payment could be made. In addition to cash, these included credit, bill of exchange and assignment in a bank (Lane and Mueller 1985: 6). Both these developments – money changing/deposit banking and the use of credit instruments – were the result of the geopolitical structure of late medieval Europe. On the one hand, political and social order was sufficient to sustain an expansion of commerce; on the other hand, monetary anarchy – especially competing moneys of account – created difficulties in making payments.

It is possible to discern in these complex circumstances the gradual development of four elements that culminated in capitalist credit-money. First, the (re-)emergence of banks of deposit in the late thirteenth century; second, the formation of public banks, especially in Mediterranean city-states in the fifteenth century; third, the widespread use of the bill of exchange as a form of private money used by the international merchant-bankers/traders during the sixteenth century; and fourth, the very gradual depersonalization and transferability of debt in the major European states during the seventeenth and early eighteenth centuries, which transformed the private promises to pay into 'money'.

In this regard, the most decisive final development was the integration of the bankers' private bill money with the coinage of sovereign states to form the hybridized, or dual, system of credit-money and a metallic standard of value. It was the late twentieth century before the latter finally disappeared to leave money in its pure credit form.

'Primitive' banks of deposit

Early medieval money-changing 'bankers' (*bancherii*), whose services were essential in the monetary anarchy of multiple and overlapping coinages and moneys of account, also took deposits of cash for safe keeping, which eventually permitted the book clearance of transfers between their depositors. However, these early banks did not issue credit-money in the form of bills and notes, and it is largely for this reason that they are referred to as 'primitive' – that is to say, non-capitalist (Usher 1953 [1934]: 264).[9]

In this regard, as we saw in relation to ancient Mesopotamia and Egypt, it is important to distinguish these two distinct bank practices – 'book' clearance of credit and debt and the 'creation' of deposits by lending. Book transfer and clearance between depositors as a means of payment come into existence when a sufficient number of deposit accounts are opened in single enterprise. Here the 'book' money exists as a currency substitute. Payment by bank transfer was, for example, countenanced by a Venetian ordinance of 1421 – *contadi di banco* (bank money), in addition to *denari contadi* (coined currency) (Usher 1953 [1934]: 263). The banker could also use some of the deposits to make loans or invest in trade, without depriving the depositors of the use of their deposits – unless of course they *all* wished to use them at the same time. Both practices augment the stock of public currency; but this is limited to the particular credit relations that actually exist between the parties involved. In other words, there exists a complex network of inter*personal* credit relations orchestrated by the bank. Transfers between accounts had to be conducted in person in the presence of the banker, as they were in the banks of the ancient and classical world (Usher 1953 [1934]; Weber 1981 [1927]). Written orders were still illegal, although they were increasingly being used. But these were restricted to very small personalized networks, as in sixteenth-century Venice, where 'the merchants rubbed shoulders with one another every day at the Rialto' (Day 1999: 37).

But accepting deposits, book clearance of credit and the lending of coined money 'merely transfers purchasing power from one person to another . . . [b]anking only begins when loans are made in bank credit' (Usher 1953 [1934]: 262). This *creation* of credit-money by lending in the form of issued notes and bills, which exist independently of any particular level of incoming deposits, is the critical development that Schumpeter and others identified as the *differentia specifica* of capitalism. The issue of credit-money, in the form of notes and bills, requires the depersonalization of debt, which enables the transferability of promises to pay. These can then circulate outside the network of any particular bank and its depositors. The transformation of the book clearance of credit transfers between depositors into depersonalized, transferable debt slowly developed with the emergence of public banks and the private bankers' bill of exchange.

Early public banks

What Weber referred to as eighteenth-century capitalism's 'memorable alliance' between financiers and states originated in fourteenth-century Mediterranean city-states. The 'primitive' deposit bankers and money-changers had to purchase licences from the city governments and perform various public functions, in return for which they received protection. In fourteenth-century Genoa, for example, bankers converted currencies for the commune, sought out forged or forbidden coins and generally supervised the circulation of the coined currency. The government required the bankers to make their records available for inspection and to produce guarantors for outstanding debts. In return, the government backed the bankers' credibility by recognizing their book entries as proof of transactions in bank lending and transfer between accounts. Most importantly, the city governments became the banks' largest clients. Public banks were established at Barcelona in 1401 and at Valencia and Genoa in 1407. Venice's Banco della Piazza di Rialto, founded in 1587, also accepted bills of exchange payable to its depositors and converted the state's debt into transferable bonds. However, the early public banks did not transform the state's debts into 'new' money by the issue of freely transferable or circulating notes and bills based on the state's promise to repay its debts (Usher 1953 [1934]; Weber 1981 [1927]).

During the late Middle Ages, monarchs in the larger kingdoms were regular borrowers from merchants and bankers, but these were, in effect, personal loans.[10] However, loans to the city-states were public, in that the debtor was the corporate government (see the general survey in Bonney 1999). This linkage of the bourgeois depositors and the city governments was the precursor of the typical capitalist mode of money creation. At this stage, the clearance of debts and credits in the banks' giro of depositors effectively monetized the city-state debts. The suppliers of goods and services to the city governments were able to draw on their bank accounts before payment from the state had been received (Mueller 1997: 42; Day 1999: 67–8).

In contrast to the conflict of interests between the sovereign and the bankers in the monarchies (see Munro 1979), these early state–bank relations were based on *intra*-class credit relations in the governing plutocracies of the Italian city-states. In effect, they were borrowing from each other, and this creation of infrastructural power depended on the solidarity and cohesion of the ruling oligarchy. Factionalism and political instability proved to be one of the chronic sources of fiscal and, ultimately, military weakness in these states. None the less, an entirely new social technology of state financing had been developed, to be integrated later with other techniques – most importantly, the bill of exchange.

The bill of exchange

The transformation of the social relation of debt into the typically capitalist *form* of credit-money began when signifiers of debt became anonymously transferable to third parties. The process may be divided roughly into two periods. First, in the sixteenth century across that part of Europe covered by Latin Christianity, forms of private money such as bills of exchange (and, later, promissory notes) were used in commerce, and existed alongside the plethora of diverse coinages of the states and principalities. Second, during the late seventeenth century, some states outside Latin Christianity (most notably Holland and England) integrated this monetary technique with public deposit banking, and began to issue *fiduciary* money. In this way, the bill of exchange, as a form of private money, gradually evolved to become part of the public currency. By means of its incorporation into a sphere of monetary sovereignty, private promises to pay now became a more extensive and stable form of public money. Again, it must be emphasized that these *particular forms* of money cannot be accounted for simply as *direct* responses to the needs of the market for more efficient exchange or of states for finance.

As we have noted, from the thirteenth century onwards, the princes of Latin Christendom not only minted their own coins, but also proclaimed, as an expression of sovereignty, their own version of the Carolingian money of account (Boyer-Xambeu et al. 1994: 6). Consequently, every coin in the promiscuous international circulation might have a different value in each jurisdiction in which it was to be found. There was now no common yardstick. As we have also noted, the extreme monetary uncertainty is evident in the absence of numerical markings on coins (Innes 1913). In other words, at the precise moment when the states' pacification of Europe allowed more extensive trade, their claims of sovereignty in both money of account and coinage created a complexity that threatened to impede it. In these circumstances, money-changers found ready employment; but their activities could do no more than ease the difficulties, and then only at the local level. The problem was resolved in the first instance by the small networks of exchange bankers, based in the Italian republics. They gave coherence to the anarchy by using their own version of the Carolingian 1: 20: 240 money of account as the basis for their bills of exchange, which were used to finance trade.

The modern bill of exchange originated in Islamic trade, and almost certainly entered Europe through the Italian maritime city-states during the thirteenth century (Udovitch 1979; Abu-Lughod 1989). Exchange by bill required two networks – one of traders and one of bankers. A trader would draw a bill on a local banker, which he would then use as a means of payment for the specific goods imported from outside the local economy. The exporter of the goods would then present the bill for payment to his local representative of the banking network. In their simplest form, the bills directly represented the value of the goods in transit. Their adoption facilitated long-distance trade, but there is nothing in these economic advantages themselves that would suggest that the bills would develop into credit-money. Indeed, this is precisely what did *not* happen across the Islamic world. Other conditions were necessary.

Without delving too deeply into the complexities, it is essential to understand that it was the particular geopolitical structure of late medieval Europe that created the circumstances in which exchange by bill could not only flourish, but also develop further into private money existing alongside the sovereign coinages. The anarchy of myriad moneys of account, and their separation from the equally varied means of payment in a plethora of monetary sovereignties, was the basis for the exchange bankers' *systematic* enrichment from the use of bills of exchange.

The bankers were able to enrich themselves and promote the use of bills through a series of exchanges that involved the *conversion of one*

money of account into another. The bankers met at regular intervals at
the fairs to fix their own overarching money of account, expressed in
terms of an *abstract* coin (*écu de marc*) upon which the private bill
money was based. Their enrichment depended on the existence of two
conditions. First, the bankers had to maintain the permanent advantage of the central fair rate of exchange of their own money of account
and (at Lyons, for example) over any other. Secondly, in order to
achieve this, they had to control the direction of both an outward flow
and an inward return of bills through their networks. In this way, they
were able also to *control* the advantageous arbitrage in which the
passage of bills unfailingly produced a profit as they were converted
from one unit of account to another (Boyer-Xambeu et al. 1994: ch. 6).

In other words, this state of affairs bore no relationship to a market
in bills, as this is understood in conventional economic analysis. The
situation outlined above, and the profit opportunities that it provided,
were the result of a *purely monetary relation* that existed between the
myriad moneys of account and their lack of any stable relationship to
the equally varied coinages. The bankers could control the direction of
a bill through the moneys of account of the myriad jurisdictions in a
way that was *always* favourable to them, as this was determined by
their own money of account at the central fair where the accounts were
settled. As described by Davazanti in the sixteeenth century, this mode
of exchange by bill was exchange *per arte*, as opposed to the *forced*
exchange that was determined by the flow of commodities (Boyer-
Xambeu et al. 1994: 130).

Leaving aside for a moment the longer-term consequences of the bill
of exchange for the development of capitalist credit-money, it would
be difficult to overemphasize the more immediate and direct effects on
economic life. Until this time, imports and exports of goods were
inextricably linked by quasi-barter exchange involving bullion. Moreover, apart from well-established bilateral trade between parties
known to each other, merchants were travellers who accompanied
their goods and means of payment. After the extension of the bill
network from the late fourteenth century onwards, they became sed-
entary, and the cities expanded.

Exchange by bill *per arte* was the means whereby the nations of
bankers enriched themselves by exploiting the unique opportunities
afforded by the particular structure of the late medieval geopolitical
structure and its monetary systems. In doing so they expanded the
early capitalist trading system. The bill of exchange system allowed an
increase in trade without any increase of coinages in the different
countries. But this was an unintended consequence of the exchange
bankers' entirely self-interested exploitation of the particular circum-

stances (Boyer-Xambeu et al. 1994: 130). The exchange banking nations had created a source of enrichment that was *relatively autonomous* from the supply and demand for 'real' exchange; but its consequence was fundamentally to transform the way in which the latter was organized and pursued.[11]

The depersonalization of debt

Exchange *per arte* – that is, the creation of credit in the bill of exchange independently of the existence of any actual goods in transit – was also known as 'dry exchange'. It entailed a dissociation of pure credit from the 'real' representation of goods. In turn, this eventually led to a further dissociation of the bill from any particular dry exchange credit relation – that is, to the growing autonomy of *depersonalized debt relations* and their eventual evolution as a *form* of credit-money. Subsequently, exchange by bill eventually became integrated with public banking, and resulted in the issue of credit-money by states.[12]

As we have noted, verbal personal contracts, based on Roman law, in both casual credit relations and more formal arrangements, conducted by the early banks of deposit, predominated until the sixteenth century (Usher 1953 [1934]: 273). These were made before a notary and witnesses, and became a matter of public record. This form of contract served to fix debt as a *particularistic social relation*; and therefore, until written contracts became the norm, the transferability of debt to the point where it served as a general *impersonal* means of payment was not possible.

The widespread use of the bill in dry exchange – *per arte* – undoubtedly hastened the transition from oral to written contracts, and opened up the possibility that the signifier of bilateral debt could be used in the settlement of a third-party debt. 'Bills were drawn for the first and fictitious destination and the option of a reimbursement in Genoa' (Lopez 1979: 16; see also Spufford 1986: xliv). This was a *pure* monetary instrument, which consisted exclusively in *a promise to pay denominated in an abstract money of account*. In this way, a further dissociation was effected: a *form* of circulating money was separated from the precious metal manifestation that it had taken in the previous 1,000 years. During the sixteenth century, bills began to leak out of the network of exchange bankers and take on the property of more general, but still restricted, means of payment. (For example, the name of the presenter of the bill was omitted when the bill was drawn and added later as necessary (Usher 1953 [1934]: 286).) But until the bills became widely transferable as means of payment to third parties *outside* the network of bankers, they remained private money.

In particular, bills were not a means of *final settlement* of debts – especially tax debts. Moreover, the elite banker 'nations' opposed the free and extended circulation of bills; it threatened their systematic enrichment *per arte*, which depended on absolute control of the directional flow of bills.

Significantly, this further development of the bill into a more generally acceptable means of payment occurred in Holland and, later, England, which were *outside* exchange bankers' *direct* sphere of influence. In Holland, by the middle of the sixteenth century, the properly constituted agent of the named payee on the bill – or *bearer* – was recognized in law. Towards the end of the century, changes to the parties involved in a contract were written on the back of a bill, and this was accepted as an order to pay (Usher 1953 [1934]: 287). From a technical standpoint, the document *itself* was now deemed to contain all the necessary information, and, in effect, signifiers of debt had become *depersonalized*. However, full transferability of such instruments of debt as means of payment outside the merchant capitalist networks and within a sovereign monetary space was not established, as we shall see, until the early eighteenth century.

During the sixteenth century, a singular form of profit making was made possible by the exchange bankers' exploitation of the diversity of moneys of account and their dislocation from the equally varied means of payment that resulted from the geopolitical structure of myriad weak states.[13] For a time, the transnational exchange bankers brought a degree of integration to the system by linking the value of the French king's *sous tournois* with their own abstract money of account – the *écu de marc*. This expressed a particular balance of power between the princes' sovereign claims, with their attendant tax advantages, and the bankers' profit-making ventures. However, this balance shifted dramatically towards the end of the sixteenth century. Two interdependent forces were involved. First, the exchange bankers' networks weakened to the point of collapse in the aftermath of typical capitalist defaults and liquidity crises, which they alone could not stabilize. Secondly, the French state reasserted sovereign control of its monetary system (Boyer-Xambeu et al. 1994: ch. 7). In 1577, the French monetary authorities effectively removed the foundations for enrichment from exchange *per arte* by the establishment of a uniform metallic standard that *reconnected* the *money of account* and *means of payment* and by the prohibition of the circulation of foreign coins. Henceforth, exchange by bills became a *financial* rather than a *monetary* relation in the sense that their value ceased to be fixed in the abstract money of account rate, but rather on the floating exchange rates of metallic coins – as in today's foreign exchange markets

(Boyer-Xambeu et al. 1994: 202). This form of exchange, and banking in general, withered temporarily in face of the absolutist monarchies' metallic money (Kindleberger 1984: ch. 6). However, the new credit-money practices moved on geographically to those states with more powerful merchant-banking classes, such as Holland and England. In the latter, credit-money and the older coinage form were eventually recombined in a further significant development.

The Transformation of Credit into Currency

Apart from later refinements, the basic *organizational* and *technical means* for producing the various forms of credit-money were, from a practical standpoint, widely available by the sixteenth century. Italian treatises on the new techniques described how the supply of precious metal coinage could be augmented. Three methods were identified: bank clearance of debt the creation of money in the form of claims against the public debt and exchange of bills *per arte* (Boyer-Xambeu et al. 1994). As we have seen, bills and promissory notes were slowly becoming disconnected from the direct representation of goods in transit or of personal debt; but they were not widely accepted as means of payment. In other words, the social and political bases for the transformation of private debt into currency lagged behind technique. Even in England, where the new forms of credit-money eventually became most extensive, the establishment of full transferability of debt was a long and gradual process, which was not completed until the eighteenth century.[14]

Moreover, it would appear that social and political structures that had provided the basis for the new capitalist credit-money – in the forms of public debt and private bills – were *in themselves* incapable of further expansion. This new 'social power' in the form of an elastic production of credit-money was impeded by the very conditions that had originally encouraged its development. For example, informal contracts by which the mercantile plutocracies of the Italian city-states lent to each other through the public banks were constantly jeopardized by the factional rivalry that was typical of this form of government. These conflicts also undoubtedly played their part in the general decline of the Mediterranean city-state republics from the sixteenth century onwards. With regard to the merchant-bankers' *private* bill money, it is difficult to see how they could have carved out the necessary monetary space for their bills, based on a sovereign jurisdiction and the necessary level of *impersonal* trust. Moreover, as we have noted, it was not even in their interests to do so, as it would have removed the circumstance from which they profited. Without a wider base, the liquidity of bills of exchange was almost entirely restricted to banking and mercantile networks, and could not evolve into credit-money *currency*.

In other words, there were definite social and political limits to the market-driven expansion of credit-money. The essential monetary space for a genuinely impersonal sphere of exchange was eventually provided by states. As the largest makers and receivers of payments, and in declaring what was acceptable as payment of taxes, states were the ultimate arbiters. They created monetary spaces that encompassed and integrated social groups whose interaction was embedded in particular social ties or specific economic interests. Until private credit-money was incorporated into the fiscal system of states which commanded a secure jurisdiction and a legitimacy, it could be argued that it remained, in evolutionary terms, a dead-end.

Rapidly shifting political boundaries, the promiscuous circulation of coins across them, not to mention competing moneys of account, were the norm. Credit-money was a product of this insecure monetary space, but, in turn, these very same circumstances could not sustain it. In this regard, it is significant that the bills of exchange were centrally important in the operation of the fairs of Champagne and Burgundy during the fifteenth and sixteenth centuries. They flourished in precisely those more feudalistic, but pacified, parts of Europe which were least favourable to the creation of a strong coinage, but just strong enough to protect the fairs. The bankers' bill-money flourished in those regions where a balance of power allowed them to function. Early capitalist monetary practices spread to these regions not only because they were on the Baltic–Mediterranean trade route, but also because the dukes of Burgundy, for example, unlike the kings of France, were not despotically powerful enough successfully to establish a monetary monopoly that integrated a money of account with metallic currency.

The two forms of money – or, rather, the structure of social relations and the interests of the producers of private bills and public coins – were antithetical and antagonistic. On a most general level, the minting of coin was both a symbol and a real source of the monarch's sovereignty. Monopoly control brought great benefits, which it was feared would be eroded if exchange by bills were to displace the coinage. But, paradoxically, the first step in the creation of stable monetary spaces that could sustain credit-money was the strengthening of metallic monetary sovereignty.

It could be said that the stringency and effectiveness of bullionist monetary policies were a good measure of the power of the medieval monarchical state. And this was nowhere more apparent than in England, where, eventually, credit-money was first successfully established as public currency. Here, mercantilist conceptions of the strength of states and related metallist monetary policy were strongly opposed to the bill of exchange. Its widespread use involved a loss of sovereign control – especially over the profits of seignorage and the manipulation of the money of account by 'crying up' and 'crying down' the coinage. At times, from the fourteenth to the mid-seventeenth century, English kings banned the importation of foreign coins and the export of bullion, ordered exporters to supply their bullion to the mints, attempted to prohibit the bill of exchange, and generally sought to limit the use of credit (Munro 1979).[15] It is significant that when Pacioli's 1494 treatise on financial practice and double-entry book-keeping was translated into English in 1588, the section on banking was omitted on grounds of irrelevance (Lane and Mueller 1985: 68). The controls on exchange and the domestic unit of account exercised by the English monarchy largely prevented the promiscuous circulation of coins and multiple moneys of account that took place in continental Europe. Consequently, both deposit banking through money changing and exchange by bill *per arte* were both less developed in England. However, the critical factor was that the new forms of credit-money could not be *entirely* suppressed. And it was precisely in this secure, socially and politically constructed monetary space that credit-money was able eventually to function as currency.

Henri III's reconstruction of the French coinage, which dealt the decisive blow to the exchange bankers' method of enrichment, was modelled on Elizabeth I's thorough recoinage in England during 1560–1 (Davies 1996: 203–8). The French stabilization collapsed in 1601; but in England, the setting of four ounces of sterling silver as the invariant standard for the pound unit of account lasted until World War I. This stability is historically unique, 'little short of a miracle, and almost inexplicable at first sight' (Braudel 1984: 356). However difficult it might be to explain, the maintenance of the standard through the centuries was indisputably the linchpin of England's fiscal and political system. As we shall see, its retention was a condition of the survival of the constitutional and fiscal settlement between sovereign, government and ruling classes after the successful resistance to the absolutist claims of James II, Charles I and Charles II in the seventeenth century. The maintenance of the standard encouraged a steady supply of *long-term* creditors for the state, and in this way provided a secure basis for the eventual adoption and expansion of the credit-money system. England eventually achieved what Venice and others had been unable to secure, and reaped the benefits. We must now examine how this critical development, involving the successful hybridization of the two forms of money (coinage and credit), was achieved in England. It occurred in two steps: the creation of a single monetary space for a national coinage, into which credit-money was then gradually introduced.

Sovereign monetary space in England

The temptations of increased seignorage by means of debasement proved too much for Henry VIII in the search to finance his costly wars. During the 'Great Debasement' (1544–51) the silver content of the coinage was systematically reduced from 93 per cent to 33 per cent, which resulted in a seignorage to the Crown amounting to over £1.2 m (Goldsmith 1987: 178; Davies 1996: 203).[16] Although the reduction of the metallic content of coins does not necessarily affect prices (Innes 1913, 1914; Braudel 1984: 356–9; Davies 1996), the debasement did discredit the monarchy and create insecurity by destroying confidence in money as a *store of value*. Like all serious monetary disorder, it threatened political and social disorder.

Elizabeth I's reforms stabilized the coinage, successfully prohibited the circulation of foreign coins and secured monetary sovereignty. English monetary policy was unequivocally monarchical and bullionist (Munro 1979). Citing the 'abuses of merchants and brokers upon bargains of exchange', Elizabeth's minister, Lord Burghley, forbade bill of exchange transactions that were not licensed and the issue of bills by unknown merchants, and placed a 1/2d. in the pound (£) tax on the discounting of bill for coin.

Other elements of state building aided the creation of monetary sovereignty. It was precisely at this time that England became a more coherent linguistic and cultural unit, in which class and state were integrated by the overarching nation (Mann 1986: 462). Significantly, the word 'nation' began to lose its medieval meaning of a group united by common kinship – as in the banking nations centred on the great fifteenth- and sixteenth-century Italian families. The emerging English nation-state became the basis for the impersonal trust that eventually enabled the forms of credit-money to become established outside the interpersonal banking and exchange networks in which, hitherto, they had been contained.

At this juncture, however, the late sixteenth-century English state had, in effect, established a form of money that was in all important aspects the same as that which had disintegrated in Rome more than 1,000 years earlier. At the very moment when the techniques for the new forms of credit-money were being disseminated across Europe by trade and treatise, the strongest states were reconstructing the ancient form as both symbol and measure of their sovereignty.[17] In the absence of further events and conditions, credit-money's development into public currency could just as readily have been inhibited by monarchical monetary policy – as it had been in France, for example. However, a century later, the Bank of England was founded, and an enduring state credit-money was issued. It was the outcome of a particular *political struggle* between the supporters of the two different forms of money – coin and credit. This outcome consisted in a remarkable coalescence of the interests of commerce and statecraft, produced by a compromise that expressed the delicate balance between too much and too little royal power.[18]

On the one hand, English kings continued to assert medieval royal monetary prerogatives. Charles I appointed a Royal Exchanger with exclusive powers over the exchange of money and precious metals; and in 1661 Charles II sought to enforce the old statutes of Edward III and Richard II licensing bills of exchange (Munro 1979: 212). On the other hand, an increasing number of the same mercantile supporters of monetary stability also advocated 'Dutch finance' – especially the creation and monetization of a national debt.[19] As I have emphasized, the techniques were by now well understood.[20] More than 100 schemes for a public bank were put forward in the second half of the seventeenth century, with the aim of regularizing state revenue and further removing it from the arbitrary control of a monarchy with absolutist pretensions (Carruthers 1996). Many were based on Amsterdam's Wisselbank (1609), which itself had been patterned closely on Venice's Banco di Rialto (1587) (Goldsmith 1987: 214).

The most important question concerned the nature of the material wealth that was to be the basis of the prospective banks' issue of credit-money – that is, for its capacity to honour promises to pay in something other than merely another promise to pay. Lessons had been learnt from the earlier experiments. The circulation of these mere promises in the form of deposits and stock held by the mercantile and affluent classes had proved to be unstable in Venice, and was viewed with suspicion. Furthermore, the Dutch had more recently experienced similar crises. Many agreed with Defoe that 'land is the best bottom for banks' (quoted in Davies 1996: 260). But, it was also beginning to be realized that mere promises to pay were, in fact, a new form of money, *sui generis*, in that they were not actually representative of any material value. As we saw in Part I, chapter 2, a credit theory of money was emerging.

> [O]f all beings that have existence in the minds of men, nothing is more fantastical and nice than Credit; it is never to be forced; it hangs upon opinion, it depends upon our passions of hope and fear; it comes many times unsought for, and often goes away without reason, and when once lost, is hardly to be quite recovered...[And] no trading nation ever did subsist and carry on its business by real stock;...trust and confidence in each other are as necessary to link and hold people together, as obedience, love friendship, or the intercourse of speech. (Charles Davenant, c.1682, quoted in Pocock 1975: 77)[21]

In England during the seventeenth century, a 'civic morality of trust' was developing that could sustain a wider credit-money economy outside the closed networks of the metropolitan mercantile and political elite (Muldrew 1998). It was a consequence of profound changes in credit relations that would seem to have occurred during the previous century. During the 1570s, bilateral personal credit, typically based on traditional oral contracts before witnesses, became commonplace for a wide range of sales and services (Muldrew 1998). For reasons that have not been fully explained, defaults soon became widespread. However, in the wake of the collapse of the credit relations, a new culture of credit based upon a currency of reputation was constructed. Given the interconnectedness of the credit relations, defaults must have had extensive ramifications: total litigation in the 1580s 'might have been as high as 1,102,367 cases per year or over one suit for every household in the country' (Muldrew 1998: 236). It is possible, but by no means clear, that such a large-scale use of the law led to the final destruction of the personal feudalistic ties of affiliation and dependence of the Middle Ages. It would appear that a process of normative reconstruction followed, in which the general quality of trustworthiness as a *public*, or *communal*, virtue replaced *personal* commitment. It entailed 'a sort of competitive piety in which virtue of a household gave it credit' (Muldrew 1998: 195). Moreover, as Muldrew emphasizes, this moral basis of trustworthiness, which could support extensive market relations and a credit-money economy, was not the result of a natural sociability. Rather, it had to be created not only by legal enactment and enforcement, but also through culture – drama, ballads and poetry. Universalistic trustworthiness, which could be *claimed by acting in a reputable manner*, replaced the obligations to honour agreements based on particularistic ties of family or kin.[22]

The dual monetary system: the hybridization of credit and coinage

By the late seventeenth century, the two forms of money – private credit and public metallic coinage – were available, but unevenly spread across

Europe. However, they remained distinct, and their respective producers – that is, states and capitalist traders – remained in conflict. As I have suggested, England's social and political structure favoured the integration of the different interests that were tied to the different moneys. Here, the balance of power was such that a compromise and a sharing of monetary sovereignty were a possibility. But there should be no presumption of the inevitability of a hybridized form of money that combined the advantages of each – sovereign coin and private credit. As ever, events proved decisive in tilting the balance away from the sovereign's monopolistic control of the supply of money.

Charles II's debt default in 1672 hastened the adoption of public banking as a means of state finance. Since the fourteenth century, English kings had borrowed, on a small scale, against future tax revenues. There was also a small market in the tally stick receipts for the loans 'which effectively increased the money supply beyond the limits of minting' (Davies 1996: 149). However, compared with state borrowing in the Italian and Dutch republics, English kings, like all monarchs, were disadvantaged by the very despotic power of their sovereignty. Potential creditors were deterred by the monarch's immunity from legal action for default and their successors' insistence that they could not be held liable for any debts that a dynasty might have accumulated.

With an impending war with the Dutch, an annual Crown income of less than £2 m and debts of more than £1.3 m, Charles II defaulted on repayment to the tally holders in the 'Exchequer Stop'. It was a critically important event in the London mercantile bourgeoisie's rejection of English absolutism. It culminated in the Glorious Revolution and the invitation to William of Orange to invade and claim the throne. The prevention of any recurrence of default was a paramount consideration, which Parliament put to the new Dutch king in the constitutional settlement of 1689. In the first place, William was intentionally provided with insufficient revenues for normal expenditure and, consequently, was forced to accept dependence on Parliament for additional funds. Second, with William's approval and the expertise of his Dutch financial advisors, the government adopted long-term borrowing. This was funded by setting aside specific tax revenues for the interest payments (Carruthers 1996: 71–83; North and Weingast 1989; the classic path-breaking account remains Dickson 1967).

The state's creditors were drawn from London merchants, who backed a proposal for a Bank of England, in order to take the financial developments a step further. They provided £1.2 m for the Bank's stock, which was then loaned to the king and his government at 8 per cent interest, which, in turn, was funded by hypothecated customs and excise revenues. In addition to the interest, the bank received an annual management fee of £4,000 and a royal charter that granted it the right to take deposits, issue bank notes and discount bills of exchange. After the failure of a Tory land bank competitor, a monopoly on banking and the right to issue further bank bills and notes to the total of newly subscribed capital was granted by royal charter in 1697. As Galbraith explains:

> When subscribed the whole sum would be lent to King William: the government's promise to pay would be the security for a note issue of the same amount. The notes so authorised would go out as loans to worthy private borrowers. Interest would be earned both on these loans and on loans to the government. Again the wonder of banking. (Galbraith 1995 [1975]: 32; see also Carruthers 1996; Davies 1996)

In effect, the *privately* owned Bank of England transformed the sovereign's *personal* debt into a *public* debt and, eventually in turn, into a *public* currency.[23] Underpinning this transformation in the social production of money was the change in the balance of power that was expressed in the equally 'hybridized' concept of sovereignty of the 'King-in-Parliament'. The institutions for the production of capitalist credit-money, and the balance of economic and political interests that underpinned it, were beginning to take shape. The state was financed by loans from a powerful creditor class that were channelled through a public bank. Each had an interest in the long-term survival of the other.

This fusion of the two moneys, which England's political settlement and rejection of absolutist monetary sovereignty made possible, resolved two significant problems that were encountered in the earlier applications of the credit-money social technology. First, the private money of the bill of exchange was lifted out from the private mercantile network and given a wider and more abstract monetary space based on impersonal trust and legitimacy. This involved an underlying fusion of modern elements such as an emerging civic morality of creditworthiness and contract law with the traditional sovereignty of the monarch.[24] Second, Parliament sanctioned the collection of future revenue from taxation and excise duty, to service the interest on loans. Here again, the *balance* between too little and too much royal power was critically important in determining the settlement between debtor and creditor. Expressed in the concept of the sovereignty of King-in-Parliament, it reduced both the factional strife that had prevented such long-term commitment in the Italian republics and also the absolutist monetary and fiscal policies that weakened the French state in the eighteenth century (Bonney 1999; Kindleberger 1984). The new monetary techniques conferred a distinct competitive advantage in the geopolitical struggles of the time, which in turn rendered England's high levels of taxation and duties for the service of the interest on the national debt more acceptable (Ferguson 2001).

From a monetary perspective, the most important, but *unintended*, long-term consequence of the establishment of the Bank was its monopoly to deal in bills of exchange (Weber 1981 [1927]: 265). This arrangement practically fused the private money and public currency. The purchase of domestic bills of exchange at a discount before maturity was a source of monopoly profits for the Bank. But it also proved to be the means by which the banking system as a whole became integrated, and the supply of credit-money (bills and notes) was influenced by the Bank's discount rate. The two main sources of capitalist credit-money that had originated in Italian banking – that is, *public debt* in the form of state bonds and *private debt* in the form of bills of exchange – were now combined for the first time in the operation of a single institution. But, most importantly, these forms of money were introduced into an *existing sovereign monetary space* defined by an integrated money of account and means of payment based on the metallic standard. The Bank's notes were at the top of the hierarchy of moneys, and were introduced widely into the economy when they were exchanged for the discounted private bills and notes.[25]

It must be stressed that during *precisely* the same period in which the Bank of England was established and the full transferability of debt was made legally enforceable, the precious metal coinage was greatly strengthened. That is to say, this process did not involve a dematerialization of money that was driven – either intentionally or teleologically – to greater efficiency. Whether from a theoretical or a practical standpoint, overwhelming intellectual opinion across Europe was behind precious metallic money throughout the seventeenth and eighteenth centuries, and beyond. In England, Locke, Hume and, later, Smith argued unswervingly in favour of a strong precious metal money. No less a figure than Sir Isaac Newton was persuaded to lend his authority to restoration of the full weight of the coinage that had deteriorated over the century since Elizabeth I's reforms. During his twenty-seven-year Mastership of the Royal Mint, which ended in 1727, the coinage was placed securely on a gold basis.[26] As credit-money became the most common means of transacting business, England *also* moved towards the creation of the strongest metallic currency in history.

The monarch had lost absolute control over money, which was now shared with the bourgeoisie. Unlike the *de facto* and informal linkage between the king's coinage and the exchange bankers' money of account and bills in sixteenth-century France (Boyer-Xambeu et al. 1994), the English state's integration of the two forms permitted a further development of credit-money. Coins and notes and bills were eventually linked by a formal convertibility in which the latter were exchangeable for precious metal coins. This hybridized nature of the system of dual monetary forms was the result of a compromise in a *struggle for control* that eventually resulted in a mutually advantageous accommodation.[27]

In addition to the main money supply of precious metal coins and bank notes, there existed other significant forms of money. On the one hand, as we have noted, inland bills of exchange continued to play an important role until mid-nineteenth century in the expanding capitalist networks, especially in industrial northern England. On the other hand, copper tokens were struck privately, throughout the country, and were used as media of exchange in local economies to augment the silver legal tender that was in short supply and minted in denominations that were too high for the routine transactions of the mass of the population. Both existed well into the nineteenth century (Anderson 1970; Davies 1996). These local monetary spaces gradually lost their identity and were very slowly but inexorably integrated into a national space. As ever, the integration was accomplished by the *money of account*, as Rowlinson has pointed out:

> By the 1830s, then, Britons could at different times and places have understood gold sovereigns, banknotes, or bills of exchange as the privileged local representatives of the pound...the pound as an abstraction was constituted precisely by its capacity to assume the heterogeneous forms, since its existence as a currency was determined by the mediations between them. (Rowlinson 1999: 64–5)

The centralization of the British monetary system and those of the states that sought to emulate her capitalist development was an inevitable consequence of the public banks' domestic and, then, international roles in the *dual* system of precious metal and credit-money. First, as the banker to a strong state, the public, or central, bank has direct access to the most sought-after promise to pay – that of the state to its creditors. The central bank's notes are at the top of the hierarchy of promises in a credit-money system. By discounting other, less trusted forms of credit for its own notes, as remarked above, it is able to achieve a *de facto* dominance, and thereby maintain the integrity of the payments system, which constitutes capitalist credit-money (Weber 1981 [1927]; Bell 2000; Aglietta 2002).[28] Second, for most of the eighteenth and nineteenth centuries, the issue of notes based on the state's promises was also given the added guarantee of convertibility into gold at a fixed rate. As other national economies placed their monetary systems on the gold standard at the end of the nineteenth century, the international relations between central banks and their management of the gold flows tended to enhance their central control of the respective domestic monetary systems (Helleiner 1999). Since the disappearance of the last vestige of precious metal money in 1971, when the USA abandoned the gold–dollar standard of the Bretton Woods international monetary system, it has been argued that central banks have lost a degree of control to foreign exchange markets (B. Cohen 2001b). But far from signalling the demise of central banking, their role in creating *credible* pure credit-money has enhanced their power and autonomy. Indeed, in pursuit of the goal of stable, pure credit-money, central banks of the major economies have gained power over the domestic systems through control of the supply of reserves and the discount rate.[29] These questions are pursued further in the following chapters.

Conclusions

The social relations for the 'manufacture' of capitalist credit-money were first successfully developed in England from the late seventeenth century onwards, and were copied, with varying degrees of success, throughout the developing Western world. Capitalist credit-money connects the state with the bourgeois classes. The institutional structure of this form of money consists in three-way debtor–creditor relations between the state, rentiers and taxpayers, which are mediated and reproduced by a public bank, an efficient bureaucratic administration and a robust Parliament. Holders of the national debt were given confidence in the state's promise to pay interest and capital by the funding of the debt with hypothecated tax revenues, collected by a vast army of bureaucrats (Brewer 1989). The terms of the settlement between state, creditors and taxpayers – that is, the levels of borrowing and tax rates – were negotiated and scrutinized in Parliament (North and Weingast 1989). For three centuries, this form of money was grafted on to the existing, but greatly strengthened, precious metal coinage, and thereby its storage of value function was given an additional guarantee. But, as I have frequently stressed, the ratio between money and goods, or money's purchasing power, was not established

directly by the market exchange ratios between precious metal and
other commodities. Rather, monetary authorities *promised* to maintain the conversion price of gold and notes that they had fixed. For
most of its history, money in capitalism was produced in a dual or
hybrid system in which public metal coinage and private credit were
integrated and transformed. As we saw in Part I, the idea of a metallic
standard ideologically naturalized the underlying social relations.
Apart from its almost entirely symbolic role in the Bretton Woods
monetary system, the gold standard has been inoperative for almost a
century.[30]

The basic elements of the pure form of capitalist credit-money are
explored further in the following chapter; but here we might note the
immense increase in infrastructural social power that the relatively
elastic production of money brought about. What was observed at the
time is now widely accepted – that is to say, England was able to defeat
France in the struggle for European dominance during the eighteenth
century because of its ability, and France's inability, to create credit-
money (Crouzet 1999; Ferguson 2001). In contrast to Patterson's
Bank of England, John Law's Banque Royale (1719) was an utter
failure. A detailed comparative analysis cannot be presented here, but
there are obvious significant differences. First, France did not have as
powerful a bourgeois mercantile class, with such an intimate knowledge of, and confidence in, 'Dutch finance', to dictate terms to the
state in the creation of financial and monetary institutions. Second,
the French state could not provide the two crucial guarantees to its
potential creditors – reliably collected tax revenues and gold standard
convertibility of notes. In Weber's terms, France remained a *patrimonial* polity in which the state was a *source* of enrichment and not a
means for the further creation of wealth. Finance was raised by the
sale of offices, and tax collection remained privatized in the hands of
tax-farmers. The beneficiaries in the traditional classes of the *ancien
régime* had no interest in monetary and financial rationalization. It
took the Revolution, and its failure, before France could attempt to
emulate her rival in the nineteenth century.

It is significant that the two most successful states of the capitalist
era – Britain and the USA – have also been the most indebted
(Ferguson 2001: 133–41). The relationship between power, success,
debt and the creation of money is complex. It involves virtuous cycles
in which debt finances successful state activity and enables further
credit to be extended on favourable terms to the borrower. Economic
activity is stimulated and taxed at a rate which gives confidence that
revenues are adequate to service the debt. On the other hand, of
course, it may equally end in disaster: ventures may fail, taxes cannot

be collected, debts cannot be repaid and a vicious cycle of decline sets in. Any outcome will be the result of many factors in which chance and contingency, as ever, will play an important part. But any successful extension of 'infrastructural' power by means of credit-money can *only* take place within a legitimate institutional framework based on an acceptable and workable settlement between creditors and debtors.

7

The Production of Capitalist Credit-Money

[T]he banker is not so much primarily a middleman in the commodity 'purchasing power' as a producer of this commodity.

Schumpeter 1934: 74

It is well enough that the people of the nation do not understand our banking and monetary system for, if they did, I believe that there would be a revolution before tomorrow morning.

Henry Ford Sr., quoted in Greider 1987: 55

[T]he overriding problem of all market-oriented societies is to find some means to maintain the working fiction of a monetary invariant so that debt contracts (the ultimate locus of value creation ...) may be written in terms of the unit at different dates.

Mirowski 1991: 579

[Greenspan] said, but as an ordinary matter, the Fed would function most efficiently by fulfilling the expectations it had created.

Mayer 2001: 225

The capitalist monetary system's distinctiveness is that it contains a *social mechanism* by which privately contracted debtor–creditor relations – for example, bank loans, credit card contracts – are routinely monetized. Private debt in its various forms (cheques, credit cards, promissory notes and so on) are converted into the most sought-after 'promise to pay' at the top of the hierarchy of promises. This the state's issue of money that is accepted in payment of taxes and final settlements. This transformation of privately contracted debts into money is achieved by complex linkages between the banking and financial system and the state and, in turn, between the state and its own creditors (bond-holders) and debtors (taxpayers). These relations are mediated by a central bank when it accommodates the banking system's private promises to pay by accepting – that is, buying – them with sovereign money. (As we noted in the previous chapter, the critical development in England was the discounting of the provincial bills of exchange by the Bank of England.) The various forms of private debt are thereby monetized – that is to say, exchanged for sovereign promises to pay that are fully transferable/acceptable anywhere within the monetary space defined by the money of account. These arrangements organize debt into a hierarchy according to criteria of risk of default – that is to say, a stratification order of debt/credit topped by the most sought-after credit – usually, but not always, a sovereign state's promise to pay. This stratification ranking occurs at every level and is organized according to differential rates of interest. The rate at which the central bank lends to the banking system as a whole is the 'base' rate. The dependent rates offered by the banking and financial system are calculated in accordance with an assessment of credit risk and profitability. For example, consumption loans to 'high-risk' borrowers may be several times greater than the basic rate. As we shall see, non-monetized forms of private credit ('near money') may achieve a limited degree of transferability – for example, endorsed cheques circulate in many economies.

The complex and constantly changing system is, as we have seen, the subject of quite divergent academic economic analyses. These tend to be driven more by theory than by a concern with the ethnography of credit-money creation – that is to say, how it actually happens. In this regard, financial journalists and, sometimes, the participants themselves are the better guides. However, as all sociologists and anthropologists should know, this method has obvious limitations. They would not be surprised to learn that one of the most knowledgeable financial writers in the USA thinks that the Federal Reserve's staff now do not have a very clear understanding of what they are doing, or even what they think that they are doing. Ironically, it would seem that as the monetary authorities have striven, in recent times, to make the system more transparent and subject to formal rules of operation, it has become less intelligible (Mayer 2001). With these caveats and difficulties in mind, the following is an attempt to set out an 'ideal type' of the social structure of monetary production in capitalist economies.

By the late nineteenth century, precious metal coinage had long since ceased to be the main *form* of money within the leading economies. Notes were convertible, as in principle were the book entries in bank accounts by which most of capitalism's business was routinely done. But the ratio of gold reserves to these other forms of money (including base metal coins) fell at a rapid rate. The guarantee was wearing thin. At the international level shortages of gold became increasingly acute (de Cecco 1974). Indeed, it is widely accepted that the gold standard did not, and could not, operate in the manner described in the orthodox commodity-money theory's specie-flow mechanism, enunciated by Hume in the eighteenth century.[1] In the first place, international transactions were denominated in sterling, and therefore it is more accurate to refer to a gold–sterling standard (Williams 1968; Ingham 1994). Second, the media of exchange and payment took the form of sterling credits produced by the City of London merchant-bankers. Like the domestic system, the international gold standard was able to operate with 'amazingly small reserves' (Bloomfield 1959: 26). None the less, the holding of reserves and the level of co-ordination required for the payments system to operate at both domestic and global levels greatly enhanced the power of central banks and the centralization and integration of monetary systems of the leading economies (Ingham 1984; Helleiner 1999). A 'pure' credit theory of money began to be considered at this time; but even the more astute writers – such as Simmel and Wicksell – did not think that the 'pure' functions of money could be performed without a precious metal guarantee (see chapters 1 and 3). However, the credibility of money is now based *exclusively* on the credibility of promises to pay. The institutional fact of money is now no more than this credibility, as it is established by the rules and conventions that frame and legitimize the acts of borrowing and lending by all the agents in the monetary system.

The Social Structure of Capitalist Credit-Money

In a 'pure' credit-money system in which private debts are monetized, the question of the production of money may be considered in terms of demand and supply for credit. But the approach taken here differs in a number of important respects from the treatment in orthodox economics. First, supply and demand cannot be seen as independent variables in which one side determines the other – as in the endogenous–exogenous money debate. As emphasized in Part I, money is not a mere commodity that is amenable to this form of analysis. For example, as we shall see, the state's demand for money – that is, its debt – is at *one and the same time* the basic source of the system's supply of money. Second, both the supply and demand for money are controlled and regulated according to criteria of creditworthiness – that is, they are socially constructed.

The private sector endogenous demand for money

By the late twentieth century, it had become clear to the monetary authorities of all major capitalist economies that central banks have very little choice, *in the short term*, but to supply funds to enable the commercial banks to balance their books and to augment their reserves after they have met the demand for loans. Apart from any other considerations, not to accede to these requests would jeopardize the liquidity of the payments system. This was recognized by the Radcliffe Report in the UK in 1959 (Smithin 2003: 44, 96), but it took the failure of monetarism for it to be officially endorsed. '[M]onetary policy can never, at least in a world where money includes deposits with private sector banks, be simply a question of the authorities deciding on the quantity of money it will allow to circulate in the economy' (Bank of England 1993). However, as we shall see, the appearance of central bank control is carefully managed, but actual control is limited to the imposition of a base rate of interest that is considered to be commensurate with stable money prices.

Within this constraint, access to the credit-money that fuels the capitalist economy is determined by an assessment of creditworthiness, by what is considered to be an appropriate rate of interest, and by as much exploitation as the level of competition in the credit market allows. Loans by the banking system are priced in accordance with a profit-maximizing strategy that includes a calculation of the degree of risk of default. First, risk is taken to increase with the length of the term of the loan; second, it is considered to vary with the purpose of the loan – investment, especially if collateral is provided, is less risky than loans for consumption; and third, the borrowers' ability to repay – creditworthiness – is assessed. Apart from the higher levels of capitalist finance, credit rating is now a formal and almost completely depersonalized procedure, based on computer database information provided by the borrower and the credit rating agencies.[2] Credit rating and the production of a stratification order of risk are a clear example of what economic theory sees as 'market failure' – that is to say, where price and, in particular, a single price will not clear the market by bringing supply and demand into equilibrium. A single interest rate considered high enough to cover all risks of default

would also deter low-risk, creditworthy potential borrowers. Moreover, no rate would be high enough to deter the reckless, desperate
and untrustworthy. Consequently, credit is 'rationed' (Stiglitz and
Weiss 1981).

Thus, there are marked inherent structural inequalities in the credit
market – clear examples of 'Matthew effects' such that 'for everyone
that hath shall be given ... ; but from him that hath not shall be taken
away even what he hath' (the following is based on Ingham 2000b). In
the upper levels of the capitalist system, credit relations may involve a
significant degree of *lender* dependency. As the adage has it: if you owe
the bank £5,000, you are in trouble, but if the sum is £50 m, the bank is
in trouble. Frequently, such high levels of indebtedness and default
need to be written off in order to preserve the payments system itself.
In 1998, the US 'hedge fund' Long-Term Capital Management collapsed with debts to the banks of over $100 bn. It was rescued, at the
behest of the US Federal Reserve, by a Wall Street consortium. Things
are different at the other end of the scale. In Britain, about 25 per cent
of the adult population does not have a bank account or access to
credit in the formal financial system. They fall prey to loan sharks'
exorbitant annual rates of interest of over 250 per cent on loans of
cash and physical coercion in their door-to-door collections. Workers
and recipients of welfare payments have to use 'cash centres' or 'cash
converters' to cash their cheques, and are typically charged an 'introduction fee' and up to 10 per cent of the value of the cheque. In the late
1990s 10 per cent of the UK population cashed more than £1.5 bn in
more than 1,000 such centres.[3]

In general terms, we may refer to three very general types of credit
relation or class position in relation to the 'social relations for the
production' of money. The top level is constituted by the basic capitalist practice of borrowing in order to make more money. A middle
level largely involves borrowing for consumption. (The degree of
prudence will vary as Dickens's Mr Micawber noted and warned.)
At the time of writing, the populations of many advanced capitalist
economies continue to add to their already historically unprecedented
levels of household indebtedness. The bottom level remains outside
the credit-money-producing circuit and uses cash and quasi-barter (see
also the discussion of local exchange trading schemes (LETS) in
chapter 9).

In many of the advanced economies, cash is a marginal form of
money, used in the criminal and informal economies, amongst other
things, to avoid participation in the fundamental monetary relation –
taxation. For obvious reasons, it is difficult to produce accurate
estimates of the sizes of informal economies, and they vary consider-

ably (see the discussion of Argentina in chapter 8). However, the
weeks leading up to the introduction of the euro in January 2002
led to the hurried disposal of large hoards of various national currencies. The movement out of deutschmarks into US dollars by East
Europeans is thought to have had a significant impact on foreign
exchange rates. By December 2001, the increased level of cash payments for luxury goods in Spain and Italy, for example, indicated that
their 'black' economies were between 20 and 30 per cent of GDP
(*Financial Times*, 13 December 2001, p. 10). The widespread circulation of *foreign cash* generally indicates a state's weakness and inability
to impose an effective taxation system that will ensure the use of its
money.[4]

The banking system and the supply of money by the 'multiplier'

During the 1920s, it was beginning to be realized that the banking
system's pyramid of debts was itself a means of producing new
money.[5] Banks accept deposits on which they pay interest, and these
debts (*liabilities* to their creditors) form *a basis* for lending. However,
banks also extend loans unmatched by incoming deposits. These
create deposits against which cheques may be drawn and are debts
owed to the bank (*assets*). These debts become money and find their
way, as deposits, into other banks in the system. Banking practice has
developed through convention and regulation to the point where only
a small *fraction* of deposits (*liabilities*) from creditor customers are
kept as a reserve out of which to pay these depositors, should they
wish to withdraw their money. As reserves earn no interest, banks
strive to operate with the smallest fraction they can. Assuming that a
bank operates with a 10 per cent fractional reserve, for every £100
deposited (liabilities), it is able to advance loans (assets) of £90. As it is
spent, this monetized debt appears in bank accounts elsewhere in the
system. In turn, further deposits are created against which these other
banks may extend loans – in the first instance, a loan of £81 (£90
minus £9 (10 per cent fractional reserve) = £81). Eventually, the
initial deposit of £100 could produce £900 of new money in the form
of loans.

   In accordance with the conventions of double-entry bookkeeping,
the totals of deposits (liabilities) and loans (assets) in the *entire system*
cancel each other. This gives the *appearance* that there exists a one-to-
one relationship between deposits and loans, as is suggested by
common sense – and, until fairly recently, endorsed by academic
opinion. However, the accountancy rules and conventions do not
capture the *dynamic* money-creating role of capitalist banking. As

the great French historian Marc Bloch observed, the 'secret' of the capitalist system consists of 'delaying payments and settlements and consistently making these deferrals overlap one another' (quoted in Arrighi 1994: 114). The time frame of the delays and deferrals that makes possible the expansion of *both* sides of the banking systems' balance sheet is established by conventional norms. There are significant cultural differences in this respect that would appear to impede the development of a truly global money market. East Asian economies – in particular Japan, as we shall see – operate with long and sometimes indefinite time frames in which debts are rolled over and extended. For the system to continue to produce money, debts must not only be repaid, eventually, but be repaid within the conventional time frame. The norms that prescribe the conventional delays and deferrals must be observed. In Keynes's phrase, the banks must 'march in step' in the construction of this systemic balance sheet of debits and credits in order to produce monetary expansion. Any disruption of the system's routines risks the collapse of the credit pyramid and the 'disappearance' of the money that is constituted by the creditor-debtor relations.[6] (As we shall see, in order that this complex system of credit and debt is not disrupted, it is imperative that every bank has access to short-term loans (overnight if necessary), usually from the central bank, in order to balance their books.)

However, not every private debt is fully monetized in this way. All money is credit, but not all credit becomes money. Private sector capitalist expansion typically involves the proliferation of debt contracts and private credit instruments with limited transferability (known as 'near money'). Usually, they will not be considered sufficiently creditworthy by the formal banking system. This is the site of an important struggle within capitalism between the creation of indigenous credit networks by firms and the banks' efforts to control the terms on which credit is created. The banks' privileged access to the state money at the top of the hierarchy gives them an advantage. As this credit is created outside the formally regulated system which has direct access to central bank money, the process is referred to as 'disintermediation'. As we shall see, this is potentially destabilizing, as, for example, in the UK's 'secondary banking crisis' in the early 1970s (for the USA, see Guttmann 1994). Today, in a similar process known as 'securitization', enterprises raise money from outside the banking system by selling claims on their assets, including future income, directly to buyers.[7] As the credit creation is not directly 'intermediated' by banks, it is frequently argued that this market-based raising of finance might bring about the 'end of banking' (see Martin 1998; Mayer 2001). However, this confuses a recurrent cyclical pattern in capitalism with a long-term secular trend. 'Disintermediation' and the issue of private debt, or 'near money', occurs in all expansionary phases of the capitalist economy. None the less, it creates instability unless it is fully monetized by being discounted by banks that, in turn, have access to the central bank's sovereign money (see the discussion of Minsky's financial instability hypothesis in chapter 8). Furthermore, the purchase of these private credit instruments is made with borrowed bank money. The question of the degree of accommodation of privately created credit is, arguably, the fundamental dilemma faced by monetary authorities.

Public sector demand for money: state debt and the creation (supply) of 'high-powered money'

If a state is viable and can tax effectively, its promise to pay its debt (demand for money) will be the most sought-after, and consequently the basis for the creation of money (supply) in the banking system. The origins of the relationships were outlined in the previous chapter. In exactly the same way as a private clearing bank's creation of money by lending to a customer, the central bank creates a deposit for the state by accepting its promise to repay the loan – usually in the form of a government bond. The state is able to pay its debts to suppliers with cheques drawn on its account at the central bank. These will first be paid into the recipients' accounts held at their commercial bank, which, in turn, presents them at the central bank for payment. As the commercial banks are required to hold some of their assets as cash deposited with the central bank as liquid reserves for crisis management, the payments mechanism increases the commercial banks' reserve holdings. Mainstream economic theory refers to this as 'high-powered money' – that is, the 'base' money for the 'credit-money multiplier' of the most sought-after promise to pay. Accordingly, government borrowing and spending will, *ceteris paribus*, increase the potential to supply credit-money – that is, the capacity of the banking system to issue new debt.

Rather than issuing new bonds, a government and its central bank might engage in 'open market operations' in an attempt to regulate the supply of money. A government might instruct the central bank to buy or sell its existing securities on the money markets. On the one hand, if the central bank buys back bonds from the private sector, the effect is to permit a possible increase in the supply of credit-money on the base of increased reserves, as in the case of the sale of new bonds. On the other hand, the central bank may be instructed to sell bonds to the commercial banks in order to reduce their reserves and limit their capacity to create credit-money through lending. In this model, cash reserves of high-powered money are held to operate exactly as bullion reserves would do under a precious metal standard. It was on these grounds that 'monetarists' argued that high-powered money could be controlled precisely enough to regulate the total money supply (exogenously determined money supply). We have seen in Part I that conceptual and methodological problems in measuring money quickly led to the abandonment of the doctrine. But these difficulties should not lead to the dismissal of the significance of so-called high powered money, as in some heterodox and post-Keynesian economics. As we have seen, it is not a question of endogenously or exogenously determined money; rather, these two terms express the two sides of the struggle over the production of credit-money that is typical of capitalism.

The experience of the late twentieth century would suggest that attempts *directly* to control the aggregate supply of money with high-powered money, or by any other method, are unworkable. The main instrument of monetary policy is now *indirect* control, through interest rates, of the propensity for indebtedness – that is, the demand for credit-money. Indeed, most central banks no longer give much weight to monetary aggregates. By its very nature, the creation of money in the capitalist system is indeterminate. Disintermediated credit creation is the norm, and the gap between the situation on the banks' balance sheets and the actual levels of debt may be considerable.[8] It would appear that '[i]n the real world banks extend credit, creating deposits in the process, and look for the reserves later. The question then becomes one of whether and how the Federal Reserve will accommodate the demand for reserves. In the very short run, the Federal Reserve has little or no choice about accommodating that demand; over time its influence can obviously be felt' (US central banker Alan Holmes, quoted in Henwood 1997: 220).

Any influence is not felt directly, but as a consequence of the fact that the central bank has the power and discretion to act as 'lender of last resort' in the event of the banks' inability to maintain the efflux and reflux of the payments system, without which the money disappears. The banks are ultimately dependent and, apart from any other consideration, have an interest in conforming to the central bank's requests concerning credit-money creation. The central bank's power derives from its production and control of the most sought-after promise to pay.[9] During the 'secondary banking' crisis in the UK in the early 1970s, for example, the Bank of England organized a 'lifeboat' for sinking banks, in return for which the survivors were invited 'to submit themselves to voluntary supervision' (quoted in Mayer

2001: 113; for further illustrations, see Mayer 2001: chs 5 and 6). Other less compliant financial firms might find themselves excluded from any rescue.

The creditworthiness of the state's high-powered money: budgets, taxes and bonds

Modern neo-chartalism, outlined in chapter 2, provides an alternative to the orthodox economic emphasis on the exogenous origins and impact of high-powered money that goes beyond merely asserting the contrary endogenous money position (Wray 1998; Bell 2000). It is acknowledged that governments can spend and create high-powered money at will, but it is argued that this could lead to excess reserves in the banking system that would eventually force down the interest rates (Bell 2000). The excess can be drained in two ways: first by taxes, and second by sales of government bonds to the banking system. In the first instance, taxpayers' cheques will debit their bank's account at the central bank. Second, government can instruct its (central) banker to offer bonds for sale to the banking system to drain an excess caused by its own spending. Thus, it is argued, Treasury bond sales are not a *borrowing* operation at all, but a means of removing excess reserves from the banking system in order to maintain interest rates.

Neo-chartalists seek to establish that the state does not in fact have *need of* its citizens' money from taxation and bond sales in order to spend.[10] But, as we noted in Part I, they appear to have missed the significance of the *political* nature of both *origins* and *functions* of the linkage between state spending, taxes and bonds in the capitalist system. These links did not originate, for example, in the function of draining excess reserves that might exert downward pressure on interest rates. Rather, they were the historical consequence of an emerging bourgeois class's resistance to the attempt of a powerful sovereign arbitrarily to control spending and taxation. Subsequently, the concern with the balance between spending, borrowing and taxation in, say, principles of sound money has become a matter of an implicit settlement between the state, capitalist 'rentiers' and the tax-paying capitalist producers and workers. Moreover, the stability of any settlement is greatly increased by its legitimization in terms of economic principles and practice. Ultimately, the political balance of these economic interests that the state is able to forge is concerned with checking its arbitrary power and establishing its creditworthiness – that is, its ability to pay its debts. This is not so much a matter of what the state is capable of in a *de facto* practical sense, but of how this is interpreted as legitimate or not by groups and classes (including the state itself) whose struggle for economic existence produces money. This is the actual function of sound money principles. Holders of Treasury bonds must be encouraged to believe that the state can pay interest and redeem the bonds.

The state and the market *share* in the production of capitalist credit-money, and, as I have stressed, it is the *balance of power* between these two major participants in the capitalist process that produces *stable* money. First, the issue of government bond issues and open market operations can only take place if the terms on which they are offered are acceptable to the state's creditors – that is to say, if they are convinced, by whatever means, that the yields will adequately cover prospective inflation. In simple terms, the rules (discussed below) by which money is produced in the capitalist system depend, ultimately, on the willingness with which a state's debt will be accepted by an independent class of rentiers. Taxation and state securities are two essential elements, or social bonds, in the capitalist state. They provide the *actual* flows of money by debt creation and destruction. This takes place according to agreed rules, expressed in a budget, that satisfy conflicting and competing interest groups and render the process meaningful and legitimate. Any disruption has very serious consequences.

The Working Fiction of the Invariant Standard

We should remind ourselves of the importance of the working fiction of an invariant monetary standard of abstract value. Inflation makes it difficult to calculate real rates of return, and the uncertainty hinders the contracting of debt for investment and the creation of value.[11] Most importantly, monetary depreciation may increase to a point where it is no longer possible to set a high enough rate of interest that will generate a positive rate of return for creditors without greatly increasing the likelihood of debtors' default. 'All permanent relations between debtors and creditors, which form the ultimate foundation of capitalism, become so utterly disordered as to be almost meaningless ... There is no subtler, no surer means of overturning the existing basis of society' (Keynes 1919: 220). Again, it is the long-term rate of interest on state debt that sets the benchmark.

Until the twentieth century, the attempt to create an invariant standard consisted in the administrative *fixing* by the state's (later central) bank of an exchange rate between nominal money and a precious metal that also had a market value. (How this affected the price level need not concern us here, beyond noting, once more, that the metallic standard was intended to generate trust in money as a store of value, rather than to establish specific exchange ratios between money and other commodities.) Today's pure credit-money standards have had to develop quite different methods for establishing credible money. These are ostensibly based on what is taken to be the objective knowledge of the economy provided by economic science, and how this is enacted by the state and its bank. The working fiction is now more clearly a function of the assessment of *both* the government's fiscal practice and its central bank's monetary policy. It is the role of the central bank to establish *credibility* in an invariant monetary standard in relation to the *creditworthiness* of fiscal policy and practice. Since the abandonment of monetarist attempts precisely to control the quantities of money in the system, credibility in stable money is assessed in relation to *procedural correctness* in arriving at interest rates that are intended to regulate the willingness to become indebted.

Current orthodoxy for establishing credibility in an invariant standard has developed out of the restructuring of the balance of power between the major economic groups and classes since the hyperinflation of the 1970s. How this new settlement was produced is discussed in the next chapter; here the basic elements of the monetary authorities' current practice are outlined (see, for example, Blinder 1999; Blinder et al. 2001; Issing 2001). It is characterized by the following general features.

The basic elements of monetary policy are generally formulated by the government, through its ministry of finance or treasury, in relation to the fiscal position – for example, the size of the budget deficit and the level of government expenditure, as discussed above. Additionally, central banks, in conjunction with the ministry of finance, construct substantive fiscal and financial rules of thumb, considered to be non-inflationary, for the state and its agencies to follow. For example, the 'Taylor rule' models interest rates as a linear function of the 'output gap' and the deviation of inflation from the explicit 'inflation target'. The issue is posed *explicitly* in the academic policy literature as an empirical question of the relative merits of rules versus discretion in the central bank's conduct of policy. Implicitly, it is a question of trust, in which simple rules have gained favour because they 'can be seen . . . as the means to ultimately ensure that credibility is earned and maintained, because they can be monitored by third parties' (Issing 2001: 42). But even their proponents do not advocate them as *prescriptive* economic policy tools, because their very simplicity does not provide a reliable economic analysis.

Most central banks now have a significant degree of independence in deciding the interest rate that is consistent with these policies and achieving monetary stability. The intention is to depoliticize monetary policy by removing it from the direct influence of those interests most likely to exert inflationary pressures, most notably governments and their electorates' demands.

The primary policy objective of controlling inflation, with a few notable exceptions, is presented as an explicit inflation target in a range usually between 2 and 4 per cent. A central bank committee consisting of some of its own officials, technically expert co-opted economists, and, in some cases, representatives of the major economic interest groups, decides, after taking into account any rules, what short-term rate of interest will best achieve the target. Monetary authorities (primarily the central bank and ministry of finance) attempt to achieve, by means of regular and frequent meetings, a record of consistency in decision making in relation to the application of their own understanding of the monetary situation and any substantive rules that might have been formulated. (However, it should also be noted that this aim for consistency is frequently jeopardized by rivalries and conflicts between the two institutions and the indeterminacy of the experts' econometric models and data.)

It is now maintained that a record for consistency of decision making is best achieved by 'transparency' – that is to say, the open communication to the public realm of a reasoned case for any decision.[12] Consistency can be accomplished only in relation to a consensus on the meaning of the monetary situation as described by economic theory and econometric models. In this situation, as we shall see, the monetary authorities are engaged in the creation of an 'epistemic community' of understanding based on theoretical economic knowledge and routine practice. (However, transparent disagreements between experts may undermine the aim of consistency; see n. 18.) In short, the manifest aim is to depoliticize monetary policy, and place it in the hands of institutionally autonomous experts whose claim to neutrality is based on the application of positive economic science.

Once the state's fiscal creditworthiness has been formally rated by credit-rating agencies such as Standard and Poor and Moody's, or judged by an IMF or OECD report, and the central bank has established its credibility, then, the 'working fictions' are traded, in the forms of currencies and government bonds, on the global money markets. As an eminent American economist recently explained, 'central banks have fully established their anti-inflation credentials and the bond markets hold them accountable by the hour just in case there is a temptation to lapse' (Dornbusch 2001: 15).

Economic theory, performativity and ideology

These current arrangements are the result of two related changes in the social structure of monetary systems at the end of the twentieth century. The first involved the expunging of inflation from the late 1970s onwards (see chapter 8). In a second change, the money markets, especially those in state bonds, became organized more impersonally, as they globalized after the 'big bang' deregulation of the major financial markets (see chapter 8). Hitherto, the buying and selling of government securities in 'open market' operations had been largely domestic affairs operated by a closed personal network, with very little public disclosure. The replacement of personal by institutional ownership and the growth of impersonal transnational markets required quite a different structure in order to operate. Formal, transparent rules and the formation of epistemic communities, based on a shared understanding of the markets' rules and the meaning of macroeconomic indicators, replaced socially embedded trading. Markets can function only on the basis of shared understandings that give meaning to changing events and circumstances (H. White 1981). These new organizational arrangements are a means of creating common definitions of the situation.

As ever, economic theory has played an important role in the reconstruction of the latest versions of the practice of sound money. In particular, rational expectations theory may be seen as an expression of the changes outlined above. In this regard, academic economics sees the relationship between theory and practice as one in which the latter is brought closer to the theoretical optimum. However, on closer inspection, it is clear that the expertise and transparency of monetary policy making is not securely grounded in the basic tenets of mainstream monetary economics.[13] To be sure, central bankers pay lip-service to the basic tenets of orthodox monetary theory, especially the long-run correspondence of the quantity of money and the level of prices. But they acknowledge that this cannot guide their practice in dealing with what they see as short-term disequilibria. It is conceded that there is no satisfactory way of constructing empirically based models of these short-run effects, or of judging the relative merits of the models (Issing 2001: 7, 21). If 'the key issue of exactly how monetary policy impacts on "real" variables over time is still only imperfectly understood' (Issing 2001: 7), how, then, do central banks and their experts actually go about their business?[14] It seems that they do as they have done for several decades. Central banks depend on accumulated *conventional* wisdom on the most important empirical signals of impending inflation.[15] These conventional signals are, of course, modelled in *ad hoc* econometric analyses, but 'a straightforward selection of the "best", if not the "true", reference model becomes a matter of *faith*' (Issing 2001: 40, emphasis added). If contemporary central banks are not applying the agreed, verified results of economic science to monetary policy, what do these acts of faith intend? What are twenty-first-century central banks doing?

Manifestly, they are attempting to establish a transparent procedural correctness that is assessed according the agreed organizational arrangements and the current macro-economic thinking. The construction of the institutional fact of stable money is established, in part, by the performativity of economic theory and practice conducted by experts (Searle 1995). The expert decisions are performative in the sense that the resulting utterances are intended to bring about the circumstances that they describe – as when Alan Greenspan defined the US Federal Reserve's role as 'fulfilling the expectations it had created'. Performativity is seen very clearly in the efficacy attributed to inflation targeting – that is to say, the belief that the mere setting of a target will bring about the intended result. It is widely held, for example, that the persistent and protracted deflation in Japan could be halted, and even reversed, if the central bank were to set a high inflation target. Moreover, it is important that the process of defining the situation – that is, the 'impression management' of the 'performance' – should be skilled (Goffman 1969 [1959]). Central banks 'must create an impression of competence . . . and quiet acquiescence' (Blinder et al. 2001: 23).

The two audiences to which central banks direct their performances are the public and the markets (see Blinder et al. 2001). 'Public' refers to *labour* and *productive capital*, and 'markets' are the *money markets* – especially the market in government bonds. These are the three major economic classes whose inflation expectations (or 'definition of the situation') will have a determinant impact on the stability of money's purchasing power. With the weakening of the alliance between the two producer classes after the 1970s, the markets are considered to be the most important of the monetary authorities' audiences, and '[s]ince this channel is dominated by expectations "convincing the markets" is part and parcel of monetary policy-making' (Blinder et al. 2001: 25). And, as we have noted, the money markets' assessment of the credibility of the commitment to stable money is now immediately decisive in its effect on the long-term interest rates of government bonds. With operational independence and transparency of deliberations established, any cut in short-term interest rates, for example, is less likely to be interpreted as a politically motivated loosening of monetary policy in response to demands from consumers, producers or the government. Consequently, the money markets are less likely to demand and force higher compensatory rates on long-term bonds. Indeed, it is a measure of the success of the new practices that recently, on occasion, long-term interest rates have fallen to a level below those of the short-term rates. (This represents a reversal of the normal ratio, in which the market risk of long-term uncertainty is expressed in higher interest rates.)

In Part I it was argued that orthodox commodity theories of money have also played an ideological role in masking the social character of the creation of money. But the very nature of recent changes in the production of money would now appear to make it more difficult to *naturalize*, and ideologically to conceal, the social construction of money.[16] However, modern independent central banks continue to attempt ideologically to *universalize* social and political relations. At the most fundamental level, this is apparent in the concepts of both neutral money and a monetary policy that implicitly denies or conceals inequalities and opposing interests in the actual process of creating money. First, it is maintained that inflation is an unambiguous cost, borne equally by all members of society, and that it is possible in principle, if not yet accomplished in practice, to theoretically establish an optimum monetary policy that would minimize these costs (Issing 2001; Kirshner 1999). Second, monetary policy is informed by an underlying meta-theoretical assumption that there exists a discoverable, *naturally* optimally efficient state of affairs in the 'real' economy, which contains natural levels of unemployment, rates of interest and so on. In this, there can be no 'real' basis for opposed interests – only cognitive error and consequent sub-optimal solutions to common problems that have a universal impact. In this conception, the struggle for economic existence can only be the struggle for rationality.[17] However, as we shall see in the following chapter, both assumptions are demonstrably false, and make it difficult to explain the rise and fall of the 'great inflation' of the 1970s.

Following Weber, we might say that the manifest aim of modern central bank practice is to establish the highest level of *formal rationality* of inflation expectations. That is to say, central bank practice, as outlined above, attempts to establish a routine and *procedurally predictable* regime of co-ordinated expectations on the part of the bank and the money and capital markets. Such credentials are established through a record of exemplary policy decisions, which are formally rational in relation to the agreed causes of inflation or economic prospects in general, as pronounced in the epistemic community of academics, policy-makers and practitioners in the financial system. However, Weber also strongly argued that any semblance of *formal* rationality in terms of predictable, routine conduct must have a *sub-stantive* basis in the predictability of the particular *power relations* that underlie the conduct. The production of capitalist credit-money is at the core of the complex economic 'battle of man with man' – that is between debtors, creditors, taxpayers and government bond-holders. The question of sound finance, like the question of the value of money itself, is part of this struggle. As Wray has pointed out, if high-powered money grew on trees, it would be worth very little (Wray 2004: 106). High-powered money is the result of the struggle between debtors' demand for money and creditors' belief that the state can service its debt, which in turn depends on tax revenues. And it is the need to work for a *taxable* income that gives it value.

Conclusions

As we shall see in the following chapter, the ability of monopoly capitalists to mark up prices, and of labour to mount successful wage claims, in the advanced economies has been moderated by the changes in the structure of power relationships that were outlined above. In short, the shift in the balance of power has been brought about by the intensification of global competition and its corollary – the weakening of trade unions and the creation of deregulated flexible labour markets. To a significant degree, central bank inflation fore-casts will be maintained to the extent that this balance of power is also maintained. This is not to say that monetary policy does not have an effect, but rather that it is as *reinforcement* of any balance of power that has been forged. The current arrangements followed on the restructuring of the balance of power during the last two decades of the twentieth century.

Arguably, the most structurally fundamental struggle in capitalism is not that between productive capital and labour, but rather between debtor (producers and consumers of goods) and creditor (producers and controllers of money) classes and centres on two rates of interest – the long and the short. (The state has its own interest as a debtor, but is also the site of the struggle.) Rates of interest represent benchmarks, or terms of reference, for 'settlements' between conflicting groups. The central banks are the main mediators of these struggles, and all the recent changes in their organization and operation express the resur-gence of money-capitalist creditor power. Central bankers are pre-sented and, in some cases, present themselves as having the knowledge and capability to control the trajectory of the economy. But in reality this control is severely constrained. First, all the evidence points to the fact that, at a given rate of interest, central banks must accommodate the private demand for money – that is, the money supply is endogenous. Second, central bank base rates seem relatively powerless to control asset prices in the money and financial markets. Indeed, it is argued that central banks are tempted to 'follow the markets' and deliver the interest rates that are 'embedded in asset prices' (Blinder 1999: 60).[18]

As we saw in Part I, the approach taken here rejects the concept of a 'natural' rate of interest that expresses the natural marginal productivity of the factors of production (see also Smithin 2003). Rather, the essence of capitalism is to be found in the calculation of, and switching between, *two possible courses of action* – the accumulation, production and control of credit-money (M-M_1) and the production of commodities (M-C-M_1) (see chapter 8, also Arrighi 1994; Minsky 1982; Keynes 1973 [1936]). Capitalism consists in the continuous comparison of money market rates and the profitability of satisfying wants by production in firms (Weber 1978: 96–7). Each side of the economy imposes limitations on, and continually threatens to perturb and impede, the operation of the other. For example, real (nominal rate minus inflation rate) rates of interest should neither be high enough to elicit a shift of capital from production, jeopardizing income generation for the servicing and repayment of debt, nor fall to a point that demotivates creditors. But the range of these limits is determined by the struggle between the two relatively autonomous sectors in capitalism's social structure. When the extremes of these limits are reached – that is, to say, in hyperinflation and debt deflation – the struggle may give way to a rebalancing of the power relations and a new settlement.

8

Monetary Disorder

[A]s long as an economy is capitalist, it will be financially unstable.

Minsky 1982:36

From a strictly theoretical standpoint, mainstream economics sees the monetary 'disorders' of inflation and deflation as short-run deviations from a long-run tendency towards an equilibrium of money and goods. This follows logically from the 'neutral veil' conception of money as a symbol of the exchange ratios of commodities. If, however, money consists in debt – promises to pay that can be contracted in a relatively autonomous manner outside the realms of production and exchange – then disequilibria are to be expected. The tenet of the long-run neutrality of money has meant that mainstream economic analysis has paid little attention to the instances of acute monetary disintegration or of chronic failures to establish viable money. These phenomena pose interesting questions about the nature of money, especially if they occur in otherwise propitious economic circumstances.

The following accounts of three examples of fundamental 'monetary disorder' are intended to illustrate in broad terms the alternative approach that was developed in Part I. None represents a thorough analysis, but each aims to draw attention to the essential social and political nature of 'disorder'. The first is concerned with the control of late twentieth-century capitalism's inflation. The facts and interpretation of the imposition of a new form of neo-liberal governance or regulation in the major capitalist states is a well-ploughed field. Here I wish to focus on the changes in the power balance of the 'struggle for economic existence' during the emergence of the inflation and its elimination. The second illustration concerns the reverse phenomenon – prolonged deflation or, more accurately, 'debt deflation'. This is illustrated with a brief examination of Japan's stagnation since 1990. Finally, the disintegration of Argentina's money after 2001 is placed in the long-term context of the state's chronic inability to forge the basic fiscal relations with its taxpayers and rentiers that underpin the production of a sovereign monetary space.

The Rise and Fall of Inflation in the Late Twentieth Century

Apart from periods of hyperinflation triggered by acute political crisis, large rises of the price level in otherwise relatively stable states are historically unusual. Indeed, even the rapid expansion of industrial capitalism throughout the nineteenth century was accompanied by a steady price level in the leading economies – the 'Victorian equilibrium' (Fischer 1996: 156–78). Soon afterwards, however, there occurred a fundamental alteration of the balance of power between the main groups and classes of the major capitalist states (Keynes 1919). There were no successful proletarian revolutions, but conflict between the two great classes of Marx's scheme was at the centre of the advance of representative democracy and the forging of social democratic settlements involving full employment and welfare. However, these developments must also be understood in the context of international relations between states, which had an impact on the production of money, at both domestic and international levels. For example, World War I's destabilization of the hierarchy of power in the international system was the proximate cause of the disintegration of the international gold standard, regardless of its internal operational weaknesses. This opened the way for the political management of money for social democratic ends.

   In the post-Cold War era it is sometimes difficult to appreciate the impact of fascism and of communism's promises of deliverance from mass unemployment and economic decline both before and after World War II. The inter-war period saw the first *systemic* failure of the capitalist system, and hastened the abandonment of faith in economic liberalism. Finance and money markets came to be seen as inherently destabilizing forces, and the free market was viewed with suspicion. In 1931 the final collapse of the restored, but by now unworkable, gold standard gave credence to the more advanced understandings of the operation of the credit-monetary system. It was soon realized that the recently discovered 'money multiplier' could stimulate an 'employment multiplier'. Keynes and his Cambridge colleagues, Myrdal and the 'Stockholm School', Kalecki, and numerous others began to create a political economy of social democracy.

The consequences of World War I may have paved the way, but the reformers' advocacy of 'cheap money' was able to triumph against 'sound money' conventions only after the normal operation of monetary systems were suspended by World War II. International money markets cannot operate in such circumstances; and domestic fiscal and monetary rules and conventions are invariably relaxed or abandoned in the face of the need for large-scale deficit finance. In the face of oblivion, the yields on government bonds and the prospects for inflation become increasingly irrelevant considerations for rentiers.

By 1945, sound money opposition to a new social democratic settlement based on full employment, welfare and 'managed' money had been moved off-stage. In the context of the heightened working-class expectations for peace and prosperity, the possibility of a return to economic breakdown, and the continued threat of Communist totalitarianism, the Keynesian welfare state came into being. As the term implies, economic analysis clearly played a part, but, as ever, this was as much rhetorical as it was a practical guide to, and influence on, practical economic decision making.[1] But it is the balance of power between the *three* great capitalist classes that I wish to emphasize. The discrediting of money-capital during the 1930s and its temporary removal from the struggle for economic existence during the war presented the opportunity to create a mode of economic regulation, including new rules for producing money, from which it was excluded (Ingham 1994).

The post-war international monetary system was intended to facilitate the managed expansion of capitalist production and international trade. It was widely held that the inter-war global economy's contraction was due, in part, to the lack of a viable means of international exchange and payment. In the absence of the uninvited financiers and money-capitalists at the Bretton Woods negotiations, the USA and the UK were able to impose the controls on the international movement of money that they considered necessary to honour a political commitment to high levels of employment (Helleiner 1994). It was intended that money's role in the international economy should be restricted to its basic functions as a neutral medium of exchange and payment. That is to say, money was not to be permitted to be a speculative commodity whose value might vary on foreign exchange markets in a way that was not determined by the 'fundamentals' of its country's economic performance. As Keynes clearly saw, the political pledge of full employment could not even be credibly made, let alone implemented, unless sovereign nation-states had control of their domestic interest rates. The rate of interest necessary to induce the level of investment to produce full employment had to be politically determined. Private owners and controllers of money could not be allowed freely to move money from one nation-state to another, either in search of higher interest rates or for fear of the supposed inflationary consequences of high levels of government spending. As Keynes explained:

> [T]here will continually be a number of people constantly taking fright because they think that the degree of leftism in one country looks for the time being likely to be greater than somewhere else.... In my view, the whole management of the domestic economy depends upon being free to have the appropriate rate of interest without reference to rates prevailing elsewhere in the world. Capital control is a corollary of this. (Keynes 1980: 149)[2]

In the relatively prosperous quarter-century after 1945, the three main economic classes – 'big business', 'big labour' and 'rentiers' – coexisted in a fragile compromise. The producer classes expanded their relative shares of national income, but the temporarily weakened rentier and financial interests at least had positive real rates of interest as consolation (Smithin 1996: 5; Rowthorn 1995). However, with steady economic expansion, two shifts occurred in the immediate post-war balance of power. On the one hand, as capitalism began to operate after the wartime corporatist controls, all three groups gradually regained power *vis-à-vis* the state. The political consequences of full employment, in which the 'labour standard' had effectively replaced the 'gold standard', meant that large monopolistic producers could not be allowed to fail. Moreover, with active encouragement from governments, the level of concentration in the economy grew rapidly. Both the corporations and their labour forces in this monopoly capital sector used the leverage to mark up their prices, and eventually set in train the cost-push–demand-pull spiral (see Part I, chapter 2). (Phelps Brown 1975; Hirsch and Goldthorpe 1978; Lindberg and Maier 1985).

On the other hand, money-capital began to resume its naturally dominant position *vis-à-vis* the producers. Capitalist expansion was, as ever, financed by debt and the creation of new money, which inevitably increased the power of the bankers. As we have noted, the increasing power of private money-capital was apparent in the growth of 'fringe' banks, outside the control of the central bank, which were involved in financing the post-war boom. At the international level, private bankers evaded and eroded the Bretton Woods regulations on international capital flows. US trade deficits had placed an enormous pool of dollars in foreign hands. The City of London bankers, by creating and exploiting loopholes in the Bretton Woods regulations, organized these expatriate dollars into 'offshore' 'euro-currency' markets. Slowly, control of international monetary flows was wrested from states (Helleiner 1994; Ingham 1994; Germain 1997).

In the early 1970s, inflation accelerated rapidly in the Western democracies. Steep increases in commodity prices, especially oil, were added to the combination of ever-expanding government expenditure and the power of monopoly capital and labour to mark up prices (Fischer 1996: 200–5). By mid-decade, inflation had increased to a level such that real interest rates and returns on financial assets were negative. And, as we noted earlier, a time came when it was no longer possible to raise interest rates high enough to compensate for money's depreciation without causing widespread default. A crisis point had been reached, and the political struggle to rebalance the forces in the economic struggle for existence began in the major capitalist states. In essence, it was to become the 'revenge of the rentier' (Smithin 1996).

The measures and the events of the 1980s in Reagan's USA and Thatcher's Britain have been thoroughly chronicled, and we need draw attention only to the main features. However, it should be borne in mind that the situation was not necessarily understood by the participants as one in which the rentiers' dominance should be restored. Clearly, not all the responses to the crisis were intended to rebalance the economic classes and groups in this way. None the less, by accident or design, this is exactly what happened. Fundamentally, the demands and expectations of the post-war era were to be reined in by sound money principles in the new guise of monetarism. The strategy began in 1979–80 with base interest rates rising close to 20 per cent in the USA and Britain. These continued despite the onset of a long world recession. Kalecki's warning in 1944 that prolonged full employment might require democratic states to 'discipline' their workforces and Marx's comments on the function of the 'reserve army' of the unemployed were noted even by political moderates.

In the USA, New Deal legislation enacted in the 1930s to alter the balance of power in favour of producers and consumers (debtors) was repealed (see Fischer 1996). In defence of victims of inflation, such as the 'fabled small saver', the interest rate ceilings and other curbs on creditor power were abolished. But of course this also benefited the country's 'wealthiest 10 per cent who owned 86 per cent of net financial wealth' (Greider 1987: 168). The power of monopolists in the supply of both goods and labour was to be checked by stronger competition policy and, in Britain in particular, by curbs on the power of trade unions and by the Thatcher government's deliberate confrontation with them. Here also, the inflationary impact of administered pricing in the public sector, in its tacit collusion with its monopolist suppliers, was to be dealt with by controlling local government expenditure and the privatization of the public sector provision of services. Eventually, the monetary policy regime in which control was placed in the hands of independent central banks was gradually adopted across the advanced economies. Evidence shows that these arrangements were first established in those countries where there existed a politically powerful coalition that was based upon money-capitalist *creditor* interests (Posen 1993: 46).

By the 1990s, a quite remarkable redistribution had taken place in favour of creditor classes. First and foremost, the adjustment is apparent in the *rising* real interest rates and *falling* real wages and profits in the production and service sectors (Henwood 1997). Since the late 1970s, the former have been at historically record high levels (Rowthorn 1995); and only in 1998 did real wages in the USA, for example, return to their 1979 level. Even when inflation rates had fallen, and economic growth had resumed, high real rates of interest persisted as evidence of the new settlement (Rowthorn 1995). Furthermore, money-capital power has had indirect, but no less material, effects. For example, in the USA during the dominance of productive capital and labour between 1950 and 1970, the rentier share of corporate surplus rose only slowly, from 20 to 30 per cent; but from the late 1980s onwards it rose to between 60 and 70 per cent (Henwood 1997: ch. 2). The shift is also evident in the growing dominance of finance *inside* the corporation during the transition from the post-war, mass-production, managerial control era, with its emphasis on growth and sales, to the current preoccupation with productivity, profitability and 'shareholder value' (Fligstein 2001). The change in corporate strategy from growth and output to a preoccupation with productivity and financial returns to investment lay behind the 'downsizing' and 'de-layering' of manufacturing that took place in the 1980s and early 1990s. Changing income differentials also show the growing dominance of the financial sector. Earnings settlements in the UK for the first quarter of 1998 showed a growth of 10.3 per cent in the financial sector, as opposed to an overall 5.6 per cent in the private sector and a mere 2.6 per cent in the public sector (Ingham 2000b). In this return to dominance of money-capital, the ratio of purely financial transactions to the production and exchange of goods and services has increased, accelerated in part by 'big bang' financial deregulation. An analysis of the US Federal Reserve's flow of funds data shows that from the 1950s to the 1980s non-financial firms' share rose from 25 to 50 per cent of GDP. However, those of the financial sector grew from an insignificant 2 per cent to more than 50 per cent of GDP (Henwood 1997; Guttmann 1994: 38). Moreover, concentration of resources in the financial sector and an increase in creditor power were accompanied by a growing indebtedness of the poor and social polarization (Fischer 1996; Arrighi 1994).

These changes in the domestic balance of power and distribution of rewards in favour of money-capital and finance were hastened by the disintegration of the Bretton Woods international monetary system and its capital controls on international capital movements. Nixon's action in abandoning the dollar–gold standard in 1971 wrought further, almost inevitable, rapid transformations in all sectors of the money market. 'Deregulation' of the restrictive practices in the closed, locally embedded stock markets, which the Bretton Woods restrictions had sustained, was the corollary of a regime of floating exchange rates. With the dismantling of exchange controls, a global market in equities/securities became possible; but first their old social and legal structures had to be swept away. 'May Day' (1 May 1975) brought about the abolition of the barriers to entry and fixed commissions on the New York Stock Exchange. Foreign investment flowed into Wall Street, and other stock markets, including the London Stock Exchange, suddenly became globally uncompetitive and restricted to poor-grade domestic securities. The US's action set off a tidal wave of responses: competitive deregulation swept around the world during the 1980s to such an extent that, by 1992, even the Japanese were pushed into a grudging, and very gradual, relaxation of their 'closed shop' stock exchange rules. As ever, the strongest players have, as intended, dominated the global financial 'levelled playing field'. During the 1980s, before the implosion of the Japanese economy, the outcome was by no means certain; but since the mid-1990s, US firms have inexorably come to dominate the global money and capital markets.

As we shall see, growth in financialization can be seen as a part of a typically cyclical phenomenon in capitalism (Arrighi 1994), not merely the result of 'irrational exuberance', as Alan Greenspan famously remarked in 1996. Often it ends with the bursting of a speculative 'bubble', which may be followed by a debt deflation in which the debts incurred during the expansion can no longer be serviced.[3] With the collapse of communication technology stock prices in 2001 and the fraud and bankruptcy of large corporations, it is again possible that such a phase will become general across the capitalist world, as it did in the 1930s (Bootle 1996; Warburton 2000; *Economist*, 22 January 2001; *Financial Times*, 3 January 2003). But such a situation has already existed in Japan for more than a decade. It is explored in the following section.

Debt Deflation and the Case of Japan

Many would consider that prolonged deflation poses an even greater threat to capitalism than inflation. Falling prices dampen 'animal spirits', inhibit the demand for credit-money, and slow the expansion of capitalist activity to the point where the system may begin to contract. Capitalism cannot 'mark time'; it is inherently incapable of reaching and maintaining a permanent equilibrium position. Moreover, it would appear that deflation is far less amenable to treatment than inflation. Interest rates and taxation are much more effective in the curtailment of economic activity than in its stimulation. In economists' terms, monetary and fiscal policy are 'asymmetric' – or, more prosaically, one cannot 'push on string'.

A persistent continuous fall in the general level of prices may produce a self-fulfilling downward spiral of expectations. For example, consumers hold back at the prospect of further price reductions, and producers cut prices in order to tempt reluctant buyers. Such a situation need not descend further into stagnation. A distinction is often made between 'dis-inflation' – that is, a steady state of the price level – and a genuine 'deflation'. There is always the possibility that the one may lead to the other, but full-blown deflation is more often the result of the collapse of an inflationary speculative 'bubble' financed by bank debt. With a collapse of prices in the speculative assets (stocks, property), it becomes difficult to service the debt without their sale, which further drives down prices. Falling prices may spread to other sectors, causing activity to slow further as expenditure and investment are cut to service the 'debt-overhang'. Stagnation results.

There is a widespread agreement in economics on this basic structure of the debt-deflation process. In fact, the analysis stems directly from work on the Great Depression of the 1930s by Irving Fisher, who, twenty years earlier, had propounded the orthodox quantity theory of money (Fisher 1933). However, orthodox analysis sees this kind of perturbation of the economy by the money side as a short-run aberration on the path towards long-run equilibrium. Deflation is a deviation from the normal operation of market forces. This may be the result of exogenous shocks – such as drastic rises or falls in commodity prices caused, for example, by natural disasters and war. Or, irrational 'manias' drive speculative asset inflation. In the long run, a reversion to 'normal' conditions and the exercise of economic rationality based on more adequate information will re-establish equilibrium. However, the heterodox economic analysis of Keynes, Schumpeter and others argues that the money side of the economy must be seen as the active autonomous force whereby capitalist economic relations are structured and projected through the *radical uncertainty* of time. Indeed, 'speculative crises' signal the historical appearance of capitalism (Weber 1981 [1927]: 286–92).

In a general sense, all capitalist activity is 'speculative' in so far as there is no certainty, for example, that all goods will find buyers. But Keynes and Weber were also pointing to purely financial speculation – that is, to the trading of claims to future income (stocks and other assets) in financial markets. In the aftermath of the Wall Street Crash of 1929 and the onset of the Great Depression, Keynes warned that '[s]peculators may do no harm as bubbles on a steady stream of enterprise. But the position is serious when enterprise becomes the bubble on a whirlpool of speculation. When the capital development of a country becomes a by-product of the activities of a casino, the job is likely to be ill-done' (Keynes 1973: 159). He did not provide a closely argued analysis of the role of bank lending in the expansion of speculative bubbles, but it plays the pivotal role in Minsky's 'financial instability hypothesis'.[4]

In the capitalist firm's balance sheet, comprising cash receipts and liabilities, 'the present, past, and future coexist in time' (Minsky 1982: 19). There are three possible sets of relations between anticipated cash flows and debt liability: hedge-finance, speculative finance and Ponzi finance. The models describe a progressive fragility. In a hedge finance enterprise, anticipated total revenues exceed running costs and cash payments in conventional accounting time periods (Minsky 1982: 21). The speculative finance enterprise has imminent repayment of principal, in addition to interest on debt, and can repay only by either using its money assets or incurring new debt, borrowed from banks or the capital markets. Ponzi enterprise, named after a Boston swindler's pyramid scheme (for details, see Kindleberger 1989 [1978]: ch. 5), describes a situation in which current earnings do not meet payment commitments 'except for some end points of the horizon' (Minsky 1982: 22).[5] Large construction projects, such as the Channel Tunnel, fall into this category, but Ponzi finance is found mainly in the financial sector, and typically involves borrowing to acquire speculative assets for resale. Under most circumstances, as the cost of debt increases with time, profitability is possible only if the asset continues to appreciate.[6] Consequently, Ponzi finance is especially vulnerable to changes in money market conditions – especially a rise in interest rates.

Following Schumpeter, Minksy sees banks as 'merchants of debt' whose interest is to encourage speculative and Ponzi finance. With the expansion of production, cash balances of the relatively secure hedge finance firms increase and permit an expansion of credit-money. Time horizons are pushed further forward; and the volume and complexity of financial relations multiplies into an investment boom (Minsky 1982: 30–2). 'Stability is destabilising' (Minsky 1982: 26). At this juncture, the expansion of investment that the stability has induced leads to higher interest rates – either as the market's response to the need to attract funds, or if they are raised by the monetary authority in order to dampen the boom.[7] Either way, speculative enterprise is transformed into Ponzi, and even the prudently hedged firms are drawn into speculative status. As the level of unserviceable debt increases, it becomes increasingly likely that rising interest rates will create defaults and a crisis. As current income is insufficient to meet the higher interest rates, assets are liquidated to realize cash for servicing debt. Investment programmes are abandoned, workers are laid off, demand and output fall, triggering debt deflation. Recession, and possibly depression, result. In short, Minsky emphasizes two propositions: 'that the internal workings of a capitalist economy generate financial relations that are conducive to instability and that the price and asset-value relations that will trigger a financial crisis in a fragile financial structure are *normal functioning events*' (Minsky 1982: 37, emphasis added). The elastic creation of credit-money through the monetization of debt has the inherent tendency to destabilize an economy.

Minsky does not, however, draw a 'Marxist' conclusion that capitalism will collapse as a result of these internal (financial) contradictions. Rather, he implies an intriguing paradox that quite correctly leaves the outcome open-ended. In his terms, a delicate balance is emerging. As capitalist finance has become more efficient in creating credit-money and managing risk, it has become more vulnerable. But at the same time, governments and monetary authorities believe that they have learned to monitor the system and to prevent 'fragility' from becoming a 'crisis'. However, there are good grounds for thinking that any permanent moderation of the extremes of the business cycle is illusory.[8] An important implication of Minsky's analysis is that bankruptcies and failures caused by the crises purge the over-indebtedness in the system and permit another cycle of the debt financing of production to begin. From a Minskian perspective, the avoidance of crises by expert monetary and financial management is merely a postponement. If debts are not expunged through bankruptcies, they remain as an 'overhang' that might be triggered into a chain of defaults. Evidence suggests that this could be a secular trend. For example, household and non-financial corporate debt in the USA, as a percentage of GDP, has doubled since the early 1960s, and has reached historically unprecedented levels. Whether this will inevitably lead to a bout of debt deflation in the powerhouse of the world economy is, arguably, *the* critical question in contemporary capitalism. Japan's unresolved debt deflation is often taken as a portent (*Economist* 2000; Warburton 2000).[9] It provides an illustration of Minsky's model and, moreover, shows the fundamental social and political nature of the creation and destruction of money.

Japan's deflation

Towards the end of the Japanese economy's ascendancy during the 1980s, it experienced rapid asset price inflation in land, property and stocks. Between 1985 and 1989, the Nikkei 225 stock market index rose from 13,000 to 38,915. Property prices increased by an annual average of 22 per cent, and it was estimated that in 1989 the property value of metropolitan Tokyo exceeded the value of that of the entire USA (Van Rixtel 2002: 171). The causes need not concern us here (see Van Rixtel 2002 for a survey of the conventional wisdom), except to note that it presents a classic example of an inflationary financial bubble. Asset prices were driven up by debt-financed demand.[10] During the 1980s, Japan's domestic credit creation was 'more reckless than anywhere else in the world' – doubling to 300 per cent of GDP (Warburton 2000: 11). Institutionalized informal links (*amakudari*) between the private financial sector and the monetary authorities in Japan created a 'regulatory forbearance' that allowed the bank-based expansion of the 'speculative bubble' to continue way beyond the early warning signs (Van Rixtel 2002: 177). And, as we shall see, the same networks have inhibited the introduction of stringent remedial measures since the crash in 1990.[11]

By early 1989, the indulgent authorities could no longer ignore the situation and raised interest rates. Real estate companies and other financial firms that had driven the asset inflation immediately experienced difficulty in servicing their massive debts. Defaults became widespread, and the scramble to sell assets to repay debt pushed prices down further. The Nikkei stock market index fell from its 1989 peak of 39,000 to 14,000 by 1992, and land and real estate prices halved during the same period (Van Rixtel 2002: 174).

The collapse of the bubble set in train a deflationary spiral that stubbornly persists. As prices fall, the real cost of debt rises, companies reduce costs – particularly labour costs, cutting aggregate demand and exacerbating the cycle. Expectations of further deflation become self-fulfilling as investment and consumption decline in mutually reinforcing descent. Every sector of the Japanese economy is affected. Towards the end of the 1990s, the pace of bankruptcies increased, and even the large *zaibatsu* conglomerates that were the engines of the post-war Japanese 'miracle' began to lay off workers and abandon their lifetime employment policy. At around 6 per cent, unemployment is relatively low by Western standards, but it continues to rise and intensify the chronic insecurity that has set in.

By encouraging investment in production and current consumption, mild inflation might break the impasse, but to date this has proved to be beyond the government's powers to induce. Orthodox measures to increase the money supply are utterly ineffective, and, moreover, with near zero interest rates and an unsustainable ratio of government debt to GDP, it would appear that the limit of conventional policy has been reached. (Interest rates cannot go lower than zero.) None the less, many orthodox economists persist in the belief that monetary policy will eventually halt deflation. For example, it is suggested that the government could drastically cut taxes and print an enormous issue of non-interest-bearing bonds that would inject high-powered money into the banking system. It is thought that in sparing future generations the burden of debt repayment, non-interest-bearing bonds would be more acceptable (A. Turner 2002). In a similar manner to modern neo-chartalism, this prescription recognizes that the state has the power to print as much money as it takes to trigger an inflationary shock to the economy.[12] 'The only limits on the ability of a government and central bank together to stimulate nominal demand are those created by the relationship between government and central bank, which the government itself defines' (A. Turner 2002). However, as we have seen, this power is conventionally limited by norms governing orthodox fiscal practice. Despite the stagnation, it is clear that the Bank of Japan is unwilling to break those that are intended precisely to prevent potential inflation. As the outgoing governor of the Bank of Japan reminded his critics, 'The central bank should be the guardian of the integrity of our country's money' (*Financial Times*, 3 December 2001). Furthermore, rentiers demand a rate of interest that is deemed to cover long-run inflation, which is 'negotiated' or 'bargained' in the market for government securities, and a level of taxation that is considered adequate to meet the interest payments.[13] In short, such a drastic measure as the issue of non-interest-bearing bonds would require a new political settlement between the state and its creditors and a new normative structure.[14] Short of wartime exigencies, such measures are rarely introduced.

Orthodox economic analysis also argues that in the current situation the Japanese banking system is disabled by the debt overhang from using the high-powered money that the government's large and growing debt provides.[15] The fall in asset prices after 1990 had an immediate effect on the banking system. Banks became burdened with bad debts, or 'non-performing' loans, and the fall in stock prices greatly diminished the value of their capital and reserves. If the banks follow the existing norms and rules that govern the ratio of lending to fractional reserves, both problems significantly reduce the capacity of the banks to extend further loans that might, in principle, stimulate the economy. (Although, of course, it must be noted that demand for investment is now very low.) The opacity of auditing practice and banking supervision in Japan has meant that estimates of the size of the 'non-performing' loans vary considerably, but they are very large. Officially, the figures is Y60,000 bn, but some put it as high as Y237,000 bn (*Financial Times*, 13 February 2002).The prescribed remedy is for banks to write off the debts and restore balance sheets to a level at which fractional reserves would permit further loans. Exasperation is often expressed in orthodox economic and monetary circles at what seems to be Japan's apparent unwillingness to take what are considered to be the necessary policy steps to activate the economy and halt the deflation ('World Bank chief hits at Japan's efforts on deflation', *Financial Times*, 17 January 2003). But the experience of the banking crisis of the late 1990s, the effects of attempts to introduce 'big bang' financial deregulation and the ensuing bankruptcies and scandals have left the Japanese elite reluctant to risk any further destabilization (Van Rixtel 2002; Murphy 2000). Writing off debts would increase bankruptcies and unemployment as banks foreclosed on companies. Given the tight networks of cross-held ownership in the upper reaches of the *keiretsu* sector of the economy, any action on the scale deemed to be necessary could effectively destroy the existing social and political structure of the economy. It is very unusual for entrenched ruling elites intentionally to undermine their own positions. Indeed, Japan is even less likely to willingly undertake such measures, given the fundamental informality (*amakudari*) of the social structure that links the economy and the polity (Van Rixtel 2002). Re-equilibrating the Japanese balance sheet by bad-debt write-offs and large-scale bankruptcies would destroy the power bases of the closely interconnected corporate and political elite (Murphy 2000).

This kind of diagnosis is acknowledged in Japan. Great efforts were made during 2001–2 to create a charismatic power base, outside the established political structure, to enable Prime Minister Koizumi to take drastic steps to restructure the economy. Banks were to be compelled to write off bad debts, and the *zaibatsu* forced to shed excess productive capacity. By 2003, it was generally agreed, in the West at least, that he had failed to overcome the established resistance in the LDP and bureaucracy. A large part of the Japanese elite fears not only for its privileged position and power, but also for social stability.

But it is doubtful whether any narrowly economic and monetary measures – however radical – would have the desired effect. Regardless of any other considerations, the long recession has created a level of insecurity that has paralysed aggregate consumer demand. The depth of the problem is a direct consequence of the particular *social structure* of the Japanese economy. After the post-war reconstruction, the basic foundation for social welfare and economic security was provided by lifetime employment in the Japanese conglomerate corporations (*keiretsu*) – not so much by the state, as in the West. But, as we have noted, the recession of the 1990s has eroded the willingness and ability of the *keiretsu* to continue this role. Regardless of the elite's reluctance to tackle the impasse, chronic insecurity resists all conventional economic policy measures to inflate the economy. As Keynes observed in the 1930s, the search for security is now sought in money as a store of value. It is doubly comforting that with deflation the value of savings increases with time – regardless of the near zero rates of interest. But this 'paradox of thrift' merely intensifies the recession.

Argentina's Monetary Disintegration

In April 2002, two well-dressed ladies in a Buenos Aires café asked how they might pay for their tea ('Argentines snowed under by paper IOUs', *Financial Times*, 11 April 2002). Dollars were to be preferred at the café's exchange rate of one to three pesos; but the waiter also offered a long list of alternatives. At the precise moment when a group of European states managed to change smoothly to a single currency, Argentina began to travel in the opposite direction and enter a period of monetary anarchy. The extent of the disintegration after the government defaulted on its sovereign debt on Christmas Eve 2001 is unusual for a developed state in peacetime – arguably, it is unparalleled in the modern era. Mexico and even Russia did not experience this level of monetary incoherence and collapse after their recent defaults.

The default broke the fixed US dollar–peso parity that had been in place during the 1990s (see below). Immediately, *two* moneys of account – a devalued peso and the US dollar – competed for the denomination of *domestic* credit–debt relations. Further confusion was added by their volatile exchange rates. Both the peso and the dollar circulated as currency, but were joined by an array of over a dozen IOUs issued by the provincial governments – *patacons* (series I, II and III), *lecops, la Riojas* and so on. To these were added luncheon vouchers, tickets and shopping mall currencies, such as Gallerias Pacifico's *pacificos*. Informal monetary arrangements, such as the *cheque volador* (flying cheque), have always played a prominent part in Argentina's large 'black' economy (Powell 2002). But the proliferation of both means of payment and, more importantly, competing and unstable moneys of account marked a new level of monetary fragmentation. All debtor–creditor relations have had to be redefined and reassembled time and again since late 2001. In a stark illustration of money's 'non-neutrality', rioting and several rapid changes of government followed within the space of a few weeks.

The current situation has interrelated, long- and short-term causes. Obviously, the country's chronic economic under-performance, its political instability and the immediate effects of the 1990s monetary policy are important. But I shall argue that the actual crisis and the character of the ensuing disintegration can be traced to the endemic frailty of the monetary system itself. Although the case cannot be established in detail, I would also suggest that Argentina's long-term economic under-performance is, to a large degree, a result of the monetary system's institutional weakness. In essence, the monetary incapacity is the result of the Argentine state's long-term inability to create and maintain stable relations between itself and its debtors (taxpayers) and creditors (rentiers/bond-holders). Consequently, the state has been unable to establish a viable sovereign monetary space in which a robust banking system could flourish and sustain an equally robust peso. To be sure, erratic and eventually stagnant economic development has reinforced the failure to develop a viable money, but the latter's feebleness also has independent social and political causes. The weakness of Argentina's money is the expression of the weakness of its state, which in turn has made it difficult to realize the potential of the country's enviable economic 'factor endowments'. The long-run development of Argentina's economy is a clear example of an underlying long-run *non*-neutrality of money. The enigmatic nature of

Argentine economic development is widely recognized (see, for example, Manzetti 1993; Lewis 1990; *Economist*, 2 March 2002). At the outbreak of World War I, Argentina ranked amongst the very richest nations in the world, ahead of France and Germany. In many ways it promised to be a South American 'USA'. Natural resources, industry, a vital immigrant population and abundant flows of money-capital sustained the growth. Its position was maintained throughout the inter-war world depression, but by 1990 it had dropped to seventieth place (*Economist*, 18 April 1992).

Recent events and the crisis

The 1980s were a dire culmination of fifty years during which annual economic growth barely averaged 1 per cent. Between 1984 and 1988, GDP increased at an annual rate of only 0.3 per cent, unemployment grew rapidly and the decade ended with hyperinflation (Bethell 1993: 61). However, by the end of the 1990s, the country was hailed as an example of the efficacy of strict modern monetary management and the economic liberal orthodoxy of free trade, privatization and deregulation. The economy grew at an average annual rate of around 6 per cent between 1991 and 1997, the highest in the Latin American region (*Economist*, 2 March 2002). The recovery was attributed to the new monetary regime, in which the peso was legally fixed at par to the US dollar. With the risk of devaluation and inflation apparently eliminated, foreign investment poured in, as it had done from time to time during the previous century, and produced rapid economic growth.

However, there were two problems with the fixed US dollar–peso parity. The first is the general disadvantage of all currency pegging, which removes the option of a flexible exchange rate policy to deal with adverse conditions, with the result that economies become hostages to fortune. Global money markets are well aware that only the weak, out of necessity, take such drastic measures as effectively surrendering monetary sovereignty. Foreign capital was initially lured by the guarantee afforded by the peg, but it none the less reacted swiftly and nervously to any unfavourable sign that might lead Argentina to abandon the arrangement, as in 1995. At this time, GDP fell by 4 per cent, and a dozen banks collapsed; but the crisis passed. With the collapse of exports and the 1998 recession, it became clear just how much the dollar peg had overvalued the peso. Most importantly, with the dollar-denominated national debt and rising government expenditure in the recession, repayment would soon become too onerous. Over Christmas 2001, Argentina became, for the time being at least, the greatest sovereign defaulter in history – to the tune of $155 billion. Inevitably, devaluation followed the default, with serious consequences for creditors at home and abroad.

The second problem was specific to Argentina, but, arguably, it was more fundamental. 'Dollarization' had merely papered over the cracks and disguised Argentina's underlying structural inability to maintain sovereign money based on an effective fiscal settlement and viable domestic banking system.[16] In some respects, the adoption of a US dollar standard was a formalization of what the Argentine elite had been practising for decades – that is, a tenuous participation in the domestic monetary system and the conversion of their assets into US dollars held offshore. In short, the apparent resolution of the peso's weakness actually exacerbated the long-standing problem.

The usual range of orthodox economic explanations of the crisis soon appeared. For example, it was widely held that fiscal laxity and the growth of government expenditure – that is, the size of Argentina's debt – are the most important factors in the débâcle. So much is obvious: if the debt had been smaller, then the problem of default would not have loomed so large. Other explanations focused on particular adverse factors – such as the late 1990s recession, 'exogenous shocks' – such as the appreciation of the dollar at a time when Argentina's main trading partner, Brazil, devalued, and so on (*Economist*, 2 March 2002). However, none of these explains the scale of the actual *monetary* anarchy that threatens to impede any solution to Argentina's *economic* problems. The current crisis is an expression of the endemic weakness of Argentina's monetary system – which was, of course, the fundamental reason for the adoption of the high-risk dollarization strategy in the first place.

As economic difficulties mounted in the late 1990s, the chronic absence of any trust between the monetary authorities and the population was again revealed. As the economy's balance of payments deficits began to threaten the ability to maintain the fixed dollar standard, the government acted in a characteristic manner. With the aim of maintaining its solvency and ability to service the debt, it sought to confiscate the banking and financial system's reserves by any means it could devise. (The central bank's governor opposed the strategy, and was removed.) Central bank reserve requirements were loosened; pension funds were coerced into buying government bonds; and banks were pressured into swapping their government bonds for low-interest loans.

As default became a possibility, Argentina's foreign creditors sold their bonds in an effort to cut their losses; and domestic depositors in the banking system rushed to withdraw their cash. To stem the sell-off, interest rates on government bonds were raised to more than 50 per cent, which further increased the need for funds to meet the mounting charges on the debt. In December 2001, in an effort to conserve the banking system's deposits for its own use, the government imposed a ceiling of $1,000 a month on withdrawals. The middle class was outraged at the confiscation of its deposits, and the ensuing shortage of cash impeded the operation of the extensive 'black economy'. Rioting and a political crisis followed the devaluation. In late January 2002, Eduardo Duhalde became Argentina's fifth president within the space of a fortnight.[17]

Despite misgivings, the IMF had continued to support the dollarization during the difficulties of the late 1990s, and in a last-ditch attempt to save the situation lent a further $8 billion in addition to the $14 billion provided in January 2001. During 2002, the Argentines asked for more, but the IMF held firm in its refusal to lend until sweeping structural reforms had been made to the monetary and political systems. The implementation of some of the conditions might conceivably improve the situation – for example, the elimination of the local provincial governments' control over their budgets and new local currencies. But such remedies presuppose that which they are intended to produce – a viable sovereign monetary space.

The failure of Argentine money

Successful money in modern capitalism consists in the institutionalization of two reciprocal relations between a state and its citizens: *taxation* and the *national debt*, denominated in the state's money of account. The two relations are linked in a settlement whose legitimacy is framed in terms of accepted norms of good fiscal practice and credibility that will be sustained. The willingness of the state's creditors to fund further national debt is to a large degree dependent on the state's capacity to secure revenue, in large part through taxation, at a level that creates confidence in the ability to pay interest on, and principal of, the debt. Today, many states' debts are funded to a greater extent than hitherto by foreign holdings of bonds through the global money markets. But the relationship of the state to domestic creditors in its fiscal constitution has been important in securing legitimacy in the most successful modern states. Argentina has failed to forge both these relations, and has become locked into a situation in which the inability to tax effectively has denied its governments access to affordable credit. This impasse was further intensified in the period from Peron to the 1990s by the related weakness of populist pandering through higher wages and fringe benefits to workers in the large state-owned sector. The legacy persists.

For at least half a century, no more than half of those Argentines legally required to pay income tax have done so (Manzetti 1993: 135; Lewis 1990: 362). The widespread non-payment does not involve surreptitious evasion so much as a widespread, blatant denial of the state's authority to collect taxes. It is a further indication of the state's weakness in relation to the Argentine capitalist classes that even if made, tax payment is the result of *ad hoc* bargaining (Lewis 1990: 270). Of course, the corporations have had good reason to mistrust the long sequence of populist authoritarian governments since Peron. In the mid-1970s, for example, it was discovered that the government owed 101 billion pesos of collected taxes to the social security system, but only 48 billion could be traced – to the Armed Forces Retirement Fund (Lewis 1990: 273).

The corollary of this level of non-payment is the large informal or 'black' economy (Powell 2002). Such sectors are to be found in all societies, but with the exception of some post-Communist states, rarely are they so open and extensive as in Argentina. Moreover, the informal operates at all levels of the economy. As in Russia, it is a 'parallel' economy, rather than merely being confined to the lower levels. In the late 1970s, a shanty town was found to have more than 30,000 relatively affluent inhabitants operating a wide range of enterprises, such as shoe and furniture factories, some of which were directly linked to foreign companies. They were illegally tapped into the nearby power lines, and were served by a well-planned network of roads (Lewis 1990: 364).

In addition to peso and dollar cash, the informal economy has its own media of exchange, such as the 'flying cheques' (*cheque volador*). As in early modern European capitalism, bilateral promissory notes between named transactors circulate, at a discount, for the payment of third parties. Dollar cheques drawn on overseas banks also circulate widely as means of payment. It is disadvantageous to hoard cash in a high-inflation economy such as Argentina's, and therefore much of the informal economy's wealth finds its way out of the country to augment the steady export of money from the legitimate sector. In effect, a majority of the population does not have to acquire the official domestic money in order to discharge their tax debt to the state. It is therefore difficult to establish the domestic value of the peso and a payments system based on a trusted domestic banking system. In the absence of a sovereign monetary space, dollarization is almost inevitable.

As I have stressed, the 'memorable alliance' with domestic capitalist classes was the foundation of the more successful modern capitalist states. The national debt became the basis for an elastic supply of credit-money upon which the capitalist system was established from the seventeenth century onwards in Western Europe. In this alliance of state and creditor, each has an interest in the strength and long-term survival of the other. States that have depended to a very large extent on foreign creditors have rarely flourished. The Argentine state has never forged a relation of advantaged interdependence between itself and an indigenous capitalist class. The result has been a chronically weak domestic banking and financial system and a fragile peso. Money generated by Argentine capitalism has customarily sought to become dollars and to find itself safely deposited in New York and London. There has been no strong domestic rentier class with an interest in, and an ability to insist effectively on, the state's fiscal rectitude.

A brief economic and monetary history

Argentina's most prosperous era, from the late nineteenth century to the 1930s, was not accompanied by the development of effective domestic banking and fiscal systems. Despite considerable balance of payments surpluses after 1890, economic development and government expenditure continued to be financed to a large extent by *foreign* investment (Bethell 1993: 64–6). The generation of wealth from the export of primary products – especially wheat and beef – did not form the basis for domestic credit-money creation for either private or public investment and consumption. Effective bank mediation of these incomes was not established.[18]

The contraction of demand for Argentine exports of beef and wheat during the world depression of the 1930s permanently altered its economy's pattern of development. Until 1914 at least, Argentina had been, in effect, economically dependent on Britain for manufactured goods and investment capital, in return for the export of agricultural staples (Bethell 1993:173). The economic dislocation and subsequent declining fortunes of the nineteenth-century landed oligarchy led to the collapse of constitutional government in 1930 in a military *coup*. This set in train the cycles of weak democracy and military dictatorship. After a *coup* in 1943, Colonel Juan Domingo Peron gradually acquired immense political power based on the support of the urban masses that had grown so rapidly during the industrialization in the 1930s. But it was a political alliance that further impeded the formation of a fiscal settlement including a bourgeois rentier class that had an interest in maintaining a capitalist monetary system.

The Peronist governments pursued a strategy of economic nationalism specifically designed to maintain political power. The state took control of the economy to accelerate industrialization by means of import substitution and to redistribute income in favour of the regime's supporters – the workers, the elite in the newly nationalized industries, employees at all levels in the rapidly expanding state apparatus, and, of course, the military itself. During the late 1940s, real wages were increased by more than 60 per cent (Manzetti 1993: 38; Lewis 1990: 182). The central bank was nationalized in 1946, in order that it could be made to respond to the increased demand for money that this strategy required. In effect, private money-capital was confiscated: all banks were required to register their deposits with the central bank, and no private bank could make a loan without its approval. Private banks making unauthorized loans had their deposits seized (Lewis 1990: 159). In all successful capitalist economies, central banks mediate the relations between the state and its creditors, but Peron effectively removed the possibility that this might develop in Argentina.

Peron's regime brought about a massive shift in the balance of power in the structure of monetary relations. Despite rapid inflation, average real family income for wage- and salary-earners increased by around 15 per cent between 1946 and 1953. For the self-employed in the industrial and mining sectors of the economy, it fell by a similar amount. But money-capital suffered more: income from commerce and finance fell 60 per cent, and rentiers' returns from interest and dividends by 50 per cent (Lewis 1990: 209). Atypically for an industrializing economy, banking's share of Argentine GDP fell by more than 50 per cent between 1945 and 1972 – from the very low comparative figure of 7 per cent. The indigenous financial sector never recovered (Manzetti 1993: 293).

The rigid control of imported manufactures was accompanied, ironically, by an accelerating outward flow of money into safe havens abroad. Isolated from any competitive constraint, there was nothing other than Peron's exhortations to prevent the industrial producers and the state employees from exercising the power he had given them to claim an ever-increasing share of the GDP. Not only did wages, salaries and government budgets increase; workers spent less and less time at work. By 1951, it was estimated that Argentine workers on average took every third day off, in addition to the extra holidays granted by the Peron government (Lewis 1990: 183). The gap between the production of goods and services and the granting of higher wages and salaries widened. And in the absence of any countervailing force in the form of a strong indigenous creditor class with a controlling stake in the money and banking system, the state was able to print the money to meet the demands.

In effect, the debtors expropriated the creditors, and the result was annual rates of inflation of at least 30 per cent and the further disaffection of the indigenous capitalist classes, most especially the rentiers and money-capitalists.

After Peron, the state lost all control of its fiscal and monetary system; it was quite unable to establish a settlement between itself, its creditors and the tax-paying citizens. Consequently, Argentina became utterly dependent on foreign loans that it was increasingly unable to service. Under pressure from foreign creditors, the state tried periodically to collect taxes and encourage the repatriation of capital. Between 1956 and the late 1980s, six amnesties, or 'whitewashes', of 'black funds' were declared (Lewis 1990: 558). On condition that illegal hoards were declared, the state offered to demand only a fraction of the original tax. The sum had to be low enough to act as an incentive to declare and high enough not to alienate the minority of willing taxpayers. These amnesties were not successful.[19] In 2001, it was estimated that more than $150 bn was held abroad, a sum equal to the total government debt at the time of the default.

The problem of the Argentine economy is to a large extent a reflection of the problem of its feeble monetary system, which, in turn, is a problem of the state. The IMF continues to insist that orthodox monetary and fiscal policies are adopted as a pre-condition for any further loans, but the absence of a settlement between the major classes precludes the deliverance of such a promise.[20] Moreover, without a domestic coalition, any such loan could do no more than offer temporary relief.

In general, the failure to establish viable monetary systems tells us much about the nature of money, but this line of enquiry cannot be pursued in any detail. Much of Africa exhibits a chronic inability to forge stable states in which promises to pay are produced in a settlement with the major economic interests (for a Weberian analysis of African patrimonial states, see Chabal and Daloz 1999). Post-Soviet Russia provides a fascinating example of monetary disorder that has much in common with that in Argentina – although for quite different reasons (Ledeneva 1998; Ledeneva and Kurchiyan 2000; Busse 2000; Woodruff 1999). Both states have found it difficult to establish the two basic monetary circuits in taxation and the government bond market that link important economic groups and stabilize the value of money. In particular, Russian capitalists, like their Argentine counterparts, maintain both a sophisticated 'virtual' economy, detached from state regulation, and a cosmopolitan orientation. Consequently, they use dollars and payment in kind, rather than roubles. All these cases of monetary failure show clearly how it is the result of a failure of the state. The inability to impose a stable money of account and a 'critical mass' of tax and bond monetary flows results in monetary anarchy in which heterogeneous forms of money coexist and remain embedded in discrete transaction networks – such as local quasi-barter exchange – at all levels of the economy.

9

New Monetary Spaces

With the arrival of electronic money, money creation will become increasingly privatized. Hayek's vision of a world of unrestricted currency competition could, for better or for worse, soon become a reality.

B. Cohen 2001b: 221

The one strategic asset we have is the fast-breaking medium of the internet and, at a time when society increasingly takes the form of a world market, our efforts at self-emancipation must be focused on the money instruments themselves.

Hart 2000: 310

In the Euro area, the traditional historical links between money creation and sovereignty will be broken to a unique extent.

Goodhart 1998: 425

The advanced modern capitalist world typically comprises separate nation-states with their own national economies and currencies. To be sure, there have been significant exceptions and deviations, but these need not detain us for the moment (Helleiner 2003). However, this 'norm' has not met with universal approval. Economic liberals and others have viewed nation-states and their separate currencies as significant, but perhaps necessary, impediments to the realization of the economic welfare that a genuinely global market would bring. These arguments are based on the assumption that it would be efficient for the world economy, conceptualized as a *single 'real' economy*, to have a *single medium of exchange*. Aside from any other consideration, such as the nation-state's tendency to protectionism, the existence of myriad national currencies brings significant transaction costs. Consequently, Hayek, for example, advocated the 'denationalization' of money, which would allow private currencies to compete to the point where the most acceptable became 'global' (Hayek 1976).

Recent developments have created a renewed interest in these relationships between the state, territory and forms of money. Economic globalization and the rapid advance in information and communication technology (ICT) would appear to be creating a more tightly integrated world economy and a consequential loosening of the typical linkages of state, economy and currency. There is discussion of the deterritorialization or denationalization of money, 'electronic money', 'virtual money', the 'end of money', all of which are seen as involving the state's loss of control over its money (Helleiner 1999, 2003; Hart 2000; OECD 2002; B. Cohen 2001b). Some believe that globalization will finally bring about the nineteenth-century liberals' hope for a genuine world market in which the international division of labour based on comparative economic advantages will expand human welfare. In principle, at least, they suggest that the increasing international factor mobility, led by the global money markets, could lead to the actualization of the neoclassical model of the 'law of one price' (Banuri and Schor 1992: 5). In the terms of Mundell's influential theory, global economic relations have set the world on a path to becoming a single optimum currency area (see the discussion in chapter 1).[1]

The argument is taken further in the contention that the computerization of economic transactions and the spread of the Internet could enable barter to become so efficient that even the 'neutral veil' of money would become redundant. With arguments based on 'new monetary economics', it is held that ICT could eliminate the inconveniences of barter that result from the 'absence of a double coincidence of wants'. 'Offers' and 'wants' of goods could be readily matched; or, in a form of 'quasi-barter', transactors could offer a range of goods – especially financial assets – as means of payment. Computerized barter in a globalized world could render state money and central banks redundant. Economics' difficulty in specifying the 'moneyness' of money will become irrelevant as any number of goods could become 'money' – as the orthodox theory has always maintained. The 'money question' would cease to exist.

Aside from these general questions, one of the most significant experiments in the history of monetary space has been gradually enacted over the past decade. No examination of the nature of money could neglect the novel way in which the relationship between money, space and sovereignty has been articulated in the European Monetary Union (see Goodhart 1998; Bell and Nell 2003). Like the conjectures on global technology and money, the orthodox theory of money as a neutral medium of exchange plays an important role.

Technology and New Monetary Spaces

It is generally believed that communication and information technology is eroding the power of nation-states – economically, culturally and politically. This is said to be occurring from two directions simultaneously – globally from the outside and locally from the inside. Transnational economic, political and cultural developments have begun to challenge the hegemony of all but the most powerful states, but localized, largely informal cultural and political movements have also expanded. In the economic sphere, the advance of transnational capitalism and global e-commerce has been paralleled by the revival of local and informal economies. Both developments make use, in part, of new forms of money, based on information communication and technology.

There are a number of different possible developments on both levels. At the globalized upper level of capitalism, for example, large transnational corporations might issue their own 'scrip' as media of exchange in Internet transactions (B. Cohen 2001b; Lietaer 2000; Weatherford 1999). In more extreme vein, as I have already indicated, others argue that Internet barter-credit transactions might even bring about the 'end of money' and, consequently, the redundancy of central banks. At the other end of the scale, the informal sectors of many modern economies have developed into organized local trading systems with their own local media of exchange. This underlying conception of money is shared by two quite diverse and opposed ideological positions, which both hold to the possibility that a 'spontaneous order' could exist without the state. Debates on money's future are part of a more general belief in the Internet as a potential force for human emancipation from the state (Hart 2000). In short, ICT has revitalized two old nineteenth-century visions: the liberal conception of a global market 'cosmopolitanism' and 'guild socialism' – now usually referred to as 'communitarianism'.

Electronic globalization: 'private' money and the 'end of money'

For some, technology promises to rectify the information and communication deficiencies that have, hitherto, impaired the perfect functioning of the market mechanism (B. Cohen 2001b). They have a vision of a truly transcendental global order: a vast moneyless market, made a reality by a barter-credit clearing system based on a fabulously more powerful successor to the Internet. These possibilities are questioned by other writers, on the grounds that states will have both the will and the capability successfully to challenge any technologically based threat to their monopolies if it is in their interests to do so (Helleiner 1999).

I agree with this second assessment, but my scepticism is also based on a slightly different, more fundamental argument concerning the nature of money. Belief in the possibility of viable denationalized e-money that emerges in the course of e-commerce is based on the common misunderstanding that we examined in Part I. Money, as opposed to a 'convenient medium of exchange', needs authoritative foundations – that is to say, some autonomous social and political bases. Narrowly market money, whether this be a sixteenth-century bill of exchange or today's e-money, remains embedded in, and restricted to, its economic network and, consequently, is only as viable as the network itself.

The most extreme interpretation of the monetary potential of ICT suggests that future generations of computers could make the Walrasian barter-credit general equilibrium model a reality. In his contemplation of the 'end of money', the then deputy-governor of the Bank of England wondered if, as a result of the 'impact of technological innovation', central banks would have disappeared by the twenty-second century (King 1999). Individuals and, more pertinently, capitalist firms might be able to settle their exchanges by the direct transfer of wealth in the form of, say, financial assets, from one electronic account to another. Computers communicating in real time could *instantaneously* verify counter-parties' creditworthiness. The realization of this possibility would make money's unique role, as the means of final settlement, redundant. If final settlement could be made without recourse to the central bank's money, the bank itself would cease to exist. Present monetary policy preoccupation with the need to limit money creation would give way to the more technically neutral regulation of the integrity of the computer systems that verify the creditworthiness of the counterparties' assets. Societies have managed without central banks and their monopoly of the supply of money in the past, and may well do so again in the future (King 1999; see also the general discussion in B. Cohen 2001b).

In fact, these kinds of payments system have existed for some time in the private 'near moneys' of the upper reaches of world capitalism (Ascheim and Park 1976). Moreover, there are numerous historical examples of moneyless systems of complex multilateral settlement with payment in kind – for example, eighteenth-century Massachusetts and present-day Russia. In essence, these are no different from King's conjecture. The quite complex economy of mid-eighteenth-century Boston had no issued currency (Baxter 1945). Farmers' and traders' debts were recorded in a *money of account* based on the English currency, which of course did not circulate. The means of payment were heterogeneous goods priced in an agreed unit of abstract value (money of account). In strict terms, such systems, including King's scenario, are not moneyless but cashless. In order to function at all, these monetary systems require only an abstract money of account.

King understands that the liquid financial assets for settlement of debt would need to be priced according to a money of account. But in his focus on medium of exchange as money's *essential* property, the question of money of account is seen to be unproblematic. In typical orthodox fashion, King simply asserts that a *commodity standard*, based on the prices of a 'basket of commodities', could produce both a unit of account and a benchmark standard of value. The money of account would simply be a 'matter of public choice', and its regulation would be no more difficult than existing weights and measures inspection. However, as we saw in chapter 1, this 'new monetary economics' position rests on two errors. In the first place, economic value is not natural like the relatively constant properties of, say, distance and weight. Indeed, it fluctuates in response to the distribution of social and economic power, and this is precisely why money of account is logically anterior and historically prior to market exchange and market value. Second, the standardization of the unit of account in relation to any standard of value has to be established by an authority. Monetary promises to pay are abstract, and they function because the question of their value is partly *removed from the free market process*. As we have seen, by promising to buy gold at a fixed price, central banks were fixing the so-called market in order to provide the stability which the market itself could not provide. The 'end of money' futurology is no more than a redescription of the nineteenth-century liberals' misunderstanding of their monetary system and, implicitly, a repetition of their vain hope of a world without politics (see the critique of the modern versions of Kantian 'cosmopolitan democracy' in Hawthorn 2000).

Doubts about the theoretical underpinnings of this extreme case do not mean, however, that the possible effects of the appearance of new and varied media of exchange and changes in the means of monetary transmission are unimportant. There are two possible developments that could fragment and erode national monetary spaces. First, it is suggested that the proliferation of limited-purpose media of exchange that appeared in the late 1980s – such as prepaid 'smart cards' for rail or air travel, mobile phone calls, cable TV and so on – could go beyond the credit card limitations (Goldschalk and Krueger 2000). At present, like credit card debt, smart card accounts must be paid for by transfers from conventional bank balances. However, the techno-logical possibility exists for balances of the different limited-purpose media to become readily exchangeable one for the other in payment for an ever-widening range of goods. The next generation of PCs will have the necessary smart card slot. For example, a mobile phone company might accept unused rail card balances as payment (Boyle 1999). Indeed, it is in the interests of companies to encourage the formation of such multilateral payment networks. It is argued that as e-commerce became more extensive, these limited media of ex-change will begin to take on the function of means of payment and final settlement, and will approach the status of private money (Lietaer 2001). The award of 'loyalty credit' for purchases of a range of goods whose suppliers comprise a linked trading network might also operate in a similar way in the production of limited media of exchange. The Internet has enabled these media of exchange to extend their scope, and in the late 1990s a number of so-called cyber curren-cies emerged – for example, beenz, ipoints and PayPal ('Dreams of a cashless society', *Economist*, 5 May 2000).

It is argued that Internet money could spread to a point where it challenged existing state moneys. 'New circuits of spending, based on alternative media of exchange, can evolve that make no use at all of a country's traditional settlement system – "rootless" money "circling in cyberspace indefinitely"' (B. Cohen 2001b: 200–1, quoting Solomon 1997: 75). The problem of the absence of trust in cyberspace money is recognized, but it is assumed that it will develop simply as a direct function of the volume of electronic commerce. In Cohen's view, this would be no different from the way in which cigarettes in prisons or chewing gum in post-war Europe became 'money' (see chapter 1 for a critique of this conception of money as no more than a convenient medium of exchange).[2]

The same technology might also enable private corporations to issue their own money. The largest global corporations' assets far exceed those of many money-issuing states, and the real goods and services of companies would back the private issue (Lietaer 2001: 79). However, there are good reasons to doubt that private corpor-ate money could ever become more than a minor adjunct to state money. Quite simply, the structure and mode of operation of what

Braudel called the 'capitalist jungle' is inimical to the creation of corporations with the necessary longevity and trustworthiness to produce money that could successfully compete with states' issue. If the pattern of the twentieth century continues, only one in three of the largest US corporations will survive the next twenty-five years (*Financial Times*, 12 April 2001). Moreover, if large corporations periodically behave like Enron and Worldcom did in the early twenty-first century, it is unlikely that private money would ever secure the necessary legitimacy. Finally, it has not been convincingly demonstrated that it would actually be in the corporations' economic interest to issue money. As the twentieth century has shown, even the dominant states whose money has been used globally have found this to be a costly burden (Ingham 1994).

However, the most important obstacle to the issue of such private money is that in order to be fungible it would have to be part of a monetary space that is circumscribed by a *dominant money of account*. Multiple currencies create transaction costs, as Charlemagne realized more than 1,000 years ago in his attempt to bring order to the monetary anarchy created by myriad competing currencies across Europe. In fact, e-money is *structurally* no different from the multiplicity of local media of exchange, corporate and government scrip and private bank money that existed in all advanced capitalist societies in the nineteenth century. As we have seen, the *heterogeneous forms* of the pound sterling money in the nineteenth century were integrated by their abstract money of account (Rowlinson 1999: 64–5). These different media were displaced not by technological innovation, but by the political interests of states in tax collection and the stabilization of their currency by participation in the international gold standard. On the one hand, states could dictate what form of money was acceptable for taxation, and, on the other, the international gold standard gave the central banks control over the issue of their convertible notes.

It is to misunderstand the nature of money to argue that '[j]ust as early forms of paper monies eventually *took on a life of their own*, delinked from their specie base, so too might electronic money one day be able to dispense with all such formal guarantees' (B. Cohen 2001a: 6, emphasis added). No money can simply take on a 'life of its own', or have a 'rootless' existence in cyberspace. To think that this is possible is the result of a preoccupation with the *form of money* and economic transactions, rather than the *social and political relations* between the issuers and the users. Money is essentially rooted in the money of account and the final means of settlement that is, of necessity, established by an authority.

Fundamentally, then, the question of new monetary spaces based on ICT is not technological, or even economic – it is political. Aside from the essential role of an authority in maintaining a money of account and means of final settlement, the extent of any developments in even very limited-purpose media of exchange will depend on the state. The European Central Bank, for example, has taken a strong stance with regard to competing private e-money. In addition to requiring that e-money conform to existing banking supervision, including the reserve requirement, the issuers of e-money are, if requested, to be legally obliged to redeem it at par against central bank euros (Issing 1999, quoted in Lietaer 2001: 216). In other words, it is the ECB's intention that any new issuers of private e-money become part of the existing banking system. Out of concern for the USA's lead in e-commerce, the Federal Reserve is, as yet, more tolerant of e-money. However, the US Inland Revenue Service has opposed the part payment of income in 'frequent flier miles' that are potentially transferable, or assignable, means of payment.

There is one final consideration that we should examine. It receives little or no attention in the literature, largely because orthodox approaches assume that money – whatever its form – is neutral in its effects. It is just conceivable that e-money might become a *transmission mechanism* for currency substitution on an extensive scale for a global financial elite. The Internet might produce a more extensive and promiscuous circulation of national currencies, as occurred in Europe before the consolidation of the state system of the eighteenth century. Or, could there be, for example, a non-bank version of the 1960s Eurodollar market?[3] The amount of globalized private investment is large and growing at a fast rate – from $1 trillion in 1981 to $4.5 trillion in 1993 (Thygesen 1995). Rather than being merely offshore, as they were forty years ago, the new markets would be in cyberspace. Currency X could be exchanged into e-money, and thence to currency Y and into other liquid financial assets. The existence of such offshore – or rather, cyberspace – wealth would lead to a further shrinkage of sovereign states' tax bases, and would affect welfare and exacerbate existing trends towards increasing inequality. Anything that enhances the fungibility of a global plutocracy's assets will tend to force national governments and their monetary authorities to act defensively. Furthermore, could this be another path to an insidious global dollarization?

In addition to economic polarization and the reduction of national tax bases, the existence of global economic elite networks would probably reinforce another trend that has a less obvious, but possibly deeper, significance. In the nineteenth and early twentieth centuries, the limitations of ICT and the relative immobility of labour in the tertiary and secondary sectors of the economy tied the economically dominant classes more closely to their particular locale. They had a stake in its economic, political and social health; but these links are becoming increasingly tenuous. It has been argued that this retreat has led to the general degeneration of local communities. But, in an ironic twist, could local community action based on local media of exchange fill the void? The very same technological possibilities are invoked as the foundation for a recovery of the 'real wealth' of the 'community' by the 'community' (Hart 2000; Lietaer 2001).

Community exchange systems and local monetary spaces

Two periods of global economic recession in the twentieth century have given rise to local self-help schemes and local moneys. In the deflation and monetary contraction during the 1920s and 1930s, local media were used to enable basic economic exchange to take place. A second wave of local moneys emerged in the 1980s, and appears to be more robust and to have continued into the 1990s economic prosperity. Many believe that these are not simply the response to economic deprivation, but represent a local challenge to globalization.

The advocacy of community money, controlled by users rather than by the banking system and monetary authority, has been prominent in populist, guild socialist and communitarian writing since the early twentieth century. (On the 1930s guild socialism, 'social credit' and 'monetary cranks', see Hutchinson and Burkitt 1997; for modern restatements, see Hart 2000; Lietaer 2001; Powell 2002). It is thought that 'community money' or 'social credit' can unlock the 'real' human and social capital of the people that is rendered impotent by the lack of money-income from the formal capitalist economy and its banking system.[4] Despite belonging to a very different ideological tradition, this conception of money is very close to the idea of the 'neutral veil'. It is maintained that 'real' capital and wealth reside only in a 'natural' substructure of economic reality comprising material and technical resources. Lacking a medium of exchange, which unemployment and the loss of income brings about, these lie idle in times of recession. Like analyses of global e-money, the crucially important questions concerning money of account and money as a store of *pure abstract value* that is a means of final unilateral payment are not considered. Secondly, the communitarian vision is essentially the same as the Hayekian liberal belief that money emerges, or could exist, 'spontaneously' – that is to say, without any need of a state or authority. For example, Hart believes that electronic transactions will dominate economic life, and that 'the sheer volume, speed and spatial dispersion of these transactions will ultimately defeat the revenue collecting bureaucracies' (Hart 2000: 316). Without the power of taxation, 'the territorial dimension of society will devolve to more local units' (p. 317). Indeed, information technology could entail the ultimate 'devolution' in personal credit by replacing state money in a 'repersonalization of economic life' (p. 323).

There are two main forms of alternative money: local exchange trading schemes (LETS) and, second, authentic local currencies – most notably 'Time Dollars' in the USA (Bowring 1998; Williams 1996; Lietaer 2001; Hart 2000; Powell 2002). For some writers, ICT raises the possibility that these local cells might become connected into strong networks that define economic spaces outside those of national moneys and currency blocs. The Internet, they argue, has the potential to transform the 'local' into the 'global' (Hart 2000).

The original local exchange trading scheme (LETS) was founded in Vancouver in 1983, and there are now more than 2,500 such schemes across advanced capitalist and developing societies. In the UK, for example, the first appeared at Norwich in 1985, but there were 450 schemes in operation by the end of the twentieth century. However, with about 30,000 participants and an annual turnover of only £2.2 m, these schemes remain, at present, very marginal to the UK economy, and the situation is not significantly different elsewhere. Strictly speaking, LETS are barter-credit networks in which offers and wants of goods and services are matched. The schemes occupy a position between simple bilateral barter and a fully developed money economy. Media of exchange credits are usually issued to participants in the form of paper chits that shadow their national currency, but sometimes signal the locality, as in 'Bobbins' in Manchester and 'Tales' in Canterbury.

After a transaction, the media of exchange are placed in local collection boxes or posted to the clearing-house where members' accounts are debited or credited. Many systems now make use of the Internet for recording and clearing transactions. LETS go some way towards overcoming the well-known impediments to barter trade that occur in the absence of a 'double coincidence of wants'. A level of multilateral exchange and separation of transactions in time is achieved, but the chits do not function beyond the direct representation of the actual goods and services to be exchanged. The successful operation of LETS requires frequent, regular trades and a very high level of velocity of the chits; they are no more than 'a convenient medium of exchange' (Keynes 1930: 2; see the discussion of prison money in chapter 1). There must be a constant readiness to trade, and to discourage hoarding, which would inhibit trading, 'demurrage' – that is, a type of negative interest or deliberate depreciation – is often employed (Lietaer 2001; Bowring 1998).[5] In other words, LETS media are not stores of abstract value and means of unilateral settlement, like full money. This has two significant outcomes. First, there are no price lists, and the terms of trade in each transaction are almost always bilateral – like pure barter. Second, as the LETS chits cannot store value, there is less incentive to drive a hard bargain, which, in turn, further inhibits the production of stable prices. Consequently, this reinforces the localization of LETS to closed circuits, and casts doubt on their ability to grow into wider networks of truly alternative monetary space. Of course, these characteristics are precisely those that are valued by some of their proponents; LETS are as much concerned with the intentional creation of co-operative behaviour and communal reciprocity as they are with producing economic welfare (Lietaer 2001).

In short, its is clear that LETS can help to combat economic disadvantage and foster social solidarity, but I would argue that their potential is limited. The unemployed are disproportionately represented, but a significant minority of LETS members are from the self-employed middle class who follow an environmental and 'alternative life-style' ethos (Williams 1996). However, there is evidence to suggest that the effects of LETS might not be as unequivocally beneficial to the disadvantaged as is generally argued. In unintended ways, they may even *increase* levels of inequality. For example, middle-class resources like tools and equipment and scarce skills and knowledge earn media of exchange credits with very little expenditure of time. Conversely, the lower classes typically offer time-consuming, labour-intensive services. Moreover, if LETS schemes were to expand and penetrate the mainstream economy as a complementary currency, as some have advocated, this would almost certainly be to the advantage of participants in the formal economy. Those with access to legal tender would participate in LETS only if it were to their advantage, and, for example, the middle classes could accumulate LETS credits at a very favourable rate of exchange with which to hire female domestic servants (Bowring 1998: 104). Unless LETS remain relatively closed and marginal to the wider economy, they could perversely intensify inequality.

The idea of an alternative value standard has long been a part of socialist egalitarian writing; but the modern version of Time Dollars was devised by the Washington law professor Edgar Cahn in 1986 (Boyle 1999). The essential idea is that Time Dollars circulate freely, as opposed to the matched offers and wants of LETS. Most local currencies are to be found in the USA, but there are signs that these are now spreading (Boyle 1999; Lietaer 2001). It is estimated that the best-known local currency, Ithaca Hours, is used by more than 2 per cent of the population of Ithaca (27,000), including 300 businesses, and by 1996 had financed $1.5 bn worth of transactions (*Wall Street Journal*, 27 June 1996). The system is organized by a group of community activists who meet twice monthly to make decisions about the supply of the Ithaca Hours notes and to draft the newspaper that lists those businesses that will accept them in full or part payment.

Some rather confused claims have been made for the 'time standard of value'. Some argue that this unit of currency does not reproduce the inequality in the formal economy, 'since every hour worked ... is equivalent in value' (Bowring 1998: 109). But of course this would be true only if an authority had forged a *monetary space* by the imposition of such a standard of value – by democratic consensus or other means. Furthermore, unless the possessors of marketable skills and commodities are willing to accept such an egalitarian non-market standard, the systems tend to reproduce the pattern of inequality of the social structure in which they are located. In fact, Ithaca Hours constitute a 'shadow' currency, in as much as each unit has a value of $10, which is around the hourly average minimum wage in the area. In some of the smaller local currency systems, where an attempt is made to maintain a genuine time standard, there is evidence that non-market exchange norms may develop. But, as in Montpelier (state capital of Vermont), lawyers charge five Hours per hour, and babysitters half an Hour per hour (*Economist*, 28 June 1997, p. 65).[6]

In any event, unless they can be used to form a basis for a parallel banking system, local currencies are limited to a medium of exchange function, and restrict their holders to a relatively passive role in the capitalist economy. Like their close relation LETS, whatever advantages they confer, they do so precisely because they are local. They are embedded in local trading networks in which money is a 'neutral veil', as in conventional economic theory. Local currencies do not give rise to the creation of pure abstract value in the form of the social relation of credit–debt, and, consequently, no money in this sense is created endogenously through the extension of bank lending. Only in a very small minority of atypical cases – as in Harvey, North Dakota (population 2,300) – have local banks accepted deposits of local money (*Wall Street Journal*, 27 June 1996). Significantly, these are lent interest-free in order not to compete with the formal banking system. Where local media are the result of the disintegration of monetary space – as in Argentina and Russia – they tend to marginalize the informal economy and reinforce the fragmentation and inequality of the wider economy. As a participant in the Argentine 'Red del Trueque' network explained, '[t]o call this (*credito*) social money is a lie. *Real* social money should give access to education, healthcare and housing' (quoted in Powell 2002: 644).

The extent to which ICT has or could produce alternative or complementary money has been exaggerated. However, there are now clear indications that the early euphoria has been tempered. E-money has not grown as expected, and there have been some recent failures of leading 'moneys'. The viability of these new forms of money is usually discussed with reference, first, to their efficiency considered in relation to user costs and benefits (Goldshalk and Krueger 2000), and secondly, in relation to the reaction of states to any encroachment on their monopoly of issue. However, I have argued that much of the conjecture and almost all the hyperbole of the early work on e-money has been the result of its conceptualization of money *exclusively* in terms of the function of medium of exchange. Many of the debates are strikingly similar in their confusion to those that arose with the acceleration of the transition from metal to paper during the nineteenth century.

Small, closed circuits of exchange are able sustain their own *media* based on *interpersonal trust and confidence*. But if the base for the confidence has no foundation beyond the economic exchanges themselves, then the media of exchange will remain what anthropologists refer to as 'limited-purpose money'. The creation of extensive monetary spaces requires social and political relations that necessarily exist independently of any networks of exchange transactions. The extension of monetary relations across time and space requires *impersonal trust and legitimacy*. Historically, this has been the work of states. Monetary space is circumscribed by the authoritative money of account that defines the abstract value that constitutes the legal means of payment for the unilateral settlement of debt. There are compelling theoretical, empirical and historical grounds for rejecting both the Hayekian conjectures on the advent of truly competitive money and also the Walrasian 'end of money' scenario. The communitarian or socialist vision of the expression of the peoples' 'real' wealth in their *own* money is equally flawed (Hart 2000: 311). Narrowly economic relations between people cannot form the basis for monetary space that enables the extension of these relations across time and space. Although the Internet extends the *technical capacity* to expand the economic exchanges to an almost infinite extent, it cannot provide the *monetary space* that would enable this to happen. The world cannot be 'run on Windows' (Hawthorn 2000). But, most importantly, the communitarian and cosmopolitan visions share a fundamentally mistaken conception of money, as no more than a symbol of 'real' wealth that resides in the physical, social and economic resources of the 'real' economy. But, as Weber observed, for money to be money, it has to be scarce and an autonomous weapon in the economic battle. These considerations are fundamentally important in the assessment of arguably the most significant monetary experiment to date – the euro.

Europe's Single Currency

The European single currency, which became fully established in 2002, is almost unique (Goodhart 2003: 195).[7] There have been other monetary unions, but possibly only one in which a common currency and independent national budgets coexisted. Furthermore, the eurozone is the first instance of a group of independently powerful sovereign states voluntarily and formally undertaking to create a new money and to relinquish a good deal of their monetary sovereignty (B. Cohen 2001a).[8]

It is generally held that monetary union is a logical counterpart to the single European, or Common, Market. 'One market – one money' is implicit in the orthodox mainstream theory of money as a 'neutral veil' over 'real' exchanges between 'factors of production'. Leaving aside the question of whether a 'common market' should be the spontaneous result of private economic actors optimizing decisions, rather than a political, contrived entity, the question for orthodox theory is whether Europe is, or could be, an 'optimum currency area'. In this view, as we shall see, the question of the coexistence of money and territory should be judged on these economic grounds. According to the theory, a region is identified as an optimum currency area if its economic factors are internally mobile and also adjust uniformly to an external shock. The labour market is usually seen as the most important, but other factors are increasingly taken into account (Coffey 1993). For example, an area may be considered optimum for a single currency if labour is sufficiently mobile to bring about uniform wage rates (Mundell 1961). These considerations raise the question of the political element of labour market differentials. Variations in the 'social wage' and welfare provision across Europe were the result of the different balances of power between capital and labour in the forging of national varieties of the post-war settlement. Similarly, differences in the UK's labour market regulation and flexibility are frequently cited as reasons for not joining the single currency. Obviously, labour market harmonization in this broad sense is inherently an even more intractable political problem than, say, the difficulties associated with the Common Agricultural Policy.

Understandably, then, the money question remained implicit for some time. Eventually, in 1969, 'economic and monetary union' (EMU) was agreed in principle by the six founder members of the European Economic Community (Coffey 1993). However, it was another twenty years before proposals for full monetary integration were put forward by the Delors Committee (1990). Soon afterwards, the member states of the European Community signed the Maastricht Treaty (1992), which contained the blueprint for the single currency monetary system of the euro and the timetable for its introduction. This was completed in the first six months of 2002.[9]

The Maastricht 'divorce'

As Bell observes (2003), the Maastricht Treaty is like a divorce contract in which the formerly unified rights and responsibilities for producing the separate sovereign moneys of the member states are now split between the independent European Central Bank (ECB) and the member states. The ECB has been given responsibility for *monetary* policy – that is to say, control of the conditions for producing money. States retain the right to conduct *fiscal* policy as decided by their independent sovereign parliaments, but within agreed limits. As we have seen, a core element in the production of capitalist credit-money is a settlement that specifies the accepted trade-off between (i) the creation of *money*, through the monetization of state debt, and (ii) the prospects for servicing the debt given by the state's *fiscal* policy and budgetary position. In short, the question is whether the state's revenue is considered adequate for servicing the level of state debt. In this arrangement, the production of high-powered money through the state's debt is limited by the terms of the settlement between important economic groups – most notably the state's creditors (rentiers) and the potential debtors in capitalist production and consumption (corporations and workers). The creditworthiness of modern states and, consequently, their ability to produce high-powered money to meet the demand from the banking system and the economy is structurally linked to the fiscal system and the money-capital (government bond) market. As we have seen, in the new settlement after the resolution of the inflationary crisis of the 1970s, the degree of political manoeuvrability in the struggle of states with the demands of their citizens has been limited by the attempt to depoliticize money with independent central banks. In effect, the Maastricht conditions take this development a step further, by the creation of a central bank outside *any* sovereign state. This has the effect of further severing the fiscal and monetary connections in the 'social relations of production' of the euro and of subordinating the fiscal to the monetary.

On the money side, the European Central Bank now has the right independently to take those measures that it considers necessary to achieve its *primary* objective of *price stability*. As we saw earlier, central banks, especially the ECB, continue to make reference to quantitative measures of the money supply, but it is now generally acknowledged that the quantity of credit-money creation can be controlled only indirectly by manipulation of the short-term rate of interest. The ECB now sets the interest rates for all the other central banks of the member states.

The Maastricht Treaty left fiscal policy in the hands of the member states, but imposed significant constraints that were intended to prevent governments from pursuing expansionary deficit spending and accumulating national debts to a level that might be deemed unserviceable. The 1997 Stability and Growth Pact forbids member states from having a budget deficit greater than 3 per cent of GDP and a debt to GDP ratio of above 60 per cent. Fiscal flexibility is further curtailed by the prohibition of member government borrowing from either the ECB or from other member country's central banks – either directly in the form of overdrafts, or indirectly through the purchase of government bonds and securities. The latter constraint is aimed at preventing individual states from monetizing their debt, in the time-honoured fashion, which would compromise the ECB's absolute control of the production of money. Now that individual member central banks cannot monetize their states' debts, budget deficits must be financed directly in the money market – like those of any *private* corporation.[10]

In essence, the eleven states in the eurozone must now secure finance *in advance* of any deficit spending, either by raising taxes or by successfully marketing their bonds. (Indeed, *ex ante*, the concept of a budget 'deficit' takes on a rather different meaning.) This situation involves a significant shift in the balance of power between the EEC member states and the increasingly globalized money market. The terms of the settlement between the main classes in the social relations of monetary production have been changed. The combined effects of the Maastricht fiscal criteria and the arguably more important reduction of the sovereign power to monetize state debt through privileged bond sales mean that the eleven eurozone states' creditworthiness is *non-negotiable*. In effect, it is based entirely on a state's 'pledge to balance its budget to get a zero *ex post* deficit, so as to protect the banks against the risk of accumulating public debt' (Parguez 1999: 72). Moreover, the new arrangements will create a more rigorous hierarchy of creditworthiness amongst the member states, who will have to compete with each other, on a scale of fiscal prudence, to sell their bonds on the money markets. The alternative source of finance is to raise taxes; but not only is this clearly subject to severe political constraints, it would not be an appropriate measure for, say, avoiding a recession.

The loss of monetary sovereignty

Renegotiations of the post-World War II 'fiscal settlements' are now widespread across the post-Bretton Woods capitalist world, but nowhere are they more institutionally fixed than in the eurozone. Here, money is no longer, in Keynes's phrase, 'peculiarly a creation of the state' (Keynes 1930: 4). Rather, 'the Euro will be a pure-private money, created at the sole request of private agents by banks obliged to comply with the targets set by the Central Bank ... sustained by the expectations of the financial markets' (Parguez 1999: 66). In other words, the euro's exchange rate will be in very large part determined by the foreign exchange markets' assessment of the credibility of the Maastricht arrangements.

With the virtual loss of their money-producing capacity and the European Central Bank's commitment exclusively to price stability, the member states' capacity to influence output and employment in a positive or expansionary direction has also been lost. It should be stressed that this does not simply involve a restraint on the potential dangers of democratic pandering to the electorate and the reappearance of the inflationary political business cycles of the 1960s and 1970s. Rather, the existing arrangements would make it more difficult to take any measures thought necessary to prevent a recession and rising unemployment. Given the existence of a world in which 'all separate nation states larger than Panama, Liberia or Liechtenstein have a single currency' (Goodhart 1996: 1084), why did the eleven European states agree to surrender their monetary sovereignty?

Justification for the single currency, as the logical counterpart to the creation of a single market, is often drawn from optimum currency area (OCA) theory (Mundell 1961). In the first place, a single currency reduces transaction costs and exchange rate risks, and thereby helps to create a single market. But others argue that avoidance of costs in changing from one currency to another – irksome as they may be – are trivial benefits. Currency conversion costs averaged less than 0.5 per cent of EU national income in the late 1980s (Eichengreen and Frieden 2001: 7). (Exchange rate considerations, as we shall see, were probably an important factor in the Delors committee deliberations, but not simply in terms of narrowly economic costs and benefits.) However, cultural and linguistic barriers to labour market mobility clearly disqualify the eurozone as an OCA. On the other hand, it is suggested that the very existence of the euro could help to foster a greater sense of European identity. However, as is frequently the case with economic theory, OCA theory plays a more important rhetorical role in pointing to the further economic advantages that a single market could bring. A single currency can be an instrument for the consolidation of a market by enhancing transparency; for example, it makes it more difficult for car manufacturers to charge different prices in different countries (Eichengreen and Frieden 2001: 7). But critics consider these to be flimsy benefits when balanced against the loss of an independent monetary policy – however constrained by the existence of foreign exchange markets' power to discipline what is deemed to be loose monetary control. Specifically, there is a fear that the Maastricht settlement will prevent the independent sovereign states of the eurozone from using government spending and borrowing to avoid a serious recession and rising unemployment.

In this regard, it is frequently argued that the Maastricht conditions and the single currency represent a triumph of economic orthodoxy – especially the monetarist preoccupation with inflation and 'sound money'. Significantly, central bankers and their orthodox economic advisors were prominent in the Delors Committee that prepared the ground for Maastricht (Godley, quoted in Bell 2003: 166). As we have noted, the Maastricht Treaty is the most stringent application to date of the post-Bretton Woods settlement between globalized money-capital and the more terrestrially located producers and consumers. Furthermore, faced with the power of the foreign exchange markets to punish perceived fiscal and budgetary weakness, it was evident that any *new* money's credibility would have to be presented and institutionally underpinned as robustly as possible. Hence, the enforcement of a rigorous rule-bound regime and the elimination of any political discretion. None the less, critics express surprise that the member states were willing to surrender so much sovereignty (Goodhart 2003).

Of course, it is possible that they were persuaded by orthodox economic theory's hegemony. The economic project of a single market will function better if money is stabilized as a neutral instrument that maximizes the efficiency of market exchanges. As we have seen with respect to technological globalization, economic liberalism holds that markets are *essentially cosmopolitan* and, if successful, render national economic interests increasingly irrelevant. Perhaps Polanyi's observation on the dominant beliefs in the early twentieth century applies again today. 'No self-respecting economist of the liberal age doubted the irrelevance of the fact that different pieces of paper were called differently on different sides of political frontiers...*different tokens* representing the *same commodity*' (Polanyi 1944: 202, 196, emphasis added).

However, it would have been remarkable if economic ideas alone had persuaded states willingly to surrender important elements of sovereignty. Aside from the fact that the exogenous control of money does enhance the political control of domestic interests – especially labour – the forfeiting of member states' monetary sovereignty makes further sense in terms of the taking of a political risk that was shaped by the logic of the European project. The original rationale for European integration was, in part, based on the judgement that independent states would need to relinquish a degree of autonomy in order to rescue themselves from the uncertainties and dangers of the post-war era (Milward 2000). In those early days, the perceived threats were a return to the deleterious consequences of intense economic rivalry – especially another war in the long sequence of Franco–German conflicts. By the 1970s, however, a further external threat to the European Union appeared in the form of the foreign exchange markets.

Whilst there may be transactions cost advantages to be gained and exchange risks to be avoided by using a single currency in a common market, it is far more important to avoid the converse, which may be politically divisive. That is to say, if currencies diverge and exchange rates move unpredictably, as they did with the disintegration of Bretton Woods and the subsequent floating exchange rates in the early 1970s, then the political foundation of a common market is all the more difficult to sustain. In very general terms, the breakdown of the post-war international monetary system had two interrelated consequences for the European project. First, the rapid appreciation of the deutschmark on the foreign exchange markets in the early 1970s threatened to destroy the European customs union – especially the Common Agricultural Policy (Guttmann 2003: 150). A defence was mounted by the fixed-rate regime European Monetary System (1979), but it proved to be unsustainable. As the foreign exchange markets became more efficient in their speculation, they began systematically to exploit currency weaknesses – perceived or real. The strong deutschmark remained relatively unscathed, but this created further political problems, in addition to the ever-present threat of disruption of the common market from the foreign exchanges. First, volatile exchange rates created the possibility of 'exchange rate politics', in which member countries pursued policies of self-protection – for example, the competitive devaluation strategy adopted by the UK, France and

Italy. Second, the credibility and stability of the deutschmark meant that Europe was falling further under the *de facto* monetary control of Germany's central bank. In the face of the political unacceptablity of a full 'United States of Europe', the original common market had attempted to cement a Western alliance and, in particular, reintegrate Germany by economic means. But the globalization of the money markets threatened three decades of political endeavour. In these terms, Maastricht was a political risk that was taken in the hope that a further surrender of the states' sovereignty would again be justified by a further rescue.

Moreover, there were additional constraints that shaped the Maastricht settlement. Full monetary sovereignty requires institutions by which monetary policy can be agreed and enforced. In other words, the absence of pan-European political sovereignty reinforced the imposition of procedural monetary *rules*, rather than the *discretionary* use of money as a tool of economic policy. Quite simply, no common institutions existed whereby the member states' different monetary interests could be reconciled politically. Even in the unitary US state, the early history of the Federal Reserve was marked by indecision resulting from the conflicts between the regional Reserve Banks (Ingham 1994). However, this does not explain the substantive stringency of the Maastricht rules; rather, these aimed to establish the credibility of the euro on the foreign exchanges.

The political risk that the Maastricht conditions might prove unacceptable in the event of a severe recession requiring a great deal of monetary discretion is not formally recognized in the economic theory that provides the framework for the novel monetary arrangements. The social relations of production of the euro are based upon the assumption that money should be a neutral medium of exchange, and that price stability is the essential key to economic success – in the long term. The question of legitimacy is not part of the equation. But, as we have seen, this analytical framework cannot provide a sufficiently robust model of what it sees as the short-run economic disequilibria that clearly might have political effects (Issing 2001). In the first place, there exists a wide range of incommensurable macro-economic models of the short run that could be readily fitted to different national or group economic interests. (Indeed, the UK Chancellor of the Exchequer bases his reluctance to join the single currency on their results.) Given the lack of European political sovereignty, this kind of economic divergence would be intolerable. (However, this is not to say that this might not occur.) Second, the orthodox theory of money has difficulty in comprehending the nature of money's role in two perennial features of capitalist economies – the disorders of deflation and monetary crisis. In the orthodox view, neither is seen as inherent in the actual structure and normal operation of a monetary system, but rather as the result of short-run *ad hoc* monetary mismanagement, or irrationality. The technocratic assumptions underlying the European monetary system may have led to an underestimation of the political risks that follow from the creation of an independent central bank constituted by formal rules, but disabled from discretionary action precisely because it lacks sovereignty.

The concept of neutral money as a symbolic medium of exchange for the market diverts attention from the fact that money consists in the social network of credit and debt of the capitalist economy. Money is constituted by the integrity of the payments system, which, if disrupted by large-scale defaults, may lead to a chain reaction and a monetary crisis. Controlling such events by acting as lender of last resort is, arguably, the most important and indispensable role of a central bank – more so than price stability (Mayer 2001; Goodhart 2003). However, there are doubts that these functions have been made sufficiently clear or robust in the ECB's constitution. Again, this is a consequence of the absence of securely established sovereignty and legitimacy (Guttmann 2003). The history of central banking, in particular in the years following the Bank Charter Acts of the 1840s in England, for example, shows very clearly that rules for the production of the necessary money to effect a stabilization have, invariably, to be abandoned in the event of default-induced crises (Kindleberger 1989 [1978]). If the Maastricht arrangements prove to be ineffective, on whose authority would the extra measures be taken?

As money is not a 'neutral veil', but rather a weapon in the 'economic battle of man with man', the legitimacy and effectiveness of any monetary system ultimately depend upon the enforcement and/or acceptability of a settlement between the major interests – that is to say, creditors and rentiers, debtor classes of producers and consumers, and the state itself (see chapter 7). The potential weakness of the euro in the face of financial crises is twofold. The first source of weakness, as we have seen, stems from the absence of an overarching European political sovereignty that could speedily and unequivocally grant the European Central Bank the power to abandon the rules that might prove to be ineffective in a crisis. The second foreseeable source has the same basis. The Maastricht settlement, with its predominantly global creditors and money-capitalists, has been imposed on the other major nationally based interests – producers and consumers. Essentially the same regime is to be found across the capitalist world. But nowhere else are the constraints based on such inflexible stringent rules, and nowhere else do they exist in a sovereignty vacuum. In

Goodhart's view, 'the defining moment for the eurozone will arrive when a (major) country is required by the treaty to take deflationary fiscal action at a time when its economy is suffering worse stagnation' (Goodhart 2003: 194). Any individual state's non-compliance with the Maastricht conditions would effectively remove the credibility and political legitimacy of the euro. The response of the global money markets cannot be assessed with any confidence, but events in the euro's novel monetary space may well help to demystify the 'nature of money' more thoroughly.

As it is constituted by real social relations, money is an active element in social life – in Weber's terms, a weapon, as I have constantly stressed. The attribution of real force and efficacy to money does not entail a metaphysical nominalism, or, more prosaically in orthodox economics' terms, a 'money illusion'. This appears to be the case only if the economic system is taken to comprise nothing of importance other than the 'real' exchange ratios of commodities, produced by individual optimizing strategies of economic agents. But this weapon, as we noted in the Introduction, is not only used despotically by the different interests in the constant economic struggle; it is also a collective resource – that is, infrastructural power. The advance of human society's organizational capacity has been accelerated by changes in the social production of money – most notably by the balance of power between money-capitalists and the state in early modern Europe. As Weber also concluded, capitalism thrives on a delicate balance of its economic interests that prevents one group from achieving monopoly dominance. He believed that too great a concentration of power in the hands of one class – labour, producers, rentiers, etc. – would inhibit the dynamism of the struggle. Following the conception of money as a neutral medium in a frictionless system of economic exchange, the Maastricht Treaty attempted to de-commission the weapon. By doing so, the European Union has temporarily enfeebled itself. The logic of the situation suggests – but of course can never determine – that it regains the power by placing its money in the hands of a sovereign body.

Concluding Remarks

Inquiry into the nature of money was one of the most serious casualties of the increasing separation and fragmentation of the social sciences that was set in train around the turn of the nineteenth and twentieth centuries. Economics' disciplinary refinement and consolidation were largely based on the meta-theory of the 'real' economy, in which money is relegated to an epiphenomenal status. Alternative approaches to the understanding of money, favoured by some of the historians and sociologists of the Historical School, were utterly rejected in the intense dispute, and were banished from 'pure' economic theory. In the subsequent division of intellectual labour, sociology failed to develop these alternative foundations, partly in the mistaken belief that money was more properly a field of economics, which also offered a satisfactory account. Thus, in a remarkable paradox, arguably the most important institution in capitalist society received far less attention than it deserved. To be sure, the questions of what money did and its cultural significance for modern society were addressed by the two disciplines, but its nature was not seen as problematic. The questions of how money was produced and how it was able to perform its functions were rarely posed. It was generally accepted that the ontology of money was adequately dealt with by the venerable theory in which money's functions were deduced from its status as a commodity. As I have argued, this entailed a serious logical category error. Such functions cannot be established in this manner; rather, they are institutional facts that can only be assigned in the construction of a social reality (Searle 1995).

Building on neglected alternative conceptions, I have argued that money is a socially (including politically) constructed promise. Regardless of its form and substance, money is always an abstract claim or credit whose 'moneyness' is conferred by a money of account. In Keynes's terms, money is what answers the description of money provided by the money of account; it is, as Simmel explained, a normative idea that 'obeys the norms that it represents' (Simmel 1978 [1907]: 122). This is most obviously so in the case of modern, inconvertible pure credit-money, but it applies equally when money is also a standard of material value – such as precious metal. Today, the 'promise to pay the bearer on demand the sum of ten pounds' printed on English banknotes would simply be met by an exchange for a note, or notes, of the same value denominated by the same money of account. Contrary to the widely held belief, the exchange under a precious metal monetary standard was essentially the same. The note was exchanged for a weight of gold that was constituted as money by its *authoritatively* fixed price in the money of account – x ounces of gold equals one pound sterling, or one dollar. The note and gold were different *forms* of the same thing – a pound, or a dollar. However, I have also argued that money is not merely socially produced – by mints, central banks, etc. – it is also *constituted* by the social relation of credit–debt. All money is debt in so far as issuers promise to accept their own money for *any* debt payment by *any* bearer of the money. The credibility of the promises forms a hierarchy of moneys that have degrees of acceptability. The state's sovereign issue of liabilities usually occupies the top place, as these are accepted in payment of taxes.

After 'moneyness' has been established by the issuer's money of account and embodied in a particular form (metal, paper, electronic impulse, etc.), only then does it take on the status of a commodity that may be bought and sold, for example, in foreign exchange markets. In other words, once money has been produced, then economic analysis is applicable; but it is essential to understand that it cannot explain the existence of money. Furthermore, economic analysis of the exchange-value of money for goods, or for another money, needs to be supplemented by sociological analysis, because the scarcity of money is socially and politically determined. At the macro level, the supply of money is structured by the rules and norms governing fiscal practice (for example, 'sound money' principles), which are the outcome of a struggle between economic interests in which economic theory plays a performative role. In capitalism, the pivotal struggle between creditors and debtors is centred on forging the real rate of interest (nominal rate minus inflation rate) that is politically acceptable and economically feasible. On the one hand, too high a real rate of interest will deter entrepreneurial debtors and inhibit economic dynamism. On the other hand, too low a rate or, more seriously, a negative rate of interest (inflation rate in excess of nominal interest rate) inhibits the advance of money-capital loans (Smithin 2003). Weber's emphasis on money's status as a weapon in the economic battle directs attention to its political nature. This element is entirely absent from all orthodox economic analysis, which, I would stress, is tacitly endorsed by the other social sciences. This lacuna is the result of the apolitical conception of politics that is to be found in the mainstream economic meta-theory and, surprisingly as it may appear to some, the Marxist counterpoint. The conception of money as a neutral instrument that underlies all modern macro-economic monetary analysis and practice by governments and their central banks derives from this foundation. Some of the errors that this can give rise to were examined in chapters 7, 8, and 9. Here, I wish briefly to elaborate the point in a more general way.

The basic elements of the meta-theoretical foundations of modern economics are to be found in Aristotle's ethics. Here, the purpose of economic activity should be the gaining of utility through production and exchange. Money should be no more than a neutral medium for the attainment of this end. The creation of and hoarding of value in the form of money, as an end in itself, was anathema. Aristotle deplored the fact that money could be a means of domination, and argued that it need not be so. For the most part, modern economics did not explicitly endorse the ethical element, but inherited, albeit unwittingly in the case of most modern practitioners, the analytical framework. By the nineteenth century it was widely accepted that money was the 'neutral veil' behind which lay a fundamental substratum of human material existence which consists in the propensities of the factors of production and the utility of commodities. In modern orthodox theory, this elementary core of the economy is modelled in terms of individually rational decisions about the marginal productivity of the factors and the marginal utility of commodities. These are mathematically formalized as supply and demand schedules of representative agents for particular commodities and in general equilibrium models of the economy as a whole. At most, money exists as an arbitrarily chosen commodity that is given a numerical value (*numéraire*) that enables the formal models to operate. Generations of orthodox economists have insisted that money does not comprise any of the essentials of economic life, and that it does not really matter. The model of the material substratum of human existence is also held to be universally applicable. Time, history and culture are analytically unimportant; they are the 'contextual tosh' from which micro-economic analysis can extract the 'rational core' (Williamson 1994).

Marx almost, but not quite, saw through the intellectual foundations that were eventually distilled into this nonsense. But his even stronger commitment to the Aristotelian conception of the essence of material life led him to make the same mistake with regard to money. Marx properly understood the significance of historical variations in the substratum of material life – in his scheme, the modes of production. He also saw that the factors of production were social categories. A piece of machinery only became capital when it was part of a social relation – that is, owned and controlled by one class and worked by another. Moreover, he saw that use-value (utility) should be distinguished from exchange-value, and that they could diverge quite markedly, especially in capitalism. But, following Aristotle, he held that these two values should be commensurate. 'Utility' *should* determine 'value', as it was thought to do in the 'natural' exchange economy of independent producers.

To his credit, Marx saw that economic theory could not resolve these questions, because it was unable to see that the factors of production in capitalism were actually social classes, and therefore that the relations between them were social relations of conflict. It was the capitalist social relations of production that led to the dominance of production for exchange with no thought for collective social utility or welfare. Following Aristotle, Marx deplored the fact that the purpose of human labour had become the pursuit of money in order to make more money. Sub-optimal welfare is to be seen, in large part, as being socially produced by the collective irrationality that results from the contradictions of the capitalist mode of production and class conflict. Marx provided a Hegelian answer to the problem. He claimed to be able to discern its 'transcendence' in the trajectory of history that would lead to the overcoming and eradication of the alienating, conflicting and unnatural social categories and consequently of the contradictions. A 'final' struggle would remove the bourgeois social relations of production to reveal the *natural material substratum* in which value could then be expressed in the only possible and true way – that is, as the unmediated and undistorted value of human labour. The politics of the economic battle would have come to an end, because the labour theory of value had been actualized. (If it had a place in 'true communism', money would be no more than the expression of these real values based on labour time.)

However, as Schumpeter understood, the substratum of the natural economy, in which money need be no more than a convenient medium of exchange, is a 'circular flow' that does not have any inherent dynamism. In most orthodox economic theory, and some versions of determinist Marxism, any source of dynamic change, such as technology, is exogenous to the model of the economy. Marx did not see, or rather admit, just how problematic was his vision of a socialist society which retained the capacity to continue dynamically to transform nature and expand human welfare. He knew full well that the bourgeoisie had played a necessary progressive and dynamic role in developing the forces of production, but there is no sustained consideration of how this might be continued in their absence. The details of the serious weaknesses need not detain us here, but Marx's 'true communism' presupposes two essential elements: first, that the products of human labour be exchanged at their 'real' values; second, that the 'true democracy', which the removal of bourgeois society would reveal, would consist in an equally 'natural' consensus on the welfare it wished to maximize. Despite the superficial antinomy, this simplistic vision has much in common analytically with the bourgeois economic theorists' late nineteenth-century solution. There is a 'real' economy in which commodities are able to exchange at their real values; and there is a *knowable* and *uncontested* future – based on either economic man's perfect information or the proletariat's objective interests. Consequently, there is no politics. Neither is there any money. In short, both models have a singularly poor grasp of modern capitalism.

The first step to a better understanding is to recognize the fact that there are two interdependent, but relatively autonomous, sides to all money economies which differ qualitatively from the mythical barter of the 'real' economy. The antagonistic interdependence between the two is a major source of capitalism's dynamic character. Obviously, technological innovation can be dynamic only if it is financed speculatively into an unknowable future. Abstract promises to pay make this possible. This is accomplished, according to Schumpeter, by a particular class, which is defined by its status as debtor – the entrepreneurs. But it is not simply a matter of debt, as Weber explains. 'If someone helps out a peasant by giving him seed and demands an increment in return, or if the same is done in the case of money loaned to a household to be returned with interest, we would hardly want to call this "capitalistic"' (Weber 1978: 96). Nor is the simple profit gained through buying cheap and selling dear or marking up a sale price in excess of costs essentially capitalistic. Rather, capitalist practice entails the continuous comparison of the rate of interest on money loans with the profitability of enterprise (Weber 1978: 97). As we have seen, Wicksell's version of the 'real' economy model posits a natural rate of interest; that is to say, both the money rate of interest and the profitability of enterprise are brought together by the 'real' marginal productivity of the factors of production. This was critically examined in chapter 1 (see also Smithin 2003). We have suggested a sociological alternative in which the two sides of the economy – entrepreneurial (and consumer) debtors – struggle with creditor capitalists over the real rate of interest. As we saw in chapter 8, this became more apparent in the struggle over inflation in the late twentieth century.

In short, the money market is the 'headquarters' of capitalism. In the most general terms, as we saw in chapter 7, this should be taken to refer to the institutional structure whereby private debts are routinely monetized by the linkages between the state's debt and the banking system, as mediated by the central bank. This system is unique to capitalism, as we saw in chapters 5 and 6. The elastic creation of credit-money through the acts of lending in the hierarchy of debtors topped by the state's liabilities, or 'high-powered money', is the means by which other dynamic elements in the capitalist economy can be actualized. However, the relations between debtors and creditors are also the source of the system's fragility – through inflation and deflation. Thus, money cannot be neutral; it is the most powerful of the social technologies, but it is produced and controlled by specific monetary interests and is also inherently unstable. Consequently, the pronouncements of central bankers and their expert committees have become the most important signals upon which the money markets make their judgements about the creditworthiness of the most important debt (the state's). These judgements establish a rate of interest on long-term state debt that is the benchmark for all the other rates upon which the rest of the capitalist system depends. In short, I would suggest that orthodox economic theory has inverted the actual relationship between the two sides. To be sure, income and revenue must be generated by the production and sale of commodities, but this takes place in conditions largely dictated by money. Finally, one should note that if the money side is not sufficiently robust in its own right, regardless of the so-called economic fundamentals and factor endowments, then, as the Argentine example shows, the performance of an economy will be impaired.

In other words, in the place of the labour theory of value and economic orthodoxy's 'real' theory, I have tentatively disinterred the social theory of value that I detect in Weber's sociology. Its development is the next most pressing task (see also Smithin 2003). Weber's heirs in their sociological orthodoxy have failed to do this; rather, they have translated his insights into a more narrowly sociological analysis of class. To be sure, this aspect of Weber's work was in many ways an extension and generalization of Marx's conflict models, but without the unremittingly materialist anchor of the labour theory of value. The complex struggles *between* and *within* and *across* the two sectors of the economy determine the production of money *and* its value. But there is no determinate outcome dictated by the reality of an objectively constituted economic substratum comprising 'natural' rates of interest, employment, etc.

In the 'socialist calculation' debate on whether efficient monetary calculation would be possible under a planned socialist economy, Weber, in typical fashion, disagreed with both sides. On the one hand, he implicitly exposed the inadequacy of the 'real' economy model that lay behind the socialists' advocacy of money based on 'labour time' (see also the discussion in chapter 9). The exchange of a socially agreed quantity of labour for specific goods would not only be barter, but also could not produce the necessary rational calculability (Weber 1978: 80). On the other hand, he also dismissed the Austrian economic theorists' argument that this was an epistemological and cognitive problem, in that we could never have sufficient information to make the calculations necessary for a viable planned economy. In a Weberian social theory of value, calculability in money terms (stable money) of the capitalist economy is the result of the underlying predictability of the clash of interests in which money is a weapon. Stable money expresses a stable, but not necessarily equal, balance of power. Finally, as I have stressed, orthodox economic theory, based on the 'real' economy, serves ideologically to mask this conflict and its essential role by naturalization and the universalization of money. In addition to the continued attempt to anchor money in the natural proclivities and propensities of the 'real' factors of production, the mainstream view asserts the neutrality of money in, for example, the universal and equally borne costs of inflation (see chapter 7). This is political, in the sense of struggle and conflict that cannot be resolved by the 'real' model – Marxist or orthodox.

However, an obvious question remains, which brings us full circle. It is one thing to say that money is socially constructed as a reality in a process of conflict and struggle; but this does not address the obvious and practically more important question, posed by both Marx and the orthodox economists, including this time Keynes, of how this might best be done. Or, more pertinently, one might ask whether this is a valid question in the sense that there exists an answer. Socialist and related communitarian solutions based on a labour theory of value, and the implicit claim in orthodox economic theory that a socially optimal outcome is the result of egotistical utility maximization, simply evade the question by bracketing the role of money. Keynes and others brought the question of the production and management of money to the forefront of political discourse during capitalism's hitherto most fragile era between the two great twentieth-century wars (as did the monetary populists and cranks whose work he, significantly, took seriously). Since then, the question has been put aside by the retrogression in economic understanding that has followed the rebalancing of power in the production of money in the wake of the 'great inflation' of the 1970s. Having posed this most intractable of questions, I propose also to close, or rather postpone, the discussion. However, I will offer two observations. First, whatever claim is made to have found the best solution to the questions of how, and how much, money is created, we can be certain that it is not the *only* one, and that it was arrived at after an essentially political struggle for economic existence between different interests. Second, without such a struggle money cannot have value.

Notes

Introduction

1 In 1878 the American economist Francis Walker decided to put the 'metaphysics' of money aside and to be guided by the simple assumption that 'money is what money does' (Schumpeter 1994 [1954]: 1086).

2 Sometimes standard of value and standard of deferred payment are presented as distinct functions. Their status depends on whether money of account is merely the numerical representation of a standard of value, such as gold, or is simply an abstract measure *sui generis*. A central argument of this book is that money of account confers 'moneyness', and therefore a commodity standard can only become money when, in Keynes's terms, it is described by the money of account.

3 The puzzle of money is apparent in the frequent use in the literature of the passage in Charles Dickens's *Dombey and Son* in which Paul asks his father, 'What is money?' Mr Dombey describes some coins, to which Paul replies that he understands that, but wants to know 'what's money after all'. See Jackson 1995 for this and a wide selection of expressions of similar bewilderment and a range of different conceptions of money.

4 In Walras's 'moneyless' model of the economy, the *numéraire* symbolizes an already existing value of an arbitrarily chosen commodity as the benchmark standard of value by which the calculation of the exchange rates between commodities can be made. See the discussion in ch. 1.

5 In essence, this is Parsons's problem in *The Structure of Social Action* (1937).

6 At the time of writing, 2003, Saddam Hussein's Iraqi state had just been overthrown by US and British forces, and looting had broken out. One TV news report contained two quite different approaches to bank looting.

In one, Iraqi bank notes were being torn and scattered in the streets. Some looters were meting out an Arab insult by striking Saddam's image on the notes with the soles of their shoes. These looters had a clearer understanding of how money gets its value than another group, who were carefully taking the notes away in the mistaken belief that they would continue to be usable. Soon afterwards, billions of US dollar notes were flown in to pay wages, as an inducement for Iraqis to return to work.

Chapter 1   Money as a Commodity and 'Neutral' Symbol of Commodities

1   Four evolutionary stages of exchange are distinguished in Aristotle's *Politics* (see Meikle 2000). The direct exchange of commodities ($C-C_1$) in barter comes first, but this is notoriously 'inconvenient' because it requires a 'double coincidence of wants'. Money greatly expands the possibilities for exchange by enabling purchase and sale to be separated in time and space ($C-M/M-C_1$, or $C-M-C_1$). Each form – either direct or money-mediated barter – is deemed to be 'natural', in that both have the 'end' of expanding use-value. In the second form, money merely provides the more efficient 'means' of performing the same function – that is, it is the later economists' 'neutral veil' or 'lubricant'. The third and fourth forms of exchange are 'unnatural' in so far as the 'end' of exchange is not utility, but only the expansion of money. On the one hand, the end of exchange with money might buy goods to sell later for a greater sum ($M-C/C-M_1$, or $M-C-M_1$). Or the possessors of money might lend it at interest – that is, usury ($M-M_1$). This 'breeding of money from money' is the most unnatural and the most despised form of exchange, because '[t]rue wealth is the stock of things that are useful in the community of the household or polis'. Exchange with the end of increasing a stock of money was considered 'wealth of the spurious kind' (*Politics* I. 1257; quoted in Meikle 2000: 159). Marx used Aristotle's analysis to produce his own similar ethical critique of capitalism, in which the first two forms of equal exchange for expanding utility, which increase human welfare, are used as the benchmarks by which to criticize the pursuit of the end of pure exchange-value. However, the 'bourgeois' classical political economists and their neoclassical successors adopted the first two forms of exchange ($C-C_1$ and $C-M-C_1$) and, from an analytical standpoint, simply ignored the others' existence ($M-M_1$ and $M-C-M_1$).

2   See Rogers's (1989) use of this distinction between the 'real' and the 'monetary'. The term 'real', as Schumpeter notes, is not very felicitous. Apart from the confusion with, for example, 'real' and 'nominal' prices, 'real' analysis is from a common-sense standpoint distinctly 'unreal' in its denial of the autonomous power and efficacy of money!

3   Note that with the introduction of an auctioneer the market now has an elementary social structure. See Hicks 1989: ch. 1, for a discussion of the *ad hoc* additions made by the late nineteenth-century economists to make

this abstract market operational – for example, Marshall's wholesale corn merchant. See also White's observation that the economic theory of the market is actually no more than a theory of 'pure' (bilateral) exchange. That is to say, economic theory cannot specify the analytical boundaries of a 'market', comprising multilateral exchanges that produce prices (H. White 1990).

4   Note also that Samuelson is saying not that it is heuristically useful to look on advanced industrial relations in this way, but that they actually boil down to simple barter.

5   It is testimony to the importance of the question of money in the *Methodenstreit* that Menger dogmatically insisted that money was nothing more than a medium of exchange. That is to say, he did not acknowledge means of payment, in the sense of final or unilateral settlement, as a distinct function (see Melitz 1974: 8). He can only have held this faintly ludicrous view out of a fear that acceptance of the distinction might have been interpreted as an endorsement of the Historical School's state theory. Here, as we shall see in the following chapter, the origins and major function of money are explained by its role in the payment of tax debts.

6   The following discussion owes much to Laidler's (1991) excellent analysis of quantity theory.

7   During the late nineteenth-century, the 'costs of production' analysis of early nineteenth-century 'classical' economics was replaced by what became known as 'neoclassical' 'marginal utility' theory. The costs of production theory had difficulty in explaining the source of the costs other than by positing an ultimate objective source of value – for example, Ricardo's labour theory of value. Marx's critical version exposed further problems. 'Marginalists' evaded the issue by substituting a subjectivist theory of value – 'preferences', 'tastes' – for objective costs. The price of any commodity was that at which the buyer was prepared to pay to gain the last, or marginal, increment of subjectively assessed utility. This was a critically important shift of emphasis, from the search for the measure of an absolute value to be found in the nature of things to relative value produced in exchange (supply and demand) based on the interplay of subjective preferences. In classical theory, the value of money was grounded in the labour theory of value – costs of production given in natural conditions of geologically determined scarcity and mining. From the marginalist perspective, the value of commodities, including money, can be established only in the act of exchange. From a purely logical standpoint, the classical theory is the more adequate theory – money is an objective number added to a natural standard of value. The incoherence in marginalism, or neoclassicism, is apparent in Walras's need to take a given commodity and *arbitrarily* assign it a value of 1 (*numéraire*) in order to create the mathematical solution.

8   Significantly, these conjectures often started with the assumption of 'an influx of bullion', which might cause people 'to expect a rise in prices, and, therefore, be more inclined to borrow for speculative investments' [which]

'would go with an increased demand for goods and a continued rise in prices' (Marshall 1926: 51–2).

9   Orthodox theory was modified during the twentieth century, to take into account the complete disappearance of precious metal money. In monetarism and later macro-economic mainstream theory, the stock of government debt (rather than the stock of gold) held by the central bank becomes 'high-powered money' upon which credit is 'multiplied'. See chapter 7.

10 'A commodity is regarded as money for our purposes if and only if it can be traded for all other commodities in the economy. Correspondingly, a money economy is one in which not all commodities are money... money buys goods and goods buy money; but goods do not buy goods' (Clower 1984 [1967]: 86).

11 As with most other features of the 'real' economy model, the 'natural rate' of interest was based on a simplified model of an agricultural mode of production that, furthermore, was shorn of any specific social relations of production. For example, Wicksell uses the analogy of waiting a further five years for trees to grow, in order to gain an increase in the overall annual output of timber, as an illustration of the natural rate of interest. In Marshall's similar example, seed-corn can be 'saved' or sown – that is, 'invested'. All such natural metaphors break down when investment capital is seen as money created by a bank's *social act* of lending and the promise of repayment (see Pixley 1999).

12 This phenomenon was described by the economist Charles Goodhart and has become known as 'Goodhart's Law'.

13 The European Central Bank's chief economist states that the characterization of money in models of modern economies is largely 'uncontroversial across all main schools of thought' (Issing 2001: 76–7). Money is held to be neutral *in the long run*; that is to say, changes in the stock of money can only affect nominal prices in the economy and leave real variables unchanged. It is widely accepted that changes in the quantity of money can have short-run effects. However, it is also acknowledged that there is no theoretical means of coming to any meaningful distinction between the short and the long run (see the discussion in ch. 7).

14 According to Innes, Smith's misinterpretation of the historical evidence was exposed in the Playfair edition of the *Wealth of Nations* in 1805 and in an *Essay on Currency and Banking* by Thomas Smith in 1832. '[I]t is curious how', Innes remarks, 'in the face of the evidently correct explanation given by those authors, Adam Smith's mistake has been perpetuated' (1913: 378).

Chapter 2   Abstract Value, Credit and the State

1   See Schumpeter 1994 [1954]: 62–4; Wood 2002: ch. 3.
2   See Keynes's discussion of Major Douglas and Gesell (Keynes 1973 [1936]: ch. 23). On 'social credit theory', see Hutchinson and Burkitt 1997. See Part II, chapter 9.

3   Galiani's distinction between *moneta immaginaria* and *moneta reale* was commonplace by the seventeenth century (Schumpeter 1994 [1954]: 296).

4   Locke wanted a state that was not controlled by any particular interest – monarch, parliament or, above all, the London financiers (Caffentzis 1989). The theory of metallic money suited his ends; it grounded money in a natural substance, whereas a theory such as Steuart's implicitly exposed its social and, therefore, malleable character. However, as we shall see, the development of the British monetary system was based on the existence of a 'national debt' and the issue of Bank of England notes. The latter's convertibility into gold at a fixed rate ensured a steady supply of creditors willing to finance the state.

5   Self-regulation soon proved to be a chimera. No sooner had the Acts been passed than they were temporarily suspended in 1847, and again in 1857 and 1866. In response to crises of confidence and the rush for cash, the legal limit on Bank of England notes had to be lifted. See Cameron 1967.

6   The following account is based on Carruthers and Babb 1996, which is one of the very few genuinely sociological analyses of the phenomenon of money, as opposed to its cultural and social effects. See also Greider 1987 on the greenback era.

7   Officialdom concurred: value 'inheres in the quality of the material thing and not in mental estimation' (*US Monetary Commission*, quoted in Carruthers and Babb 1996: 1576).

8   Like Attwell in Birmingham in the 1830s and Gesell in the 1930s, some late nineteenth-century Americans went even further, and argued that inflation, by inducing people to spend their money quickly, was a benefit, in that it stimulated economic activity.

9   Innes's original essays together with commentaries and related articles are to be found in Wray 2003.

10   'The general belief that the Exchequer was a place where gold or silver was received, stored and paid out is wholly false. Practically the entire business of the English Exchequer consisted in the issuing and receiving of tallies and the counter-tallies, the stock and the stub, as the two parts of the tally were popularly called, in keeping the accounts of the government debtors and creditors, and in cancelling the tallies when returned to the Exchequer. It was, in fact, the great clearing house for government credit and debts' (Innes 1913: 398).

11   But, the young Keynes reviewed the 1913 article favourably in the *Economic Journal* in 1914 (Keynes 1983: 404).

12   This was far less intellectually unified and coherent than is implied by the term 'school' (see Schumpeter 1994 [1954]), but work of its members on money is a significantly radical departure from the classical and neoclassical commodity theory.

13   The dematerialization of money coincided with the social question of welfare and employment. Changes in the form of money were also related to political developments such as the advance of representative

democracy and the growth of international conflict and competition. These empirical questions are discussed in chapters 7 and 8.

14 See Schumpeter's discussion of R. Hawtrey's *Good and Bad Trade* (1994 [1954]: 1117–22. Hawtrey reviewed state theory in the *Economic Journal* 35 (1925). The 1905 German edition of Knapp's *State Theory of Money* could have influenced Hawtrey's *Currency and Credit* (1919), which deals with the logical origins of money in money of account. This was in turn reviewed very favourably by Keynes (1983: 16). Keynes had also reviewed favourably a German popularization of state theory (1983: 400–30).

15 The case of Schumpeter, who had of course experienced the state theory controversy and its place in the *Methodenstreit* at first hand, is a little different. Throughout his career, Schumpeter held firmly to the Walrasian model of the 'real' economy, because of its mathematical sophistication, which he thought conferred scientific prestige. But at the same time, he argued that 'practically and analytically, a credit theory of money is possibly preferable to monetary theory of credit' (Schumpeter 1994 [1954]: 717). Moreover, his analysis of the fundamental institutional structure of capitalism in *The Theory of Economic Development* and *Business Cycles* does not follow Walras (see Ingham 2003). He never really resolved the contradiction, and he was, therefore, a 'reluctant creditist' (Earley 1994). None the less, despite himself, his work contains a clear heterodox analysis of the bank creation of credit-money by lending – that is, 'loans make deposits', rather than pre-existing deposits being simply collected and lent on by banks acting as mere intermediaries. See Part II, chapter 7.

16 In a letter to his future wife Lydia Lopokova (18 January 1924), he referred to his research as 'purely absurd and quite useless'. But, none the less, he was 'absorbed to the point of frenzy' (Keynes 1982: 1–2).

17 Keynes provides a withering dismissal of the mainstream focus on money as a commodity. 'Something which is merely used as a convenient medium of exchange on the spot may approach to being Money, inasmuch as it may represent a means of holding General Purchasing Power. But if this is all, we have scarcely emerged from the stage of Barter' (Keynes 1930: 3).

18 See the discussion of Cannan's cloakroom analogy in chapter 1 (Schumpeter 1994 [1954]: 1113–14).

19 On one level, the endogenous–exogenous debate was a faintly absurd controversy. As we shall see in Part II, the distinctiveness of the capitalist mode for producing money is that it necessarily entails *both* an exogenous state and the endogenous factors involved in the financing of production.

20 Some post-Keynesians depart even more radically from economic orthodoxy and argue that fractional reserves have no real impact on the creation of credit-money (Rogers and Rymes 2000; Wray 1998).

21 This essentially empirical question could have some light shed upon it by enthnographic methods. But the absolute dominance of statistical

methods in the analysis of monetary aggregates rules this out. For example, all attempts to resolve the pivotal question of the direction of causation between *nominal* (demand for money) *wages* and the *money supply* have been made by means of econometric models. Largely for the same reasons that monetarism failed as a mode of practical reasoning and economic policy making, this exercise has produced inconclusive results.

22 Cencini quotes R. S. Sayers: 'No asset is in action as a medium of exchange except in the very moment of being transferred from one ownership to another, in settlement of some transaction' (Cencini 1988: 71). This formulation makes sense of the paradox of thrift and the deflationary consequences of hoarding. Saved money, as a store of value, eventually loses value through its deflationary effect on wealth creation.

23 Indeed, its iconoclasm is evident in the charge, from a strong supporter of monetary circuit theory, that Wray's current chartalism cannot be reconciled with his earlier post-Keynesianism, and that he is best described as a 'funny monetarist' (Rochon 1999: 298). This is a quite serious misunderstanding of Wray's work. There are clear theoretical and intellectual links between the state theory and the credit theory of money, as I have suggested.

24 More prosaically, according to Gertrude Stein, 'Men can count, and they do, and that is what makes them have money' (*Saturday Evening Post*, 22 August 1936, quoted in Jackson 1995: 13).

25 After a lifetime of distinguished orthodoxy and, at times, explicit criticism of monetary heterodoxy, Hicks, for example, eventually embraced a similar position (Hicks 1989: ch. 5). He argued that money had just the two functions, as the measure and standard of value and a means of final payment. Hicks was one of the first and most effective critics of Keynes (Hicks 1937). Eventually, he thought that 'the evolution of money is better understood if one starts with *credit*' (quoted in Smithin 2003: 29–30, original emphasis).

26 It should be noted that the construction of a network of credit relations in the private sphere, even with its own money of account, is not incompatible with state theory. Most notably, the Free Banking school have used the examples of eighteenth-century Scotland and nineteenth-century New York to argue the case for a purely market-based banking system that operates effectively without a central bank. However, there is a tendency to conflate private with market in these analyses. In both examples, the private bankers established their own regulatory authority. See also Part II, chapter 6, on the bill of exchange in early capitalism.

27 Orthodoxy has held that monetary policy based on these heterodox ideas has been responsible for some of the most significant monetary crises in history. The collapse of John Law's Banque Royale in early eighteenth-century France, the German hyperinflation of the early 1920s and the inflationary end to the post-war boom in the 1970s have all been

attributed to application of unsound theories of money. This charge
cannot be dealt with in detail here; but there are good reasons to question
the orthodox indictment. In each instance, social and political dislocation *preceded* the monetary crises and inflation. Indeed, these examples
may be used in support of the state theory of money. Without exception,
weak states have weak monetary systems (Goodhart 1998).

Chapter 3   Money in Sociological Theory

1   The question of 'primitive money' became a central issue in the sterile
    formalist–substantivist debate on the applicability of deductive economic
    theory to pre-modern societies (see ch. 5, n. 9). The 'formalists' defined
    money as a commodity that functioned as a medium for market exchange,
    and concluded that 'primitive' non-market societies could not, therefore,
    possess money as such (Hart 2000). For references to the same dispute in
    the historiography of Greece at the turn of the twentieth century during
    the *Methodenstreit*, see Davies 1996.
2   A recent article in the *Journal of Classical Sociology* entitled 'The soci-
    ology of the sociology of money' makes no reference to the intellectual
    relationships between economics and sociology, and argues that the
    'sociological study of money can . . . be appropriated by the new cultural
    studies' (Deflem 2003: 67).
3   The deficiencies in the understanding of money have more general conse-
    quences for the entire Marxian economic theory of profit and surplus
    value, but these questions cannot be pursued here.
4   The quite inordinate and misguided emphasis on *The Protestant Ethic and
    the Spirit of Capitalism* has led to a serious distortion of his work (see
    Ingham 2003).

Chapter 4   Fundamentals of a Theory of Money

1   A recent attempt to analyse the monetary anarchy in post-Soviet Russia
    (Seabright 2000) is seriously hampered by the use of the orthodox concep-
    tion of money as a medium of exchange.
2   This process has been referred to as 'disembedding' (Giddens 1990), but it
    is best seen as the substitution of impersonal trust (or legitimacy) for
    personal trust (Shapiro 1987).
3   'All forms of credit, from the bank note to book credits, are essentially the
    same thing, and in all these forms credit increases the means of pay-
    ment . . . The external form of the credit instrument is quite irrelevant . . . if
    it actually circulates' (Schumpeter, *The Theory of Economic Development*,
    quoted in Earley 1994: 337). As Earley notes, if one's credit card begins to
    'circulate', it is time to call the bank's 'hotline'.

4   The theory of money as a neutral medium over real exchange that circulates with variable velocity is evident in the late nineteenth-century Cambridge economist Edgeworth's parable. Two men take a barrel of beer to sell at the races. As the men become thirsty on their journey, one of them asks the other if he may buy a share of the beer with the only threepenny piece they have between them. As the day gets hotter, both men become thirstier and the transactions multiply. Eventually, the velocity of circulation of this 'vehicle' of a single coin, as it passes from one to the other, is able to finance the sale of the entire barrel (quoted in Robertson 1928: 62–3). It is interesting to note the contrived equilibrium conditions of symmetrical, dyadic trade in the example. It is more important, however, to realize that the transactions – symmetrical or not – did not need the coin. They could have been recorded in money of account to be settled at a later date by an acceptable means of payment.

5   'Once the state imposes a tax on its citizens, payable in a money it creates, it does not need the public's money in order to spend; rather the public needs the government's money to pay taxes. This means that the government can buy whatever is for sale in terms of its money merely by providing its money' (Wray 2000: 59; Bell 2000).

6   Weber also cited Knapp's arch-enemy von Mises and Knapp as the other major influence on his understanding of money (Weber 1978: 78); and doubted whether the 'the substantive theory of money in relation to prices... belongs to the field of economic sociology at all' (Weber 1978: 79). The following hundred pages or so of *Economy and Society* indicate, however, that Weber was not entirely convinced by his own attempt at *rapprochement*!

7   They could be excused, given the level of state expenditure in the late nineteenth century. None the less, Schumpeter, (1994 [1954]), not to mention Knapp, did see the significance.

8   Strictly speaking, macro-economic forecasts can only be hypothetical, not probabilistic, statements, as they claim to be. Rather, such forecasts are radically uncertain in the sense used by Keynes, and are therefore open to quite different interpretations.

Chapter 5   The Historical Origins of Money and its Pre-capitalist Forms

1   After his bouts of 'Babylonian madness', Keynes, for example, whimsically put the question aside and moved on. '[Money's] origins are lost in the mists when the ice was melting, and may well stretch back into the paradisaic intervals in human history of the interglacial periods when the weather was delightful and the mind free to be fertile of new ideas in the Islands of the Hesperides or Atlantis or some Eden of Central Asia' (Keynes 1930: 13).

2 In their important critique of orthodox economic theories of money, Heinsohn and Steiger (2000) follow Keynes in linking money with contract, and mistakenly conclude that money has its origins in private property. However, I argue that the idea of money – that is, money of account – is anterior to contract and price lists (Keynes 1930; Hicks 1989; Grierson 1977). See also Weber: 'From an evolutionary standpoint, money is the father of private property' (1981 [1927]: 236).

3 As Marx implied from a somewhat different perspective, the 'real' relation between the individual and society is inverted in their 'appearance' as monetary relations in the market. The paradoxical dualism of modern money lies in the fact that it is an *'ensemble de relations sociales'* that can be privately appropriated (Aglietta and Orlean 1998: 16).

4 In *La Violence de la monnaie* (1982), Aglietta and Orlean link a theory of money to Girard's (1972) speculative anthropology in *La Violence et le sacré*. Girard locates the origins of social order in the collective exclusion of outsiders, which is later repeated in symbolic representation by sacrifice.

5 A follower of Knapp's state theory argued, for example, that these contributions were standardized into a form of 'food money' owed to the temple (Laum, *Heiliges Geld* (1924), quoted in Hudson 2003). The derivation of the modern word 'money' from the Roman temple of Juno Moneta, where precious metal coinage was struck during the Punic Wars, shows the close link between money, the refining of precious metals and religion in early civilizations (Hudson 2003).

6 It is significant that the transition from sacrifice to money of account does not appear to have taken place in early meso-American societies, such as the Mayan (Sharer 1994). The existence of money in ancient American societies is clouded in more mist than Keynes's 'Eden of Central Asia'. This question cannot be explored here beyond the observation that these were very tightly controlled societies in which an elite's direct domination of a 'mass' was based almost exclusively on coercion. There was no land rental system as in Mesopotamia, and no scale of *Wergeld*-type payments.

7 In barter, '[t]he parties concerned in any transaction are comparing their individual needs, not values in the abstract, and can balance these out against the particular merits or defects of the goods involved' (Grierson 1977: 19).

8 Sociology's analytical foundation rests on a rejection of the assumption to be found in 'real' economic analysis that there exists a substratum of social and economic order that is in the 'nature of things' (see Parsons 1937). Most notably, this was expressed in Durkheim's insistence that the idea of contract presupposes an anterior moral order: 'all in the contract is not contractual ... wherever a contract exists it is the work of society not that of individuals' (Durkheim 1960 [1893]: 189, 194).

9 The nature of ancient and classical economies and their relation to modern capitalism was a central issue in the *Methodenstreit*. The economic theorists insisted on the trans-historical universality of *homo*

economicus and the applicability of modern economic theory to the ancient world in which historical differences are merely the context in which utility maximization takes place. The dispute infiltrated social anthropology during the 1920s, and was revived in the substantivist–formalist debate, during the 1950s and 1960s, on the interpretation of 'primitive' economies. The economic theorists, or formalists, argued that 'thick' ethnographic description did not constitute explanation. Some anthropologists agreed. For a rejection of the notion that primitive media of exchange could have been a precursor of modern money, see Dalton 1976. These dichotomies – 'primitive-modern' and 'formal-substantive' – ruled out historical or evolutionary analysis. Opposition to these positions was mounted by Polanyi and his colleagues, who argued that it was mistaken to identify the economic spheres of all types of society with the market. As the historian Pearson remarked, 'something must have happened in over four thousand years of economic transformation, but the conceptual twilight of orthodox economic theory is utterly incapable of illuminating this process' (Polanyi et al. 1957: 10).

10 The following account is based on the most recent interpretations by Hudson (Mesopotamia) and Henry (Egypt) in Wray 2004. Henry argues that the development of money accompanies the transition from an egalitarian subsistence to an unequal surplus economy.

11 Esnuuna's Laws (*c*.2000 BC) begin with the establishment of the equivalencies, and Hammurapi's Laws (*c*.1750 BC) ruled that all debts denominated in silver shekel could be paid in barley. Assurbanipal's coronation prayer cites shekel equivalencies of wool, barley and oil (Hudson 2004: 7).

12 Modern financial techniques originated in the risk analysis that accompanied early capitalist trade in the sixteenth century. They were based on significant changes in bookkeeping technique and advances in the mathematics of chance and probability. For a popular account, see Bernstein 1996.

13 As it did in the eastern European Communist Comecon after World War II.

14 More recently it has been asserted on the basis of little evidence that the early electrum 'coins' were privately issued, and that it is unlikely that they were acceptable to mercenaries (Redish 1992).

15 Kurke, in a study of classic Greek culture, argues that the issue of coin represented the assertion of the state's ultimate authority to regulate all spheres of behaviour in which a general-purpose money operated – economic, social, political and religious (1999: 12–13). The state's coin symbolized the merger of different domains of value under the final authority of the *polis*. It is argued that the use of coins exerted a democratic influence by wresting control from the traditional elites, who practised gift exchange and the allocation of resources by norms of reciprocity.

16 'A cycle of imperial expenditure and commerce kept most Roman coins in perpetual circulation', and, for example, between AD 132 and 135, during the Roman control of Egypt, the total number of coins in circulation was five times greater than that collected in taxes (Harl 1996: 86, 255–6).

17 There was not enough gold to operate the classic late nineteenth-century gold standard, but the crucial difference was that capitalist banking in the City of London was able to provide an adequate supply of credit-money.

18 One gold aureus = 33 labour days; one silver denarius = 1.32 labour days; one copper sestertius = 0.33 labour days; one copper quadrans = 0.12 labour days (Goldsmith 1987: 58).

19 Some recent historical sociology has unwittingly and implicitly incorporated mainstream economic assumptions. Neither Mann (1986) nor W. G. Runciman (1995) refer to the distinctiveness of the Roman economy's pre-capitalist monetary and financial system. Indeed, Runciman's 'puzzle' is mistakenly based on the assumption that classical Rome was capitalist in every respect except a formally free labour market. See the critique in Ingham 1999.

20 In other words, there was no market in debt. As Weber noted, negotiable instruments were 'indispensable for a modern capitalistic society' (Weber 1978: 681). The personal character of debt was institutionalized in the face-to-face validation of debt contract in highly ritualized oral contracts and verification by witnesses (see the discussion in ch. 6).

Chapter 6   The Development of Capitalist Credit-Money

1 Arrighi's *Long Twentieth Century* (1994) is a brilliant exception that is based on a theoretical synthesis of Smith, Marx, Weber and Braudel and emphasizes the essential financial character of capitalism from its earliest stages.

2 Schumpeter gave greater prominence to the particular monetary structure of capitalism than almost all his contemporaries, and seems to have had a direct influence on the French school (Braudel 1984: 475–6).

3 In fourteenth-century Venice, for example, '[w]hen the Great Council voted that 3 *lire a grossi* should be the base salary of the watchmen to be appointed by the Signori di Notte, the councillors were probably thinking less about the metallic content of *grossi* than about the salary of the noble Signori di Notte themselves, which was about 6 *lire a grossi*' (Lane and Mueller 1985: 483).

4 Basically, three kinds of coin were struck: (i) 'black' money – that is, debased silver pennies that turned black when rubbed; (ii) 'white' money, which shone when rubbed; (iii) the 'yellow' money of fine gold (Spufford 1988: xx).

5   As late as 1614, in the Low Countries, for example, more than 400
    varieties of coins were circulating (cited in Lane and Mueller 1985: 12).
6   Some large payments did involve weighing (Spufford 1988, 2002; Lane
    and Mueller 1985); but this was, in effect, payment in kind. Weighing, as
    opposed to counting, transformed the coin into a commodity.
7   The frequent and arbitrary changes in both the nominal values and
    metallic content and the constantly changing issues of coin from myriad
    mints meant that 'none but an expert could tell what the values were'
    (Innes 1913: 386). Aside from any other consideration, how, under these
    circumstances, could the metallic content of money be a determinant
    of the prices of other commodities? Fischer points out that the long-
    standing orthodox explanation of sixteenth-century inflation as a result
    of South American silver discoveries has failed to note that prices rose
    first (Fischer 1996: 75).
8   Monetary policy also involved periodic renegotiations, in recoinages, of
    the terms of exchange between possessors of coin and bullion and the
    sovereign mints. In part, these aimed to maintain the nominal value of
    the coin above its bullion value, in order to pre-empt the operation of
    Gresham's Law, according to which 'bad money drives out good'.
    Money whose high precious metal content is undervalued in nominal
    terms in relation to either its bullion value or, in a bimetallic standard,
    another coin ('good money') is withdrawn from circulation or melted
    down for bullion, leaving coins which have a greater money value than
    their bullion value ('bad money').
9   'Primitive' deposit banks were very similar to the financial institutions
    which existed in Rome during the late Republic, but there is no evidence
    to suggest *direct* historical continuity. Money changing and personalized
    credit relations were maintained throughout Islam during the centuries
    that followed the fall of Rome, a period of monetary dislocation in
    Europe. But the stricter prohibition of usury than in Christendom
    would appear to have inhibited the development of the kind of deposit
    banking that reappeared in late twelfth-century Italy (Udovitch 1979;
    Goldsmith 1987; Abu-Lughod 1989). Rather, it would seem that 'primi-
    tive' deposit banking was learned anew, and grew from the large-scale
    routine money changing that followed the reactivation of the mints and
    the flood of diverse coins into the cities. The term *bancus* emerged only in
    medieval Europe, and derives from the Latin for bench or table, used by
    the money-changers.
10 The situation was different in the European dukedoms and kingdoms.
    Here the emphasis was on bullion, not banking. Sovereigns sought to
    control both money of account and the issue of coinage, by controlling
    the flow of precious metal. In the main they looked on their merchants
    and bankers as competitors whose book transactions evaded taxation
    and reduced their seignorage profits from minting.
11 Moreover, banking nations made some of the earliest more general
    contributions to the development of capitalist practice, which were

later employed in industrial production. They set up business schools that specialized in languages and used arithmetic based on Arabic numerals to replace the cumbersome Roman system of counting. The zero was especially important in the development of double-entry bookkeeping, which made possible the control of the two-way flow of bills of exchange (Boyer-Xambeu et al. 1994: 23–4).

12   As we have already noted, the same line of development did not occur in its Islamic region of origin. The question of the relationship between credit instruments and economic growth cannot be pursued in detail here. But it should be noted, for example, that medieval Byzantium's bullionist policies and the esteem in which the gold *bezant* was held, as a symbol of wealth and hoarded store of value, probably retarded economic development (see Bernstein 2000: 58–65).

13   French kings, for example, were among the most despotically powerful of the embryonic states (Mann 1986); and they proclaimed monetary sovereignty with their own money of account and twenty royal mints. But there were also more than 200 baronial mints in France. If multiple coinages and several units of account existed within the same jurisdiction, the area could not be considered politically homogeneous (Boyer-Xambeu et al. 1994: 108–11).

14   Aside from any other consideration, the very slow pace of the diffusion of the new 'social technology' of credit-money makes it difficult to accept economic 'efficiency-evolution' explanations of these developments.

15   An attempt to ban the use of bills in England seriously disrupted the wool trade in 1429, and all parties lost economically (Munro 1979: 196).

16   Henry needed the bullion to pay his foreign mercenaries in France. English coins were not as acceptable as payment in kind with silver.

17   As in the Roman system, there was some separation of the forms and functions of money. The integrated money of account and silver standard coin was the accepted means of payment or settlement. However, the smallest 1/2*d.* coin was the value of an hour's wage labour and, therefore, too large for petty transactions. These were conducted, as in Rome, by base metal media of exchange issued by cities and private agencies (Goldsmith 1987: 179). Again like Rome, gold coins were used as stores of value.

18   On the general significance of this balance of power in the development of capitalism, see Moore 1966; Weber 1981 [1927]; Collins 1980.

19   But it should be noted that mercantile interests were not unequivocally opposed to the monarch's medieval metallism. Parliament consistently enforced the policy of sound metallic money, but insisted that the monarch not exploit his monopoly minting powers. But it should be emphasized that this was not simply, or even primarily, an economic issue. Sound money was also seen as part of the wider project to build a strong modern state. The balance between the benefits of the collective security of a strong state and the costs to particular economic interests of any

particular monetary arrangements is expressed in a settlement between the major groups in a system of monetary production.

20   In his *Quantulumcumque concerning Money* (1682) the polymath Oxford professor of anatomy and founder member of the Royal Society, Sir William Petty, answered his own rhetorical question 'What remedy is there if we have too little money?' with 'We must erect a bank, which well computed, doth almost double the effect of our coined money' (Petty 1682, quoted in Braudel 1985: 475).

21   But, however 'fantastical' it might be, this trust could be cultivated, for 'it very much resembles, and, in many instances, is near akin to that fame and reputation which men obtain by wisdom in governing state affairs, or by valour and conduct in the field' (Charles Davenant, in Pocock 1975: 77).

22   Weber argues that the extension of market relations required the removal of an ethical dualism which was typical of traditional societies (1981 [1927]: 312–13). Here, norms of hospitality and an ethic of fairness governed intra-communal relations, whereas outsiders were cheated and ruthlessly exploited. See also Collins 1980.

23   In Weberian terms, this monetary dimension of the transformation of the state from patrimonial to bureaucratic and rational-legal is of central importance, but has not been given the attention it deserves. It is widely acknowledged that the modern state is identifiable as a system of power whose existence remains independent of those who happen to have control of it at any particular time (see Bonney 1999: 3). Its debts are similarly depersonalized in a national debt. This raises further conceptual problems (see D. Runciman 2000).

24   Conservative groups argued that public banks were consistent only with republics, and that the Bank of England effectively gave control of the kingdom to the merchants. The traditional monarchists would have agreed with Marx's later judgement that the state had been alienated to the bourgeoisie.

25   The existence of the national or public debt and the establishment and expansion of the bill of exchange business hastened the introduction of the law merchant (*lex mercatoria*), concerning the transferability or negotiability of debt, into common law and, thereby, into society at large. Bills, promissory notes, certificates of deposit and other financial instruments used in the mercantile economy had achieved a degree of transferability in practice and law by the late seventeenth century, particularly in the Low Countries (Usher 1953 [1934]). Even in 'backward' England, as early as the late fourteenth century, 'merchants customarily settled their debts by "setting over" their financial claims to others' (Munro 1979: 214). With the establishment of the Bank of England, the pace of legal change accelerated until the Promissory Notes Act of 1704, by which all notes, whether payable to 'X', or to 'X or order', or to 'X or bearer', were made legally transferable (Carruthers 1996: 130; Anderson 1970). These legal changes gave credit-money a monetary

space that was, for the first time, coextensive with the public sphere, as
opposed to private transactions.

26   Between 1695 and 1740, £17 m of gold, as opposed to £1.2 m of silver,
was minted: 'the gold standard had practically arrived, silently a century
or more before its legal enactment' (Davies 1996: 247). This established a
stable store of value upon which a vast superstructure of credit-money
could be confidently erected. But this did not involve a ratio between
money and goods based on their exchange-values as commodities (precious metal and X). The price of gold was *fixed* by the promise of the
state's bank to purchase gold at a given price and to convert its notes at
that rate.

27   However, the very same metropolitan interests that had made it possible
to adopt the techniques of 'Dutch finance' also inhibited its immediate
further development. The Bank of England's monopoly of joint-stock
banking, until this grip was relaxed in 1826 and then abolished in 1844,
stifled any expansion of the private London banks (which pre-dated the
Bank's monopoly) and, arguably, retarded the growth of the private
'country' banks (Cameron 1967: 18–19, also Davies 1996). Nevertheless,
the latter grew rapidly after the middle of the eighteenth century. By the
1780s there were more than 100 country banks, and the number had
increased to more than 300 in 1800 (Cameron 1967: 33). Some estimates
suggest that bank money had significantly exceeded the metallic coinage
by the second half of the eighteenth century (Davies 1996: 238).

28   The practices were classically codified in Bagehot's *Lombard Street*.
Although it may seem to be an elementary point, it must be stressed
that the 'money' in such a credit-money system is actually *constituted* by
the system of payments through the transfer of credits (see Part I, chapter
4). If this cannot be accomplished effectively, the 'money' disappears.
The hoary question cannot be pursued here, but all the historical evidence suggests that the disappearance of money in this way can be
avoided by the *authoritative* provision of an integrating money of account and a trusted supply of credit at the acme of the hierarchy of
credit. As a last resort, this can be injected into the system in the event of
defaults that threaten money's existence (see Part II, chapter 7).

29   The two developments are connected. The efforts to enhance the domestic power of central banks over the supply of credit-money is the corollary of the loss of direct control over exchange rates on the international
markets (Aglietta 2002).

30   None the less, it still has strong support in parts of the orthodox economic
establishment – for example, by the Nobel prize-winner Robert Mundell.

Chapter 7   The Production of Capitalist Credit-Money

1   For example, a country's balance of trade deficit would lead to a net
outflow of gold that would reduce the money supply and thereby deflate

prices. Cheaper exports and dearer imports would restore the trade equilibrium – as if by an 'invisible hand'.

2   The 'moral economy' of debt in which a public 'competitive piety' gave a household credit has been transformed in the modern world (Muldrew 1998: 195).

3   It should be noted that the structure of the monetary system itself exerts an independent 'Matthew effect' on inequality. Money is not merely a neutral measure of existing inequality (see Ingham 2000b).

4   It is significant that the strong city-state of Singapore has plans to abolish cash and replace it with electronic money which will be integrated with formal identification, tax liability and so on (OECD 2002).

5   As Schumpeter stressed, banks do not simply gather money from 'small pools' to lend on; rather, they also create it by lending. However, as late as 1970, US holding company law defined a bank as an institution which 'agglomerates the transaction balances of a community to lend it at interest to its commercial enterprises' (quoted in Lietaer 2001: 306).

6   The representation of the process of money creation as balanced credits (loans = assets that are owed to the bank) and debts (deposits = liabilities that the bank has to its depositors) in double-entry form also helps us to understand the otherwise counter-intuitive conclusion that money would *disappear* if everyone paid their debts. That is to say, the *simultaneous* repayment of all loans (assets) would also cancel the deposits (liabilities) on the other side of the balance sheet that are the source of money. As we have noted, Bloch grasped the fact that capitalism would collapse if all debts were simultaneously repaid in full. (We should also note that capitalism is, of course, equally, and more obviously, endangered when *nobody* repays his or her debt within the time specified by the norms of the system.)

7   This is also known as 'financial engineering'. In the 1990s, Citicorp, for example, converted future credit card interest payments into marketable bonds. In the USA, the securitization market grew from $400bn to $2,000bn between 1985 and 1995.

8   As Goodhart's Law implies. See Mayer on Alan Greenspan's task of 'explaining how in a world where banks do a minor share of financial intermediation, the Federal Reserve by increasing the rates they must pay for overnight money affects the course of the real economy' (Mayer 2001: 225).

9   On the basis of the experience of the nineteenth century, Bagehot famously recommended, in his *Lombard Street*, three rules for halting a bank panic. The Bank of England should 'lend freely' on 'good collateral' at 'penalty rates of interest'. Many neoclassical economists would argue that this safety net makes the banks less risk-averse and, consequently, the whole system more crisis-prone ('moral hazard'). See Kindleberger 1989 [1978].

10   As we noted in chapter 2, neo-chartalists are following Lerner's idea of
     functional finance, and are concerned to establish that a government can
     act as a non-inflationary employer of last resort.

11   However, the actual *costs* of inflation have proved impossible to quan-
     tify. Indeed, prominent anti-inflation economists have conceded that
     there is no evidence to suggest that inflation below 20 per cent has a
     negative impact on economic growth (Barro and Gordon 1983: 104). See
     the survey of the literature in Issing 2001: 16–18; Kirshner 1999).

12   At present, the European Central Bank is a notable exception.

13   In a recent survey of the literature, the European Central Bank's chief
     economist confirmed the status of these assumptions: 'The one to one
     relationship between money and prices is one of the few results that have
     remained undisputed over time and across economists' (Issing 2001: 9,
     76–7). Long-run correspondence between the quantity of money and
     prices is only a *theoretical* possibility, and one that can be established
     only in terms of the tautologous quantity equation (see Part I, chapter 1).
     Most importantly, from the standpoint of economic practice, the equa-
     tion itself does not specify – beyond the notoriously imprecise and
     unoperational concepts of quantity and velocity – any policy instruments
     that might bring about the long-run equilibrium.

14   Furthermore, as the different models carry highly different alleged impli-
     cations for monetary policy, economic analysis would appear not to
     provide a secure basis for policy-making (Issing 2001: 7).

15   First, they look for signs that the economy might be running near to full
     capacity that could provide opportunities to exploit supply shortages by
     raising prices. Second, central banks pay very close attention to supply
     costs, especially the trajectory of wage settlements. Third, rises in asset
     prices are thought to convey two signals. On the one hand, they are
     thought to be a possible inflationary trigger through a 'wealth effect' on
     consumer spending. On the other hand, in so far as it is an expression of
     rentiers' expectations of long-run inflation prospects, the 'yield curve' is an
     indicator of the credibility in the money markets of central bank policy.

16   However, the transparency of central bank policy formulation in order to
     establish credibility in the dialogue with the global money markets might
     serve further to ideologically denaturalize money, and thus to weaken the
     very institutions it is designed to strengthen. Open disagreement con-
     forms to the norm of transparency, as orthodox economic analysis
     prescribes, but exposes the fact that economic data are subject to differ-
     ent and legitimate expert interpretations. There has been criticism that
     the transparent lack of unanimity in the Bank of England's Monetary
     Policy Committee did not provide the certainty that the markets require.
     These differences of opinion have led to the discussion of the social
     psychology of committee decision making and how this might lead to
     systematic policy errors. For example, an expert might not wish to
     concede the superiority of a competing argument. In short, conformity
     to orthodox economics' model of rational decision making based on a

positivist conception of social science might further expose the actual fragility of group consensus and the social construction of money itself. It is perhaps significant that the European Central Bank, which faces a more difficult task in trying to establish the credentials of the European Community's new euro currency in the face of potentially greater national differences, has opted not to disclose the minutes of its deliberations.

17   The actors in macro-economic models are referred to as 'representative agents', who act according to the 'economic man' assumptions. That is to say, they share the same cognitive understanding of the world as the economists who construct the models. In this way, economists can present themselves as arbiters of the common good (see Persson and Tabellini 1990).

18   In this regard, central bankers are in an unenviable position. They have less power than they claim and are credited with, but they are expected to be able to avoid both inflation and deflation. Alan Greenspan's charisma was carefully constructed during the boom years of the 1990s, but almost vanished within a few weeks of the bubble bursting in the first years of the twenty-first century.

Chapter 8   Monetary Disorder

1   An enormous literature exists on this 'Golden Age' of capitalism, the efficacy of economic ideas and the quite wide variations in their implementation. For a concise account, see Smithin 1996.

2   This observation on the general relationship between domestic economic management and international money markets was later formulated in the 1960s as the Mundell–Fleming model, comprising (1) independent monetary policy (control of domestic interest rates), (2) fixed exchange rates, (3) international capital mobility. Any two can coexist, but not all three. The option of (1) and (2) was chosen at Bretton Woods. With its disintegration and subsequent floating exchange rates, (1) and (3) obtain.

3   In the financialization phase, the productive sector becomes increasingly involved in purely financial deals. For example, Enron started life as a supplier of energy, and ended its days playing the derivatives markets in the same commodities.

4   Minsky (1991) considers his hypothesis to be an interpretation of Keynes's *General Theory* and of Fisher's debt-deflation theory of great depressions. His work is dismissed by orthodoxy because it contradicts two of its tenets. First, economic agents are seen, in this view, to be *fundamentally* 'irrational' by repeatedly engaging in speculative manias. Second, the persistent and repeated dissociation of the money and commodity sides violates the primacy of the 'real' economy. These objections are found in the essays in Kindleberger and Laffarge 1982. A more positive assessment of Minsky's work is found in Dymski and Pollin 1994, especially Isenberg's article on the Great Depression and the evidence in favour of Minsky's interpretation.

5 In the consumer sector, for example, credit card holders would be in a position of having to take out additional longer-term loans to make the payments necessary to avoid having credit withdrawn. One 'ultra' Ponzi scenario would involve multiple card holding and borrowing from one to pay off another. In *Rosalie Goes Shopping*, a German satirical film set in Midwest USA, a housewife reaches the end of her credit limits on the thirty or so credit cards that she has used to pay interest of one to the other. She then persuades the bank to lend her 1 m, then 2 m, dollars.

6 There are exceptions, such as 'short selling' in a falling market. Dealers sell assets for future delivery that they do not own, in the expectation of being able to buy them later at a lower price. It is argued that this exacerbates the 'bear' market, and at the time of writing (early 2003) there are calls for its prohibition.

7 If interest rates do *not* rise during an investment boom, this implies 'that a flood of financial innovation is taking place' (Minsky 1982: 33) by which the financial system creates its own 'inside' or 'near' money that eludes the authority's control, as we noted in the previous chapter. Although Minsky does not discuss this aspect in detail, such an expansion of credit outside the monetary authority's control is doubly destabilizing. On the one hand, it increases the level of Ponzi finance; on the other, it creates an unregulated fringe of even more fragile credit relations.

8 During the technology stock bubble at the end of the twentieth century, opinion shifted from the consideration of 'irrational exuberance' to the idea that a 'new economy' had been constructed. Information and communication technology, it was argued, were able to create limitless productivity gains that had eliminated the boom and bust of the business cycle. Note that this conception of the business cycle is implicitly grounded in a 'real' economy model in which money is neutral.

9 As the following account implies, there are good reasons to think that the USA's social and political structure would be resistant to a deflationary impasse like Japan's. This interesting question cannot, however, be pursued here.

10 Furthermore, as is typical of inflationary expansion, new credit instruments were 'financially engineered' by a rash of 'fringe', or 'non-bank', firms that soon emerged (Van Rixtel 2002: 171).

11 All societies develop informal networks, linking the public and private sectors, for the conduct of business, but these are particularly robust in Japan and a basic element of social structure. There are a number of terms: for example, *jinmyaku* refers in general to personal relationships between the public and private sectors, *amakaduri* ('descent from heaven') to retired Ministry of Finance and Bank of Japan bureaucrats' acceptance of position on the boards of private banks (see Van Rixtel 2002: esp. ch. 3).

12 As we have already noted, proponents of the new orthodoxy have also argued that the monetary authorities should set an inflation target of,

say, 3 per cent, and hope that this will produce the necessary rational expectations.

13 A. Turner (2002) also observes that government's limitless power to create money is 'deliberately disguised by conventional arrangements'.

14 The situation is of course reminiscent of the 1930s, when Keynes lambasted the hidebound conventions of British Treasury officials.

15 In 2002, the Bank of Japan increased base money by 25.7 per cent, but the supply of bank credit-money barely responded, rising by just 3.3 per cent (*Financial Times*, 17 February 2003).

16 It is significant that foreign banks have dominated Argentina throughout its history.

17 Further measures after the devaluation and confiscation of deposits astonished foreign observers and enraged the middle-class bank depositors. In early 2002, the new Argentine government imposed a 'pesoification' of all bank deposits and liabilities, seized the banks' dollar reserves, changed the bankruptcy law to weaken creditors' right to claim debtors' assets, and invoked an old Peronist economic subversion law further to intimidate the banks ('Argentina on the road to ruin', *Financial Times*, 1 May 2002).

18 Under pressure from the Bank of England, after the Baring crisis of 1891, Argentina adopted stringent domestic fiscal measures as a condition for a loan to refinance the state and the banking system. In 1899 Argentina adopted the gold standard administered by a Conversion Board. Unlike with the other participants, there was no central bank to oversee the 'manufacture' of credit-money by monetizing private debts between banks and borrowers. The Currency Board was so eager to appease foreign creditors with its metallist monetary orthodoxy that it effectively negated some of the advantages of large balance of payments surpluses. As the gold reserves grew from 38 million gold pesos in 1903 to 263 million in 1913, the Currency Board increased the legal reserve requirement for note issue from 23.1 per cent to 72.7 per cent (Bethell 1993: 73). The money supply in the form of notes increased, but not nearly as much as it might have done, and money creation by bank lending remained low. Moreover, during this period of prosperity and stability, the state's fiscal position continued to deteriorate. Between 1900 and 1912, expenditure increased by 118 per cent, but revenue from taxation by only 59 per cent (Bethell 1993: 74).

19 Such has been the periodic seriousness of the fiscal situation that official devaluations of the peso, before the dollar peg, appear to have been motivated by the need to attract hitherto undeclared hoards (Lewis 1990: 363).

20 The IMF insists that the level of political and fiscal devolution is a major cause of Argentina's high level of public expenditure. Since the Participation Law of 1853, the provincial governments have been responsible for the largest proportion of social expenditures and receive a share of the central government tax revenue, such as it is. This exacerbates the

situation in so far as central government cannot, in principle, control the balance of expenditure and revenue across the whole economy. However, it is not fundamental, except perhaps in so far as the power of the provinces is an expression of the inability of a metropolitan bourgeois class to tame the provincial landowners.

Chapter 9   New Monetary Spaces

1   It is sometimes suggested that the dollarization of global trade would seem to support such a view (see Helleiner 1999); but whether this occurs as a result of narrowly economic forces is very doubtful. Ultimately, it is a question of how markets are created. Do they develop spontaneously in the course of 'truck, barter and exchange'? Or are they made possible by states and their money, as I suggested was the case in the classical empires of Greece, Rome and Britain. This very large question, or rather package of questions, on the nature of globalization cannot be dealt with here, beyond the observation that the money question is, as ever, central. Obviously, the dollarization of independent nation-states, by either formal or informal means, is at least as much the consequence of US hegemony as it is of a market-driven reduction of transaction costs (see Helleiner 2003). The USA's share of world trade, for example, would not in itself warrant such a widespread use of the dollar.

2   See the extreme economic liberal view that '[u]ltimately, the competition for the standard of value should be no different to the competitive market of multiple providers we see for toothpaste and shoes' (Mantonis, *Digital Cash and Monetary Freedom*, quoted in Denny 1999.)

3   At this time, US deficits led to the accumulation of very large foreign holdings of dollars, which, in conjunction with loose regulation in the City of London, produced an unregulated foreign exchange market that eventually put pressure on the post-war Bretton Woods system (Ingham 1994; Helleiner 1994).

4   During the 1930s, Major Douglas was the most prominent advocate whose ideas were acknowledged by Keynes. Working as an engineer for Westinghouse in India, Douglas observed that much needed hydro-electric projects failed to go ahead despite their viability, plentiful cheap labour and the existence of low-priced materials and equipment. Lack of finance was usually given as the reason for not starting a project. But on enquiring, Douglas learned from the Comptroller General of India that money and the currency were plentiful; it was bank credit that was in short supply. Money, he argued, was only a 'ticket' (or credit) that granted permission to participate in the economy. Banks should have no more right to decide what should be produced than a ticket office to decide on the right to travel or the traveller's destination. 'Real', or 'social', credit, which is the 'effective reserve energy belonging to the community', should replace bank credit.

5   In the 1930s, Gesell argued that deflation could be combated by the deliberate depreciation of saved or hoarded money by overstamping with a lower denomination. This would encourage spending. See Keynes's discussion (Keynes 1973 [1936]: 353–8).

6   As with LETS, the relatively narrow range of goods and services on offer reduces the liquidity of local currencies. In the words of a participant of the Montpelier, Vermont, scheme: 'You can only have so many massages and aromatherapies in your lifetime' (*Economist*, 28 June 1997, p. 65). Where local currencies are authentically complementary and expand, they will, at some stage or other, attract the attention of the state's tax authorities.

7   Goodhart used his seminal paper on the two concepts of money – 'chartalism and metallism' – to analyse the nature of the single European currency (Goodhart 1998; see the discussion in Bell and Nell 2003). In general, I agree with Goodhart's analysis, but I believe that it would be theoretically more complete if, in addition to establishing the chartalist case by historical analysis, it had given more attention to the question of the logical necessity of an authoritative money of account. As I have argued, the metallist (or commodity) theory of money cannot provide an explanation of the source of the 'moneyness' of money – that is, money of account. Goodhart explains that he qualified EMU uniqueness after Flandreau pointed out that the pre-1914 Austro-Hungarian Empire had a single currency, but separate national budgets (Goodhart 2003: 195, n. 1).

8   The seven others listed by B. Cohen (2001) joined together out of weakness. Belgium–Luxembourg Economic Union (1922), the African CFA Franc Zone (1959), the South African Common Monetary Area (1986), East African Community (1967), East Caribbean Currency Area (1965), Latin American Union (1865), Scandinavian Monetary Union (1873).

9   It should be noted that the euro existed as a functioning money of account for the denomination of prices and debts for two years before its embodiment in circulating notes and coins. It was 'imaginary', but performed all the functions apart from being a circulating medium of exchange. For these two years, I set the following question in the final examinations in the Faculty of Social and Political Sciences: 'What does the existence of the "cashless" euro tell us about the nature of money?' Not a single student chose to answer it!

10 The theoretical rationale comes from the idea that privileged government financing, in which the central bank, in effect, cashes the state's cheques by paying for any bonds that it issues, crowds out private finance. This is based on the questionable orthodox economic assumption that there exists a finite loanable fund of money. As I have stressed, such a position does not acknowledge the relative autonomy and efficacy of the money side in capitalism.

References

Abu-Lughod, J. 1989: *Before Hegemony: The World System, AD 1250–1350*. Oxford: Oxford University Press.

Aglietta, M. 2002: Whence and whither money? In *The Future of Money*, Paris: OECD, 31–72.

Aglietta, M. and Orlean, A. 1982: *La Violence de la monnaie*. Paris: PUF.

Aglietta, M. and Orlean, A. (eds) 1998: *La Monnaie souveraine*. Paris: Odile Jacob.

Allington, M. 1987: Numeraire. In J. Eatwell, M. Milgate and P. Newman (eds), *The New Palgrave*, London: Macmillan, vol. 3, 686–7.

Anderson, B. 1970: Money and credit in the eighteenth century. *Business History*, 12 (2), 85–101.

Andreau, J. 1998: Cens, évaluation et monnaie dans l'Antiquité romaine. In Aglietta and Orlean 1998: 213–50.

Arena, R. and Festre, A. 1999: Banks, credit, and the financial system in Schumpeter: an interpretation. In H. Hanusch (ed.), *The Legacy of Joseph A. Schumpeter*, vol. 2, Cheltenham: Edward Elgar.

Arrighi, G. 1994: *The Long Twentieth Century*. London: Verso.

Ascheim, J. and Park, Y. 1976: *Artificial Currency Units: The Formation of Functional Currency Areas*. Essays in International Finance, 114, Princeton: University of Princeton Press.

Asimakopoulos, A. 1988: The aggregate supply function and the share economy: some early drafts of the *General Theory*. In O. F. Hamouda and J. Smithin (eds), *Keynes and Public Policy after Fifty Years*, vol. 2: *Theories and Method*, Aldershot: Edward Elgar, 67–92.

Bank of England 1993: *Economic Briefing*, August.

Banuri, T. and Schor, J. (eds) 1992: *Financial Openness and National Autonomy*. Oxford: Oxford University Press.

Barkai, H. 1989: The old historical school: Roscher on money and monetary issues. *History of Political Economy*, 21 (2), 179–200.

Barro, R. and Gordon, D. 1983: Rules, discretion and reputation in a model of monetary policy. *Journal of Monetary Economics*, 12, 101–21.

Baskin, J. and Miranti, P. 1997: *A History of Corporate Finance*. Cambridge: Cambridge University Press.

Baxter, W. 1945: *The House of Baxter: Business in Boston 1724–1775*. Cambridge, MA.: Harvard University Press.

Bell, S. 2000: Do taxes and bonds finance government spending? *Journal of Economic Issues*, 34 (3), 603–20.

Bell, S. 2001: The role of the state and the hierarchy of money. *Cambridge Journal of Economics*, 25, 149–63.

Bell, S. 2003: Neglected costs of monetary union: the loss of sovereignty in the public sphere. In Bell and Nell 2003: 160–83.

Bell, S. and Nell, E. 2003: *The State, the Market and the Euro*. Cheltenham: Edward Elgar.

Bernstein, P. 1996: *Against the Gods*. London: John Wiley and Sons.

Bernstein, P. 2000: *The Power of Gold*. New York: John Wiley.

Bethell, L. 1993: *Argentina since Independence*. Cambridge: Cambridge University Press.

Blinder, A. 1999: *Central Banking in Theory and Practice*. Cambridge, MA: MIT Press.

Blinder, A., Goodhart, C., Hildebrand, P., Lipton, D. and Wyplosz, C. 2001: How do central banks talk? In *Geneva Reports on the World Economy*, 3, Geneva: International Centre for Monetary and Banking Studies.

Bloch, M. 1954 [1936]: *Esquisse d'une histoire monétaire de l'Europe*. Paris: Armand Colin.

Bloch, M. 1962: *Feudal Society*. London: Routledge and Kegan Paul.

Bloomfield, A. 1959: *Monetary Policy under the Gold Standard, 1820–1914*. New York: Federal Reserve Bank.

Bonney, R. (ed.) 1999: *The Rise of the Fiscal State in Europe, c.1200–1815*. Oxford: Oxford University Press.

Bootle, R. 1996: *The Death of Inflation*. London: Nicholas Brearley.

Bowring, F. 1998: LETS: an eco-socialist alternative. *New Left Review*, 232, 91–111.

Boyer-Xambeu, M. T., Deleplace, G. and Gillard, L. 1994: *Private Money and Public Currencies: The Sixteenth Century Challenge*. London: M. E. Sharpe.

Boyle, D. 1999: *Funny Money*. London: Harper Collins.

Braudel, F. 1984: *Civilisation and Capitalism. The Perspective of the World*, vol. 3: London: Fontana.

Braudel, F. 1985: *Civilisation and Capitalism*, vol. 1: *The Structures of Everyday Life*. London: Fontana.

Brewer, J. 1989: *The Sinews of Power: War, Money and the English State, 1688–1783*. London: Unwin Hyman.

Buchan, J. 1997: *Frozen Desire: An Inquiry into the Meaning of Money.* London: Picador.

Busse, E. 2000: The embeddedness of tax evasion in Russia. In Ledeneva and Kurchiyan 2000: 129–43.

Caffentzis, G. 1989: *Clipped Coins, Abused Words and Civil Government: John Locke's Philosophy of Money.* New York: Autonomedia.

Cameron, R. 1967: *Banking in the Early Stages of Industrialization.* Oxford: Oxford University Press.

Carruthers, B. 1996: *City of Capital.* Princeton: Princeton University Press.

Carruthers, B. and Babb, S. 1996: The color of money and the nature of value: greenbacks and gold in post-bellum America. *American Journal of Sociology,* 101 (6), 1556–91.

Cencini, A. 1988: *Money, Income and Time: A Quantum-Theoretical Approach.* London: Pinter.

Chabal, P. and Daloz, J-P. 1999: *Africa Works: Disorder as a Political Instrument.* Oxford: James Currey.

Clower, R. 1984 [1967]: A reconsideration of the microfoundations of money. In D. Walker (ed.), *Money and Markets,* Cambridge: Cambridge University Press, 81–9.

Coffey, P. 1993: The European monetary system and economic and monetary union. In P. Coffey (ed.), *Main Economic Policy Areas of the EC – After 1992,* Dordrecht: Kluwer Academic Publishers, 3–37.

Cohen, B. 2001a: Beyond EMU: the problem of sustainability. In B. Eichengreen and J. Freiden (eds), *The Political Economy of European Monetary Unification,* Boulder, CO: Westview Press, 179–204.

Cohen, B. 2001b: Electronic money: new day or false dawn? *Review of International Political Economy,* 8, 197–225.

Cohen, E. 1992: *Athenian Economy and Society: A Banking Perspective.* Princeton: Princeton University Press.

Collins, R. 1979: Review of M. Mayer, *The Bankers. American Journal of Sociology,* 85, 190–4.

Collins, R. 1980: Weber's last theory of capitalism: a systematization. *American Sociological Review,* 45, 925–42.

Collins, R. 1986: *Weberian Sociological Theory.* Cambridge: Cambridge University Press.

Cook, R. 1958: Speculation on the origins of coinage. *Historia,* 7, 257–62.

Crawford, M. 1970: Money and exchange in the Roman world. *Journal of Roman Studies,* 60, 40–8.

Crouzet, F. 1999: Politics and banking in revolutionary and Napoleonic France. In R. Sylla, R. Tilly and G. Tortella, *The State, The Financial System and Economic Modernization,* Cambridge: Cambridge University Press.

Cutler, A. et al. 1978: *Marx's 'Capital' and Capitalism Today,* vol. 2. London: Routledge and Kegan Paul.

Dalton, G. 1976: Primitive money. In G. Dalton (ed.), *Tribal and Peasant Economies,* Austin: Texas Press, 27–42.

Dasgupta, P. 1988: Trust as a commodity. In D. Gambetta (ed.), *Trust: Making and Breaking Cooperative Relationships*, Oxford: Blackwell, 66–81.

Davies, G. 1996: *A History of Money*. Cardiff: University of Wales Press.

Day, J. 1999: *Money and Finance in the Age of Merchant Capitalism*. Oxford: Blackwell.

de Cecco, M. 1974. *Money and Empire*. Oxford: Blackwell.

de Vroey, M. 1984: Inflation: a non-monetarist interpretation. *Cambridge Journal of Economics*, 8 (4), 381–99.

Deflem, M. 2003: The sociology of the sociology of money: Simmel and the contemporary battle of the classics. *Journal of Classical Sociology*, 3 (1), 67–96.

Denny, C. 1999: Electric Currency could Trash Cash. *Guardian*, 4 November.

Dickson, P. 1967: *The Financial Revolution in England*. London: Macmillan.

Dodd, N. 1994: *The Sociology of Money*. Cambridge: Polity.

Dornbusch, R. 2001: *Financial Times*, 28 August.

Douglas, M. 1986: *How Institutions Think*. London: Routledge.

Dowd, K. 2000: The invisible hand and the evolution of the monetary system. In Smithin 2000: 139–56.

Dunbar, N. 2001: *Inventing Money*. London: John Wiley.

Durkheim, E. 1960 [1893]: *The Division of Labour in Society*. Glencoe, IL: Free Press.

Dymski, G. and Pollin, R. (eds) 1994: *New Perspectives in Monetary Macroeconomics: Explorations in the Tradition of Hyman P. Minsky*. Ann Arbor: University of Michigan Press.

Earley, J. 1994: Joseph Schumpeter: a frustrated 'creditist'. In G. Dymski and R. Pollin 1994: 337–51.

Eichengreen, B. and Frieden, J. 2001: *The Political Economy of European Monetary Union*. Boulder, CO, and Oxford: Westview Press.

Einaudi, L. 1953 [1936]: The theory of imaginary money from Charlemagne to the French Revolution. In F. C. Lane and J. C. Riemersma (eds), *Enterprise and Secular Change*, London: Allen and Unwin, 229–61.

Einzig, P. 1966: *Primitive Money*. London: Pergamon Press.

Ellis, H. 1934: *German Monetary Theory 1905–1933*. Cambridge, MA: Harvard University Press.

Fama, E. 1980: Banking in the theory of finance. *Journal of Monetary Economics*, 6, 39–57.

Ferguson, N. 2001: *The Cash Nexus: Money and Power in the Modern World 1700–2000*. Harmondsworth: Penguin.

Fine, B. and Lapavitsas, C. 2000: Markets and money in social theory: what role for economics? *Economy and Society*, 29 (3), 357–82.

Fischer, D. 1996: *The Great Wave*. Oxford: Oxford University Press.

Fisher, I. 1911: *The Purchasing Power of Money*. New York: Macmillan.

Fisher, I. 1933: The debt-deflation theory of the Great Depression. *Econometrica*, 1, 333–57.

Fligstein, N. 2001: *The Architecture of Markets*. Princeton: Princeton University Press.

Friedman, M. 1969: *The Optimal Quantity of Money and Other Essays.* Chicago: Aldine.

Friedman, M. and Schwartz, A. 1963: *A Monetary History of the United States, 1867–1960.* Princeton: Princeton University Press.

Galbraith, J. 1995 [1975]: *Money.* Harmondsworth: Penguin.

Ganssmann, H. 1988: Money – a symbolically generalized medium of communication? On the concept of money in recent sociology. *Economy and Society*, 17, 285–315.

Gardiner, G. 1993: *Towards True Monetarism.* London: Dulwich Press.

Germain, R. 1997: *The International Organization of Credit.* Cambridge: Cambridge University Press.

Giddens, A. 1990: *The Consequences of Modernity.* Cambridge: Polity.

Gilbert, E. and Helleiner, E. (eds) 1999: *Nation-States and Money.* London: Routledge.

Girard, R. 1972: *La Violence et le sacré.* Paris: Grasset.

Goffman, E. 1969 [1959]: *The Presentation of Self in Everyday Life.* London: Penguin.

Goldschalk, H. and Krueger, M. 2000: Why e-money still fails. *Third Berlin Internet Workshop*, <www.paysys.de>

Goldsmith, R. 1987: *Premodern Financial Systems.* Cambridge: Cambridge University Press.

Goodhart, C. 1996: European monetary integration. *European Economic Review*, 40, 1083–90.

Goodhart, C. 1998: The two concepts of money: implications for the analysis of optimal currency areas. *European Journal of Political Economy*, 14, 407–32.

Goodhart, C. 2003: A reply to the contributors. In Bell and Nell 2003: 184–96.

Graziani, A. 1990: The theory of the monetary circuit. *Économies et Sociétés: Monnaie et Production*, 24 (7), 7–36.

Greider, W. 1987: *Secrets of the Temple: How the Federal Reserve Runs the Country.* New York: Simon and Schuster.

Grierson, P. 1977: *The Origins of Money.* London: Athlone Press.

Guttmann, R. 1994: *How Credit Money Shapes the Economy.* New York: M. E. Sharpe.

Guttmann, R. 2003: Money as a social institution: a heterodox view of the euro. In Bell and Nell 2003: 138–59.

Hahn, F. 1982: *Money and Inflation.* Oxford: Blackwell.

Hahn, F. 1987: Foundations of monetary theory. In M. deCecco and J. Fitoussi (eds), *Monetary Theory and Institutions*, London: Macmillan, 21–43.

Harl, K. 1996: *Coinage in the Roman Economy, 300 BC to AD 700.* Baltimore: Johns Hopkins University Press.

Hart, K. 2000: *The Memory Bank: Money in an Unequal World.* London: Profile Books.

Hawthorn, G. 2000: A world run through Windows. *New Left Review*, 5, 101–10.

Hawtrey, R. 1919: *Currency and Credit*. London: Longmans.

Hayek, F. 1976: *The De-nationalisation of Money*. London: Institute of Economic Affairs.

Heichelheim, F. 1958 [1938]: *An Ancient Economic History*. Leiden: A. W. Sijthoff.

Heinsohn, G. and Steiger, O. 2000: The property theory of interest and money. In Smithin 2000: 69–100.

Helleiner, E. 1994: *States and the Reemergence of Global Finance*. Ithaca, NY: Cornell University Press.

Helleiner, E. 1999: Denationalising money?: Economic liberalism and the 'national question' in currency affairs. In Gilbert and Helleiner 1999: 141–57.

Helleiner, E. 2003: *The Making of National Money*. Ithaca, NY: Cornell University Press.

Henry, J. 2004: The social origins of money: the case of Egypt. In Wray 2004: 79–98.

Henwood, D. 1997: *Wall Street*. London: Verso.

Hicks, J. 1937: Mr Keynes and the classics. *Econometrica*, 5, 147–59.

Hicks, J. R. 1982 [1955]: Inflation and the wage structure. In *Money, Interest and Wages: Collected Essays in Economic Theory*, vol. 2, Oxford: Blackwell, 29–43.

Hicks, J. R. 1989: *A Market Theory of Money*. Oxford: Oxford University Press.

Hilferding, R. 1981 [1910]: *Finance Capital*. London: Routledge and Kegan Paul.

Hirsch, F. and Goldthorpe, J. (eds) 1978: *The Political Economy of Inflation*. London: Martin Robertson.

Hoover, K. 1996: Some suggestions for complicating the theory of money. In S. Pressman (ed.), *Interactions in Political Economy*, London: Routledge, 204–16.

Hopkins, K. 1978: *Conquerors and Slaves*. Cambridge: Cambridge University Press.

Hopkins, K. 1980: Taxes and trade in the Roman Empire 200 BC to AD 400. *Journal of Roman Studies*, 70, 101–25.

Hudson, M. 2004: The archaeology of money: debt vs. barter theories of money. In Wray 2004: 99–127.

Hutchinson, F. and Burkitt, B. 1997: *The Political Economy of Social Credit and Guild Socialism*. London: Routledge.

Ingham, G. 1984: *Capitalism Divided?* London: Macmillan.

Ingham, G. 1994: States and markets in the production of world money: sterling and the dollar. In S. Corbridge, N. Thrift and R. Martin (eds), *Money, Power and Space*, Oxford: Blackwell, 29–48.

Ingham, G. 1996a: Money is a social relation. *Review of Social Economy*, 54 (4), 507–29.

Ingham, G. 1996b: Some recent changes in the relationship between economics and sociology. *Cambridge Journal of Economics*, 20, 243–75.

Ingham, G. 1998: On the 'underdevelopment' of the sociology of money. *Acta Sociologica*, 41 (10), 3–18.

Ingham, G. 1999: Capitalism, money and banking: a critique of recent historical sociology. *British Journal of Sociology*, 50 (1), 76–96.

Ingham, G. 2000a: 'Babylonian madness': on the sociological and historical 'origins' of money. In Smithin 2000: 16–41.

Ingham, G. 2000b: Class inequality and the social production of money. In R. Crompton, F. Devine, M. Savage and J. Scott (eds), *Renewing Class Analysis*, Oxford: Blackwell, 66–86.

Ingham, G. 2001: Fundamentals of a theory of money: untangling Fine, Lapavitsas and Zelizer. *Economy and Society*, 30 (3), 304–23.

Ingham, G. 2002: New monetary spaces? In *The Future of Money*, Paris: OECD, 123–45.

Ingham, G. 2003: Schumpeter and Weber on the institutions of capitalism: solving Swedberg's 'puzzle'. *Journal of Classical Sociology*, 3 (3), 297–309.

Innes, A. M. 1913: What is money? *Banking Law Journal* (May), 377–408.

Innes, A. M. 1914: The credit theory of money. *Banking Law Journal* (January), 151–68.

Issing, O. 1999: *Annual Hayek Memorial Lecture*. London: Institute of Economic Affairs.

Issing, O. 2001: *Monetary Policy in the Euro Area*. Cambridge: Cambridge University Press.

Jackson, K. 1995: *The Oxford Book of Money*. Oxford: Oxford University Press.

Jones, R. 1976: The origins and development of media of exchange. *Journal of Political Economy*, 84 (4), 757–75.

Keynes, J. M. 1919: *The Economic Consequences of the Peace*. London: Macmillan.

Keynes, J. M. 1930: *A Treatise on Money*. London: Macmillan.

Keynes, J. M. 1973: *The Collected Writings of John Maynard Keynes*, vol. 14, ed. D. Moggeridge. Cambridge: Cambridge University Press.

Keynes, J. M. 1973 [1936]: *The General Theory of Employment Interest and Money*. In *The Collected Writings of John Maynard Keynes*, vol. 7, ed. D. Moggeridge, Cambridge: Cambridge University Press.

Keynes, J. M. 1980: *Collected Writings of John Maynard Keynes*, vol. 25, ed. D. Moggeridge. Cambridge: Cambridge University Press.

Keynes, J. M. 1982: *Collected Writings of John Maynard Keynes*, vol. 28, ed. D. Moggeridge. Cambridge: Cambridge University Press.

Keynes, J. M. 1983: *Collected Writings of John Maynard Keynes*, vol. 11, D. Moggeridge. Cambridge: Cambridge University Press.

Kindleberger, C. 1984: *A Financial History of Europe*. London: Macmillan.

Kindleberger, C. 1989 [1978]: *Manias, Panics, and Crashes*, rev. edn. London: Macmillan.

Kindleberger, C. and Laffarge, J.-P. (eds) 1982: *Financial Crises*. Cambridge: Cambridge University Press.

King, M. 1999: Challenges for monetary policy: new and old. *Bank of England Quarterly Bulletin*, 39, 397–415.

Kirshner, J. 1995: *Currency and Coercion.* Princeton: Princeton University Press.

Kirshner, J. 1999: Inflation: paper dragon or Trojan horse? *Review of International Political Economy*, 6 (4), 609–18.

Klein, P. and Selgin, G. 2000: Menger's theory of money: some experimental evidence. In J. Smithin 2000: 217–34.

Knapp, G. F. 1973 [1924]: *The State Theory of Money.* New York: Augustus M. Kelley.

Kraay, C. 1964: Hoards, small change and the origin of coinage. *Journal of Hellenic Studies*, 84, 76–91.

Kuhn, K. 1970: *The Structure of Scientific Revolutions.* London: Routledge.

Kurke, L. 1999: *Coins, Bodies, Games and Gold.* Princeton: Princeton University Press.

Laidler, D. 1991: *The Golden Age of the Quantity Theory.* London: Philip Allan.

Lane, F. and Mueller, R. 1985: *Money and Banking in Renaissance Venice,* vol. 1: *Coins and Money of Account.* London and Baltimore: Johns Hopkins University Press.

Laum, B. 1924: *Heiliges Geld.* Tübingen: J. C. B. Mohr.

Ledeneva, A. 1998: *Russia's Economy of Favours: Blat, Networking and Informal Exchange.* Cambridge: Cambridge University Press.

Ledeneva, A. and Kurchiyan, M. (eds) 2000: *Economic Crime in Russia.* The Hague: Kluwer Law International.

Lerner, A. 1943: Functional finance and the Federal debt. *Social Research*, 10, 38–51.

Lerner, A. 1947: Money as a creature of the state. *American Economic Review*, 37 (2), 312–17.

Lewis, P. 1990: *The Crisis of Argentine Capitalism.* Chapel Hill, NC, and London: University of Pittsburg Press.

Leyshon, A. and Thrift, N. 1997: *Money/Space.* London: Routledge.

Leijonhufvud, A. 1973: Life among the Econ. *Western Economic Journal*, 11 (3), 327–37.

Lietaer, B. 2001: *The Future of Money.* London: Century.

Lindberg, D. and Maier, C. (eds) 1985: *The Politics of Inflation and Economic Stagnation.* Washington, DC: Brookings Institute.

Lopez, R. 1979: The dawn of modern banking. In Center for Medieval and Renaissance Studies, University of California, Los Angeles, *The Dawn of Modern Banking*, New Haven: Yale University Press, 1–27.

Maier, C. 1978: The politics of inflation in the twentieth century. In Hirsch and Goldthorpe 1978: 37–72.

Mann, M. 1986: *The Sources of Social Power.* Cambridge: Cambridge University Press.

Manzetti, L. 1993: *Institutions, Parties, and Coalitions in Argentine Politics.* Pittsburg and London: University of Pittsburg Press.

Marshall, A. 1926: *Official Papers of Alfred Marshall*, ed. J. M. Keynes. London: Macmillan.

Martin, P. 1998: A long goodbye. *Financial Times*, 24 November.

Marx, K. 1970: *A Contribution to a Critique of Political Economy*. Moscow: Progress Publishers.

Marx, K. 1976: *Capital*, vol. 1. Harmondsworth: Penguin.

Marx, K. 1981: *Capital*, vol. 3. Harmondsworth: Penguin.

Mayer, M. 2001: *The Fed*. New York: Free Press.

McLuhan, M. 1964: *Understanding Media*. London: Routledge.

Meikle, S. 2000: Aristotle on money. In Smithin 2000: 157–73.

Melitz, J. 1974: *Primitive and Modern Money*. Reading, MA: Addison-Wesley.

Menger, K. 1892: On the origins of money. *Economic Journal*, 2 (6), 239–55.

Mill, J. S. 1965 [1871]: *Principles of Political Economy*. Toronto: University of Toronto Press.

Milward, A. 2000: *The European Rescue of the Nation-State*, 2nd edn. London: Routledge.

Minsky, H. 1982: The financial instability hypothesis. In C. P. Kindleberger and J-P. Laffarge, (eds), *Financial Crises*, Cambridge: Cambridge University Press, 1–39.

Minsky, H. 1986: Money and crisis in Schumpeter and Keynes. In H-J. Wagener and J. Drukker (eds), *The Economic Law of Motion of Modern Society*, Cambridge: Cambridge University Press, 112–22.

Minsky, H. 1991: The financial instability hypothesis: a clarification. In M. Feldstein (ed.), *The Risk of Financial Crisis*, Chicago: University of Chicago Press, 1–21.

Mirowski, P. 1991: Post-modernism and the social theory of value. *Journal of Post-Keynesian Economics*, 13, 565–82.

Moore, Barrington Jr. 1966: *The Social Origins of Dictatorship and Democracy*. Harmondsworth: Penguin.

Mosler, W. 1997: Full employment and price stability. *Journal of Post-Keynesian Economics*, 20 (2), 167–82.

Mueller, R. 1997: *Money and Banking in Renaissance Venice*. vol. 2: *The Venetian Money Market: Banks, Panic and the Public Debt*. London and Baltimore: Johns Hopkins University Press.

Muldrew, C. 1998: *The Economy of Obligation: The Culture of Credit and Social Relations in Early Modern England*. London: Macmillan.

Mundell, R. 1961: A theory of optimum currency areas. *American Economic Review*, 51 (3), 657–65.

Munro, J. 1979: Bullionism and the bill of exchange in England, 1272–1663. In Center for Medieval and Renaissance Studies, University of California, Los Angeles, *The Dawn of Modern Banking*, New Haven: Yale University Press, 169–240.

Murphy, T. 2000: Japan's economic crisis. *New Left Review*, 1 (2nd ser.), 25–51.

3

North, D. 1981: *Structure and Change in Economic History*. New York: W. W. Norton.

North, D. and Weingast, B. 1989: Constitutions and commitment: the evolution of institutions governing public choice in seventeenth century England. *Journal of Economic History*, 49 (4), 803–32.

OECD 2002: *The Future of Money*. Paris: OECD.

Orlean, A. 1998: La Monnaie autoréférentielle: réflexions sur les evolutions monétaires contemporaines. In Aglietta and Orlean 1998: 359–85.

Parguez, A. 1999: The expected failure of the European Monetary Union: a false money against a real economy. *Eastern Economic Journal*, 25, 63–76.

Parguez, A. and Seccareccia, M. 2000: The credit theory of money: the monetary circuit approach. In Smithin 2000: 101–23.

Parsons, T. 1937: *The Structure of Social Action*. Glencoe, IL: Free Press.

Parsons, T. 1950: *The Social System*. New York: Free Press.

Parsons, T. 1991 [1953]: The Marshall Lectures. *Sociological Inquiry*, 61, 1–59.

Parsons, T. and Smelser, N. 1956: *Economy and Society*. Glencoe, IL: Free Press.

Persson, T. and Tabellini, G. 1990: *Macroeconomic Policy, Credibility and Politics*. London: Harwood.

Phelps Brown, E. H. 1975: A non-monetarist view of the pay explosion. *Three Banks Review*, 105, 3–24.

Pigou, A. C. 1949: *The Veil of Money*. London: Macmillan.

Pixley, J. 1999: Beyond twin deficits: emotions of the future in the organizations of money. *American Journal of Economics and Sociology*, 58 (4), 1091–1118.

Pocock, J. 1975: Early modern capitalism: the Augustan perception. In E. Kamenka, and R. S. Neale, (eds), *Feudalism, Capitalism and Beyond*, London: Edward Arnold, 37–91.

Polanyi, K. 1944: *The Great Transformation*. Boston: Beacon.

Polanyi, K. et al. (eds). 1957: *Trade and Market in the Early Empires*. New York: Free Press.

Posen, A. 1993: Why central bank independence does not cause low inflation; there is no institutional fix for politics. In R. O'Brien (ed.), *Finance and the International Economy*, vol. 7, 41–65.

Powell, J. 2002: Petty capitalism, perfecting capitalism or post-capitalism? Lessons from the Argentine barter experiments. *Review of International Political Economy*, 9 (4), 619–49.

Radford, R. 1945: The economic organization of a POW camp. *Economica*, 12, 189–201.

Redish, R. 1992: The development of coinage. In J. Eatwell amd M. Milgate (eds), *New Palgrave Dictionary of Money and Finance*, London: Macmillan, 376–8.

Robertson, D. 1928: *Money*. London: Nisbet.

Rochon, L.-P. 1999: *Credit Money and Production: An Alternative Post-Keynesian Approach*. Cheltenham: Edward Elgar.

Rogers, C. 1989: *Money, Interest and Capital*. Cambridge: Cambridge University Press.

Rogers, C. and Rymes, T. 2000: The disappearance of Keynes's nascent theory of banking between the *Treatise* and the *General Theory*. In Smithin 2000: 257–69.

Rowlinson, M. 1999: 'The Scotch hate gold': British identity and paper money. In Gilbert and Helleiner 1999: 47–67.

Rowthorn, R. 1995: Capital formation and unemployment. *Oxford Review of Economic Policy*, 11 (1), 26–39.

Runciman, D. 2000: Is the state a corporation? *Government and Opposition*, 35 (1), 90–104.

Runciman, W. G. 1995: The 'triumph' of capitalism as a topic in the theory of social selection. *New Left Review*, 210, 33–47.

Samuelson, P. 1966 [1958]: An exact consumption-loan model of interest with or without the social contrivance of money. In J. Stiglitz (ed.), *The Collected Scientific Papers of Paul A. Samuelson*, vol. 1, Cambridge, MA: MIT Press, 219–33.

Samuelson, P. 1973: *Economics*, 9th edn. New York: McGraw-Hill.

Schmandt-Besserat, D. 1992: *Before Writing*, vol. 1: *From Counting to Cuneiform*. Austin: University of Texas Press.

Schmitt, R. 1975: *Monnaie, Salaires et Profits*. Paris: PUF.

Schumpeter, J. 1917: Money and the social product. *International Economic Papers*, no. 6. London: Macmillan.

Schumpeter, J. 1934: *The Theory of Economic Development*. Cambridge, MA: Harvard University Press.

Schumpeter, J. 1994 [1954]: *A History of Economic Analysis*. London: Routledge.

Scott, J. 1997: *Corporate Business and Capitalist Classes*. Oxford: Oxford University Press.

Seabright, P. (ed.) 2000: *The Vanishing Rouble*. Cambridge: Cambridge University Press.

Searle, J. 1995: *The Construction of Social Reality*. Harmondsworth: Penguin.

Shapiro, S. 1987: The social control of impersonal trust. *American Journal of Sociology*, 93 (3), 623–58.

Sharer, R. 1994: *The Ancient Maya*. Stanford, CA: Stanford University Press.

Sherman, S. 1997: Promises, promises: credit as a contested metaphor in early capitalist discourse. *Modern Philology*, 94 (3), 327–48.

Simmel, G. 1978 [1907]: *The Philosophy of Money*. London: Routledge.

Skidelsky, R. 2000: *John Maynard Keynes*, vol. 3: *Fighting for Britain*. London: Macmillan.

Smith, A. 1986 [1776]: *The Wealth of Nations*. Harmondsworth: Penguin.

Smithin, J. 1996: *Macroeconomic Policy and the Future of Capitalism: The Revenge of the Rentier and the Threat to Prosperity*. Cheltenham: Edward Elgar.

Smithin, J. (ed.) 2000: *What is Money?* London: Routledge.

Smithin, J. 2003: *Controversies in Monetary Economics: Revised Edition*. Cheltenham: Edward Elgar.

Solomon, E. 1997: *Virtual Money*. New York: Oxford University Press.

Spufford, P. 1986: *Handbook of Medieval Exchange*. London: Offices of the Royal Historical Society.

Spufford, P. 1988: *Money and its Use in Medieval Europe*. Cambridge: Cambridge University Press.

Spufford, P. 2002: *Power and Profit: The Merchant in Medieval Europe*. London: Thames and Hudson.

Sraffa, P. (ed.) 1951: *The Works and Correspondence of David Ricardo*, vol. 1. Cambridge: Cambridge University Press.

Stiglitz, J. and Weiss, A. 1981: Credit rationing in markets with imperfect information. *American Economic Review*, 73, 912–27.

Thygesen, N. 1995: *International Currency Competition and the Future Role of the European Single Currency*. London: Kluwer Law International.

Trautwein, H-M. 1993: A fundamental controversy about money: post Keynesian and new monetary economics. In G. Mongiovi and C. Ruhl (eds), *Macoeconomic Theory*, Aldershot: Edward Elgar, 16–31.

Turner, A. 2002: Europe's best defence against deflation. *Financial Times*, 4 November.

Turner, B. 1999: *Classical Sociology*. London: Sage.

Udovitch, A. 1979: Bankers without banks: commerce, banking and society in the Islamic world of the Middle Ages. In Center for Medieval and Renaissance Studies, University of California, Los Angeles. *The Dawn of Modern Banking*. New Haven: Yale University Press, 255–73.

Usher, A. 1953 [1934]: The origins of deposit banking: the primitive bank of deposit, 1200–1600. In F. C. Lane and J. C. Riemersma (eds), *Enterprise and Secular Change*, London: Allen and Unwin, 262–91.

Van Rixtel, A. 2002: *Informality and Monetary Policy in Japan*. Cambridge: Cambridge University Press.

von Mises, L. 1934 [1912]: *The Theory of Money and Credit*, tr. H. E. Bateson. London: Jonathan Cape.

Warburton, P. 2000: *Debt and Delusion*. Harmondsworth: Penguin.

Weatherford, J. 1997: *The History of Money: From Sandstone to Cyberspace*. New York: Three Rivers Press.

Weber, M. 1951: *The Religion of China*. New York: Macmillan.

Weber, M. 1978: *Economy and Society*. Berkeley: University of California Press.

Weber, M. 1981 [1927]: *General Economic History*. New Brunswick, NJ: Transaction Publishers.

White, H. 1981: Where do markets come from? *American Journal of Sociology*, 87 (3), 517–47.

White, H. 1990: Interview. In R. Swedberg, *Economics and Sociology: Conversations with Economists and Sociologists*, Princeton: Princeton University Press, 78–95.

White, L. 1990: Competitive money reform: a review essay. *Journal of Monetary Economics*, 26, 191–202.

Wicksell, K. 1907: The influence of the rate of interest on prices. *Economic Journal*, 17, 213–20.

Wicksell, K. 1935 [1915]: *Lectures in Political Economy*. London: Routledge and Kegan Paul.

Wicksell, K. 1962 [1898]: *Interest and Prices*. London: Royal Economic Society 1936. Reprinted New York: Augustus Kelly, 1962.

Williams, C. 1996: Informal sector responses to unemployment: an evaluation of the potential of local exchange trading schemes. *Work Employment and Society*, 10 (2), 23–35.

Williams, D. 1968: The evolution of the sterling system. In C. Whittlesey and J. Wilson (eds), *Essays in Money and Banking*, Oxford: Clarendon Press, 266–97.

Williamson, O. 1994: Transaction cost economics and organization theory. In N. Smelser and R. Swedberg (eds), *The Handbook of Economic Sociology*, Princeton: Princeton University Press, 77–107.

Wood, D. 2002: *Medieval Economic Thought*. Cambridge: Cambridge University Press.

Woodruff, D. 1999: *Money Unmade: Barter and the Fate of Russian Capitalism*. Ithaca, NY: Cornell University Press.

Wray, R. 1990: *Money and Credit in Capitalist Economies*. Aldershot: Edward Elgar.

Wray, R. 1998: *Understanding Modern Money*. Cheltenham: Edward Elgar.

Wray, R. 2000: Modern money. In Smithin 2000: 42–67.

Wray, R. 2004: Conclusion. In Wray 2003: 228–68.

Wray, R. (ed.) 2004: *Credit and State Theories of Money*. Cheltenham: Edward Elgar.

Zelizer, V. 1994: *The Social Meaning of Money*. New York: Basic Books.

Index

CPSIA information can be obtained at www.ICGtesting.com
Printed in the USA
BVOW080509061212

307451BV00021B/822/P